Religion and Judgment

THE CENTURY PHILOSOPHY SERIES

Justus Buchler and Sterling P. Lamprecht, *Editors*

WILLARD E. ARNETT
Chatham College

Religion and Judgment

An Essay on the Method
and Meaning of Religion

 New York

APPLETON-CENTURY-CROFTS
Division of Meredith Publishing Company

112509

To Patricia Rae Arnett

Preface

The philosophy of religion, as distinguished from religious philosophy, has only rarely received its proper due. It arose primarily in two forms: as a rational protest against the dogmatisms of the creeds and sects, and as a "scientific" attempt to explain every aspect of religion in terms of nonreligious complexes and interests. But with the ascendancy of modern science, philosophy has increasingly drawn both its method and substance from the procedures and results of scientific inquiry and has in some quarters become essentially indifferent, and in others genuinely opposed, to any serious concern with the fact and character of religious experience, activity, and claims. And so inquiry into religion has lately been left largely either to the religiously committed, with all the exclusiveness this normally implies, or to the sociologist and psychologist with bizarre interests in the irrational and abnormal among men. Even that great classic of religious psychology, *The Varieties of Religious Experience* by William James, approached both the religious person and the religious experience as notable deviations from the normal.

If the results of such inquiries have usually been disappointing, they have not been surprising. Those committed to the absolute truth of particular sects and traditions have found various, if generally devious, ways of confirming their own beliefs, no matter how narrow and exclusive; and the sociologists and psychologists have not lacked elaborate (though no doubt often sophistical and absurd) arguments to support their claims that religion is generated and sustained by specific cultural and economic developments, by ignorance and fear, or as magical and irrational efforts to deal with the unknown, the uncertain, and the fearful.

The approaches of both the sectarians and the social scientists, however, important and reliable as they often are in relation to particular movements and projects, apparently leave the most basic and generic aspects of religion untouched. The sectarian

v

evaluates religions other than his own in terms of their approximation to his perspective and so tends to identify all religion with
specific manifestations which may nonetheless disappear without
any radical effects on religion as such. And the approach of the
social scientist, though not without important exceptions, regards
religion as primarily the complex symptoms of social disorganiza-
tion, ignorance, insecurity, and fear—symptoms which will presumably all disappear when society is better organized and
individuals become less desperate or more knowledgeable and
rational.

In contrast to such approaches, this essay is based on the
assumption that religion can in fact be understood only as an
irreducible feature of existence or as a form of man's openness to
an existence which may be judged religiously, and that religion
is essentially one, though it appears in many varieties. The religions
are therefore regarded as complex groups of phenomena which,
although they may be examined and partially understood in terms
of other human attributes and activities, are not any more subject
to being fully explained in such terms than are the arts or the
sciences or even man himself. In other words, the fundamental
theme of this essay is that religion is one of the very basic ways
in which man exists and judges—or recognizes and evaluates
appropriately—certain critical aspects or dimensions of his own
character, situation, and possibilities. Thus no religion may be
regarded as having a monopoly on religious truth, even as no art
and no science provides the standards or the criteria by which
other arts and sciences may be judged. One religion may of course
have virtues and faults or powers and dangers which another does
not have, and may, like an art or a science, mismanage in some
respect its own capacities or misinterpret its own achievements.
Also, certain aspects of any religion may be understood in terms
of the influence of particular events and doctrines or as the result
of certain social, economic, and psychological factors. But religion
as such is only *conditioned* or *modified*, and *not caused*, by such
factors. Religion, I claim, is generically a mode of judgment necessitated, even as the science of physics or the art of painting is, by
the fact that certain dimensions of existence can presumably be
discovered, or apprehended, and communicated in no other way.

There is of course no reason to pretend that all this has been proved in the pages which follow. Philosophical argument is always less than proof, though it is not for that reason any less valuable and necessary. Or as C. I. Lewis has said, the philosopher can offer proof "only in the sense of so connecting his theses as to exhibit their mutual support, and only through appeal to other minds to reflect upon their experience and their own attitudes and perceive that he correctly portrays them."[1] In this sense the book does indeed offer argument—and proof in so far as the argument succeeds.

Thus the book is intended primarily as a contribution to the philosophical understanding of religion and not as a survey of the literature of the field. And the uses I have made of the work of Ernst Cassirer, John Dewey, William James, C. S. Peirce, George Santayana, and A. N. Whitehead are integral parts of both theory and argument. Each of these men has focused on at least one, and in most cases several, important and apparently permanent elements of religion, although each has also neglected certain other fundamental features of it. None of these men was sectarian; and none was wholly insensitive to the fact that there are evidently aspects of existence which can be articulated and communicated only in religious terms—though Cassirer, Dewey, and Santayana were convinced, each in his own manner and degree, that religion in its traditional forms has had its day. So the pages which follow attempt to show also, at least by indirection, how the claims of these men, and to a lesser extent the claims of others also, are related, either positively or negatively, to a theory or vision of religion as an integral and permanent part of the life of judgment through which man recognizes, and in quite crucial respects modifies, the conditions of his existence. The general view which I defend is not attributable to any of them, though it owes much to each. Even the claims with which I disagree most thoroughly are among the indispensable elements of the argument.

The view that judgment may, contrary to much current philosophical thought, characterize any of the manifold forms of man's saying, making, and doing is due mainly of course to the influence of the highly important work of Justus Buchler of Columbia

[1] C. I. Lewis, *Mind and the World Order*, p. 23.

University. The excellence of his philosophical argument, to the effect that the great diversity in modes of judgment is the most distinctive characteristic of man, can be properly acknowledged only as one of the most original and suggestive contributions to contemporary philosophy. No doubt my use of his concepts departs in many respects from, and is much less profound than, his own achievement. Nonetheless, the book would have been vastly different except for this influence.

To recognize all the debts, personal and intellectual, incurred in the writing of these pages is strictly impossible. But the special interest and help of a number of persons must be duly noted. Among many students whose interest and questions have done much to form my thought, a few have taken a special and enduring interest in the progress of the work; these include Lesley Wells Brooks, Ruth M. Jones, Joan Bailey, Dorothy Evans Fulton, and Betty Bennett Morrow. I am also grateful to President Edward D. Eddy and the trustees of Chatham College for a semester's leave of absence to complete the work. And Pamela E. Johnson must be thanked for her careful help with the proofs and the index.

Among friends and colleagues, Harold D. Hantz of the University of Arkansas read one of the earliest drafts, and, in addition to encouragement, provided me with a set of critical notes which guided the revision of several sections. H. S. Thayer of City College, New York, read a later version and suggested important additions. And no doubt I have profited more than I know from discussions with Thelma W. Taylor and Frank A. Hayes of Chatham College.

Above all, however, I am grateful to Justus Buchler who as my professor, friend, and editor, as well as philosopher, has always taken a genuine and critical interest in my work. His encouragement, incisive criticism, and suggestions as he read different versions of this book were indispensable to its present form.

Of course no one other than myself is responsible for the faults which remain, especially since in several instances I have stubbornly refused to heed the advice of my friends and critics.

W. E. A.

Chatham College

Contents

3. ON RELIGION AND MORALITY

4. ON RELIGION AND ART

5. ON RELIGION AND TRUTH

Contents

I

On Man in the World

From time immemorial man has known that he is the subject most deserving of his own study. . . .

MARTIN BUBER

If to see more is really to become more, if deeper vision is really fuller being, then we should look closely at man in order to increase our capacity to live.

PIERRE TEILHARD DE CHARDIN

ON MAN'S SEARCH FOR HIMSELF

But I do not yet know clearly enough what I am, I who am certain that I am.

RENÉ DESCARTES

No matter what else may be said, whether by scientists, theologians, poets, or philosophers, man rarely ceases to be deeply troubled and puzzled by himself. Instead, the more he achieves in knowledge and skill, the greater the reasons for anxious wonder and even for a sense of awesome destiny. Increased knowledge and greater control over objective powers and processes, far from alleviating concern about his own ultimate powers and potentialities, often only serve to deepen and confound the mysteries of his existence. Man's own being, vision, hopes, and possibilities for both good and ill seem always greatly to outrun his knowledge.

Yet all claims to knowledge and all inquiry assume, if they
do not seek, an answer to the question of what man is. For any
claim (e.g., that the sun is the center of the universe, that the
universe has no center, or that life and knowledge itself are ultimately products of only chemical and physical forces) presumes
that man is a knowing creature, or that he is somehow so constituted that *what is* does not altogether elude him, and seeks to
establish his place in nature, or to provide a scheme in terms of
which his existence and experience can be interpreted. When he
posits a claim to know anything at all, man's profound concern
to know himself is there in the background.

But although the collective knowledge of twentieth-century
man about himself and the universe he inhabits is vast compared
with what other creatures know (if other creatures may properly be
said to know at all) or with what man knew not more than a few
hundred years ago, the candid and honest mind must surely recognize that man's search for himself, prolonged, tortuous, and rewarding as it has undeniably been, is still radically incomplete.
In spite of the profound relevance of various descriptions and
definitions, such as that he is "a little lower than the angels" or
"a rational animal" or "a being that knows it must die" or "an
animal among other animals," and in spite of the many illuminating and valuable discoveries in biology, anthropology, and
psychology, man remains in fundamental respects—in his totality
if not in every detail—a mystery to himself.

Yet many ignore or deny this mystery, in practice if not also
in theory, in order to be confident in approaching difficulties that
must be resolved one way or another, whether intelligently or not.
This confidence or bravado, however, when not based altogether on
illusion, is often at best only a product of trial, error, and habit,
and not of insight or understanding. What man is and why he does
the things he does, when he takes an uncompromising look at himself, are surely ultimately as puzzling as the origin of the universe
and the extent of time and space. As John Scotus Erigena claimed
in the ninth century, man knows *that* he is but does not know
what he is and is therefore presumably uncircumscribed and an
infinite puzzle to himself. Man, the creature whose knowledge is

most magnificent, is nonetheless unknown (and perhaps unknowable) to himself.

At least the individual does not know himself as an object and is notoriously ignorant of his own prejudices and predilections. And if one person may be said to know others by observing what they do and say, the result is not wholly unlike that of observing an eye. For what is observed is not the eye seeing but only the structures and processes without which sight is presumably impossible. We cannot, even with the help of mirrors and microscopes, see the eye seeing. A person seeking to know another may observe the intricate permutations and processes of the flesh, but the most ordinary dimensions of the spirit, the modes in which a man lives, enjoys, suffers, and seeks to know himself as a person are never fully revealed to either observation or the most careful analysis. And as Martin Buber has repeatedly emphasized, it is perhaps only in the choice to speak to one who also chooses to listen that one person is ever significantly revealed to another.

So the existence of the individual, and not only that of the universe and mankind, is, so far as human knowledge is concerned, largely gratuitous and inexplicable. The individual not only did nothing (for he could have done nothing) to originate himself but cannot finally offer even vaguely satisfactory accounts of his own origins and possibilities. He is of course more or less aware of economic, political, artistic, and religious facts and traditions which seem to converge to make him what he is in any given situation. Also each individual is presumably in part the product of biological heredity and psychological needs and desires. Yet all such observations, important as they no doubt are in many respects, are *post facto*. Nothing in them makes personal existence—the lucid and creative duration of a sensitive and searching individual self—either necessary or even conceivable. As far as man's knowledge is concerned, each person is a miraculous and novel event. And not only the sources but also the manner and the degree in which the life of one person may touch and change the lives of others are largely obscure.

In brief, the existence of man, though subject to enormities of ugliness and sorrow, is splendid and awe-full, and only the ignorant or arrogant presume to know, without serious doubt and wonder, just what, how, or why he is. Yet thoroughgoing scepticism concerning him is neither possible nor necessary. For each individual is also evidently related to and dependent on distinguishable and enduring universal powers and conditions and shares with a group social and cultural traditions which possess characteristic structures and qualities. So even as the eye may be judged by its structures and qualitative functions in comparison with the structures and functions of other eyes, the individual may judge himself or others in comparison with the attributes and actions of other persons and groups. On such a comparative basis alone much that is highly important can presumably be discovered about both the individual and mankind.

But not only comparative judgments are possible by and about man. In spite of the severe limits of his knowledge, he is nonetheless aware of ideals and possibilities as well as actualities. He in fact recognizes the ideal—which promises no immediate or certain realization—and manipulates the actual to achieve the possible. So even the general reliability of comparative discriminations and judgments by no means implies that the standards of personal excellence are only norms derived from the average character of individual persons in specific cultures and situations. The history of intellectual and moral progress, to whatever extent such progress has occurred, seems clearly and directly related to the effort to achieve the ideal implicit (as Aristotle long ago suggested) in the actual. There is or seems to be a direction in which excellence lies, a particular mark for each person that may be hit or missed. And both the moral and the aesthetic sense of man, in their most effective and profound manifestations, are evidently inseparable from the apprehension of the ideal and the untiring efforts to make it actual in one way or another. Thus in metaphysical systems as different as that of Plato, Aristotle, G. E. Moore, and John Dewey, it is nevertheless the ideal that both inspires and in large measure guides moral perception and effort. Presumably, then, no matter what the ultimate decision concerning the ontological status of the ideal itself, there can be little, if any, doubt that man is significantly revealed in the ideal judgments which he passes on himself.

There are then at least two important dimensions to man's search for himself: the comparative or empirical, and the ideal or normative. Each of these has many, if not infinite, implications in the perhaps endless search of man for himself. And in the philosophy of religion perhaps more than in any other area of inquiry, each dimension must be carefully accorded its due and proper weight.

ON MAN AND THE WORLD HE BUILDS

We do not learn who man is by learned definitions; we learn it only . . . when he projects something new (not yet present), when he creates original poetry, when he builds poetically.
MARTIN HEIDEGGER

Many religions and philosophies have emphasized man's ultimate, and perhaps complete, dependence on powers which he neither understands nor controls—on Moira, matter, fate, or God. Human events and prospects have no doubt often justified such judgments. Yet it also seems clear, and equally important as the fact that the individual is a mysterious culmination of past and uncontrollable events, that man cannot be at all understood except as the source and harbinger of the very substance of his own future. For in the pursuit of the possibilities of excellence, the individual person may change substantially the face and course of a community, a nation, or even, presumably, the earth and mankind. This happens in the case of no other creature. No other fact about man is so awe-full; no other fact is so marvelous. This in itself justifies moral concern and action, or is at least a fundamental reason for a radical emphasis on personal excellence and social responsibility. Nature cares for other creatures, provides them with a suitable habitat, or else destroys them. But man qua man must forever build and rebuild his own dwellings, both physical and spiritual. He must care (in both senses of this ambiguous word) not only for himself but for others—including both his ancestry,

from whom he has received so much, and his posterity, to whom
he must in turn pass on his heritage and his own achievements.
On man's own workmanship, not on an inevitable and beneficent
order of nature, depends whether or not he and those who come
after him will have a world fit to live in. Thus man's responsibility
to man, in spite of all the violent denials of it, is deep and ineradicable.

Indeed it may be said, and not at all metaphorically, that man
is, among other things, the only creature who must build the
world in which he must live and who in so doing determines in
many respects his own character and destiny. For to say that man
builds the world in which he must live, means not simply that he
adopts attitudes towards things and events or that he raises cities,
changes the course of rivers, and cultivates the fields. He does these
things, and they are not unimportant. But the world in which man
lives is also comprised of traditions in morals, in the arts, in science,
and in religion. And his self-directed energies may either establish
and sustain or radically transform not only his physical but also
his intellectual and spiritual landscapes. He builds poetically, imaginatively, and logically, giving distinctive form and substance to
many facets of the world, including himself. Whether or not his
world is fit for his habitation depends, therefore, largely on himself
and no less on what is done in one area than on what is done in the
others. Art and religion, whether for better or worse, no less than
science and technology, influence in many ways the shape of his
world. A desiccated world of the spirit, the prophets and the moralists have always claimed, is no less uninhabitable by man than a
world that fails to produce nourishment for his body. And indeed
moral and spiritual sickness, no less effectively than violence and
the slow erosion of time, have evidently often wrecked his most
splendid achievements.

Each person *must* in fact live to some extent in a world
created by his own decisions, his modes of thought, and the tastes
and skills which he develops or fails to develop. The individual
may *choose* to live almost completely in his own world—in a world
of fancy or in a world of thought. But neither the semiprivate
world in which the individual must live nor the fanciful world in
which he may choose to live is the chief theme here. That which

men share, their common and inextricable roots in nature and culture, is equally as important for philosophy and religion as either the egocentric predicament or individual capacities and private interests. The many things men have in common, including their religious needs and interests, are clearly as important, if not greater, than individual differences. There are features of the shared world, of nature and culture, that no person, try as he may, can escape. For even if man is, as Pico della Mirandolo claimed in the fifteenth century, more fortunate than either the animals or the angels primarily because he has the freedom to make of himself what he will, the individual has this self-creating attribute only in common with others and must also share many of the consequences of the choices made by others.

Man, the harbinger of the future, creates, reforms, and alters and so determines crucial aspects of the world in which he must live. The quality and direction of cultures, as well as the attributes of individual persons, are modified when public modes of thought and behavior are changed or when that which men possess in common changes its character. A person, be he scientist, poet, prophet, or artisan, may work changes not only in his own world but also in the world that men share by changing the common heritage.

ON MAN AND NATURE

We forget that nature itself is one vast miracle transcending the reality of night and nothingness. We forget that each one of us in his personal life repeats that miracle.

LOREN EISELEY

Man is most obviously a product of *nature*. But to say this is not to explain the origin of man or even to deny either the existence of the supernatural or that man may in important respects transcend nature. In any case the nature which sustains man can by no means be limited to atoms in motion, to the aspects of existence that can be described in the terms of current physics and chemistry, or as some form of matter and energy. The term "nature" has in fact no substantial limitation and is used here only as a unifying term to suggest that nothing that exists is ever clearly and wholly independent of all else. In David Hume's perhaps uncharacteristic words, "The parts hang all together, nor can one be touched without affecting the rest, in a greater or less degree."[1] Or as A. N. Whitehead emphasized repeatedly, "Any local agitation shakes the whole universe. The distant effects are minute, but they are there."[2] Nature is the sum total of the dynamic factors which may influence and be influenced by the changes in each other. Consequently God, if He may be said to exist at all, is either a part of nature or is (as long tradition claims) unchanged by anything that occurs in nature.

But although any event may influence in one way or another any other event, this need not imply that nature is a tightly-knit system of invariable and uniform action and reaction. Certain entities in nature—perhaps most notably men—are apparently in some degree independent or self-determining and may choose or direct their own modes of action and reaction. Thus culture, although in many respects a product of nature, may be at least distinguished from nature to the extent that, and only because, there is a looseness that allows culture to assume various forms according to the decisions of men and more or less, but never absolutely, independent of the larger and less variable processes. And man himself may be distinguished from nature only because and to the extent that his own freedom and the looseness in nature allow and ordain the individual to choose in some respects his own character and destiny.

Of course no argument can prove conclusively the actuality of freedom, or that nature is so constituted that man's own undetermined and radically unpredictable choices influence the course and character of certain events and situations. But it is hardly reasonable to maintain on the one hand that man's judgments re-

<hr/>

[1] David Hume, *Dialogues Concerning Natural Religion*, New York, Hafner, 1948, p. 77.
[2] A. N. Whitehead, *Modes of Thought*, New York, Putnam, Capricorn Books, 1958, p. 188.

flect the essential character of existence, and on the other that his sense of freedom and effective choice are altogether illusory. And certainly the assumption that, in spite of the impressive regularity discovered by scientific investigation, he is nonetheless free is still immensely less paradoxical than the belief that, though completely immersed in a strict and pervasive causal order, he can yet both predict and radically affect the future. If all things were equally necessary and predictable, man would be ultimately as helpless as the flowers of the field. In a world of many parts and contingent events, however, his freedom of conduct and his moral choice and responsibility must be regarded as basic facts. These facts effectively separate him in important respects from the massive and inexorable or regular movements described by the so-called laws of nature.

But the looseness in nature is clearly not all, and man is not wholly free. His existence is obviously and intricately interwoven with both the microscopic and the macroscopic. His life is apparently dependent on both sub-atomic (whether determinate or indeterminate) and astronomical features of the world. Nothing is more evident than his dependence on the sun, and nothing is more important, it is said, than the chemical balance in his blood and brain. Both freedom and dependence, paradoxical as the two may appear in conjunction, are surely highly significant if not the absolutely necessary conditions of man's existence. The features of the world on which he depends, in addition to posing certain and constant threats, also render his biological, social, and intellectual existence possible. But his freedom is the fulcrum of the power required to manipulate things and events and is both the necessary condition and the perfection of his moral and intellectual life. It is clearly freedom and not dependence that makes the life characteristic of man—a life of significant concern and decision—possible. For it is obviously freedom that makes intelligence effective, as well as morally necessary, and progress (as well as tragedy) possible. Nothing indeed can be conceived as genuinely significant, either morally or practically, except insofar as it is a factor in the decision-making of a being that possesses some degree of foresight and freedom. So without freedom the existence of man, to the extent that something similar to him would be at all possible, would be only another and trivial fact within the massive and inexorable movement of the whole. But with freedom, man is himself the originator of novel, remarkable, and presumably enduring developments in nature.

ON JUDGMENT

Mankind is that factor in nature which exhibits in its most intense form the plasticity of Nature.
                                      A. N. WHITEHEAD

Man may now be said to be the creature who, by the exercise of freedom, constructs the world in which he must live. His freedom, however, is actualized only in his judgments. In other words, he builds the world in which he must live by or through the judgments he must make. But judgment, at least in some primitive sense, is a distinctive capacity not of man alone but of all living creatures. The characteristic processes and events of life are instances of accepting or rejecting, of turning materials to diverse uses and thus variously modifying both the self and the environment. Judgment occurs in its most elementary forms when an organism simply responds in some way to its environment or to itself. But when the organism is aware that conditions admit alternative responses, or that the responses themselves are appropriate or inappropriate, necessary or unnecessary, successful or unsuccessful, judgment may be said to become deliberate.

Among the plants and lower animals the processes of judgment, of acceptance and rejection, though surely not clearly mechanical, are largely if not wholly automatic. There is of course obviously a plasticity in plant and animal structure and behavior which permits training or conditioning in sundry ways. But apparently plants and animals, when left to themselves, do not deliberately behave in radically novel or unprecedented ways. Conditioning or training which results in unique developments may be imposed on them by unusual circumstances or by man when he desires their products or services or is interested in their behavior patterns and capacities. Man himself may also be conditioned or trained to behave in specific and generally predictable ways: to stand up when certain music is played on public occasions, or to rush out of classrooms when bells ring, or to give only his name, rank, and serial number when captured by an enemy in wartime.

A distinctive feature of man's judicial capacity, however, is that he can generally resist the patterns that are imposed on him or that he judges not only automatically and habitually but also reflectively and freely. So although it may be said that all living things are in some measure free, or capable (in Aristotle's terms) of voluntary action, only man's freedom is a radical freedom— a freedom at the very heart of his existence—and no other creature is held morally responsible for its acts. The awesome dignity and the dreadful responsibility of man for himself are thus respectively the reward and the terrible burden of the freedom at the heart of his existence.

Man not only judges but he also judges deliberately. Deliberate judgment and radical freedom are in fact inseparable, since only the conditions that make deliberate judgments possible can support such freedom. And so the problem of how freedom is possible is nothing other than the complex and immense task of describing man and the manner of his being in the world. Summarily it may be said that as a product and possessor of memory and culture, he lives not only in a specious present but also with the success and failure and joys and sorrows of the past; that deeply sensitive to the quality and direction of the processes that constitute, surround, and pervade his own existence, he lives in and with the promises and the threats of the future; and that aware of the actual, the ideal, and numerous possibilities, his life is always a complex of unavoidable and irreversible decisions. Thus the many dimensions of his awareness combined with the manifold possibilities in nature and his own diverse powers of language, art, and reason are the sources of the genuine alternatives necessary for radically free and effective judgment.

And so as Justus Buchler has most cogently claimed, man may also be regarded as the creature that judges in many modes.[3]

[3] Justus Buchler, *Nature and Judgment*, New York, Columbia, 1955.

Unlike the animals whose behavior patterns or judgments are severely limited by structure and the absence of complex symbolic and conceptual capacities, man is capable of judgments that are richly diverse in both mode and function. Through the various arts, the different forms of science, and the many forms of religion, as well as through individual actions and social organizations, man employs his powers to judge in many ways and uses his freedom to build the world in which he must live. For man judges, as Buchler insists, not only when he makes verbal claims that may be said to be true or false but also in every action, product, and word which may be said to be a "situational recognition" of the universe or of *what is*. Each act, product, and word bears witness to the world from a specific perspective or predilection and may in turn become a part of the enduring circumstances in which man must live. The poet, the physicist, the painter, the economist, and the prophet may each judge a windstorm, a legal decision, or an economic crisis in his own and relevant manner. And the actions, products, and words of each will often be, not only momentary recognitions of an actual situation or of *what is*, but may also become significant elements of the shared world in which each and others must continue to live and judge.

The responsibility of each person for both himself and others is of course inseparable from his capacity to judge in many modes. For although a person may habitually judge in the modes or terms of a specific cultural, moral, religious, or scientific tradition, he is not normally bound to do so. The individual may judge other persons by the color of their skin or the sound of their voices. A man often judges without critical inquiry or guided only by a first and unexamined impulse. But he is not bound to do so. A person is not bound to judge exclusively in any particular manner or mode because other manners and modes may be assimilated, or developed, and used. Freedom inevitably requires the individual to be a person created in part by his own decisions; but freedom is sustained and extended only by judgments which are guided by careful deliberation or inquiry and supported by actual and complex circumstances.

But although man achieves, maintains, and increases his

radical and characteristic freedom only through deliberate judgment, he is never a wholly independent spectator of existence.
Rather, he discovers and judges the structures, processes, and
qualities of a world in which he dwells and which also dwells in
him. The so-called and celebrated "objectivity" of the sciences is
the result, not of some extraordinary detachment or independence of scientific minds, but of general consent to certain judicial
(methodological and existential) principles. Indeed, man's independence and consequently his judgment and freedom is perhaps
never altogether as great as it appears. Yet his envisagement of
himself as a spectator—beautifully and terribly an outsider in his
own world—is surely not simply or wholly illusory. As a creature
that may look both to the past and the future, deliberate before
he commits himself to irreversible or irreparable actions, and
control many of his own functions and some features of his environment, man cannot be at all adequately conceived except as
a being that may in a measure transcend his temporal involve-
ments and the physical processes which surround and support
him. Nature, like a parent, is both demanding and permissive.
Therefore, while plant and animal behavior contributes primarily
to the preservation of the individual or the species, human judgments may be self-effacing, sacrificial, and even self-destructive.
The individual person may of course choose survival; but he may
also choose death or some object of worth which can be attained
only by obvious and severe risks to survival.

But if man's transcendence of nature is measured by his freedom, his freedom plainly depends on the scope and reliability of
his judgments. And the scope and reliability of judgments are
apparently increased, not only by improving methods of extending
and validating particular modes and instances of judgment, but
also by developing the capacity to judge in several modes, from
different perspectives, and for various ends or purposes. No one
mode of judgment is ever clearly or intrinsically superior to all
others in all instances; and the reliability of any judgment is
evidently related in some measure to its implicit recognition that
circumstances, problems, and goals may be judged from different
perspectives and in several ways. The person who speaks or understands only the language of the sciences can presumably never

judge appropriately the problems and complexes recognized and articulated by the arts and religions. And the judgments of the prophet or the artist who is unfamiliar with the sciences may surely result in catastrophes which some acquaintance with the methods and discoveries of science might prevent. Similarly, to judge all activities and products in moral terms or to refuse to make moral judgments at all may be equally shortsighted and disastrous. The world is many-dimensioned, and man's limited knowledge of it and his freedom in it are inseparable from the capacity to judge in many modes. For all he ever knows is the flickering candlelight of judgment in various forms, invading the darkness of existence.

ON JUDGMENT, LANGUAGE, AND NATURE

We feel the earth below us, we see the sky above; the ways of expressing ourselves that derive from that situation could be changed only if the actual mode of our insertion into the universe could be changed.

GABRIEL MARCEL

Distinctively human experience and judgment, many philosophers from Plato and Aristotle to Ernst Cassirer have insisted, are inseparable from language. "In the beginning was the Word," proclaims *The Gospel According to St. John*; and regardless of its ultimate metaphysical meaning and truth, no claim about the phenomenal nature of man is more evidently true. Without language the most remarkable and distinctive powers and activities of man would to all appearances not exist at all. For all activities which require complex processes of deliberation and choice, and of course all conceptual and most symbolic capacities, are apparently related either directly or indirectly to, if not completely dependent on, some form and degree of linguistic achievement. Indeed, the various forms and dimensions of human freedom are so utterly inseparable from the uses and powers of language

that the arbitrary denial of freedom of speech and press is tanta-
mount to the denial of the judicial capacities which distinguish
man from animal. The prelude and in large measure the consummation of tyranny, whether political or intellectual, is the cur-
tailment of freedom in the uses of language.

Language is manifestly not simply a passive reaction to the
pressures of an external world—not something that man suffers
or has imposed on him—but it is rather his own most special way
of discovering, creating, and modifying the world in which he
must live. Yet his control over language, contrary to the widespread notion that linguistic decisions are ultimately arbitrary,
is far from absolute. For language is evidently no less a product
of complex existential conditions than are the ocean waves and
the green of the grass. So the freedoms—including the freedom
to say and mean what one will—which the various forms of
language demand, support, and extend are neither absolute nor
arbitrary. In spite of persistent and persuasive claims to the contrary, neither the syntax nor the meaning of language is appreci-
ably independent of either the order (the logic or structure) or
the content (the substance and processes) of existence. The fact
that the logical and symbolic burden of one language can be
largely translated into others, which at least superficially are
utterly different, is surely evidence that neither syntax nor meaning, no matter how formal and abstract, is without ground in the
actual and objective character of being.

Therefore to conceive language, as Thomas Hobbes and
many later empiricists have, as an exception to the general scheme
of existence and the chief, if not only, source of judicial error and
absurdity is a profound and serious philosophical mistake. Unable
to account for language by his general metaphysical principles or
as simply a product of matter and motion, Hobbes declared that
language is a gift of God which, in spite of all the advantages it
brings to man, is also the principal source of confusion, deceit,
and absurdity. Linguistic claims but not "natural sense and imagination," he said, may be absurd or false. Words are only "wise
men's counters, they do but reckon by them." Fools alone con-
fuse mere "counters" with genuine "money" or regard words as
indispensable or as the very substance of human reason and exist-

ence. Language has, according to Hobbes (and many later empiricists have agreed with him), no part at all in the basic or
causal order of nature. Thus nothing ontologically distinctive or
fundamental but only a convenient dexterity is added to man's
existence by the symbols and functions of language. Language,
according to Hobbes, may note and record but can never influence
the inexorable course of matter in motion. And man devoid of
language is and can do essentially all that he is and can do with
it, even though with it he can reason with greater facility and
promote absurdities that are impossible for dumb animals. The
animal that speaks, this view implies, is different only in degree
from the animal that cannot speak.[4]

Hobbes' view of language, in spite of the fact that his general
view of man and nature is generally recognized as woefully oversimplified and inaccurate, is still amazingly influential. The current
notions that truth and falsity are attributes of language only, that
philosophical problems are essentially linguistic absurdities or
puzzles, and that philosophy is simply a second-order activity or
analysis of the methods by which primary existents are presumably
discovered and described (rather than being itself a fundamental
approach to critical questions about primary facts) are all directly
related to the supposition that language merely reflects and never
embodies or alters in any particular the essential content and
causal order of existence. This view is of course as old as the
claim of Democritus (who disagreed with the Greek philosophers
who insisted that *logos*, language or reason, is the very substance
of man) that "Speech is the shadow of action." However, the
modern version is more emphatic, if not more consistent, in adding
that the shadow is very often the shadow of nothing and, perhaps
more often than not, terribly distorted and misleading if not altogether illusory. Language, it is now accordingly suggested by those
who follow Hobbes in the matter, is judicially (or cognitively
and ontologically) significant only insofar as it reflects or conveys
and is checked against the observable objects, relations, and
processes which are presumed to be altogether independent of
linguistic forms and distinctions. Except in such "verified" in-

---

[4] Thomas Hobbes, *Leviathan*, Chap. IV. There are many editions of this
work which was first published in 1651.

stances, it is claimed, language is most apt to be or reflect emotional or perhaps aesthetic illusions or other serious distortions of the actual objects of judgment.

A view of language could hardly be more naïve or uncritical. For judged only by its most obvious characteristics, language is clearly both a mode of action and in many cases a guide of actions that are not linguistic. The bonds (or relations) between language (signs, concepts, and symbols) on the one hand and non-linguistic structures, relations, and qualities on the other are of course exceedingly complex and by no means always obvious. No doubt linguistic usage often seems to be the most "unnatural," the most unpredictable, and transcendental of human powers and activities. Surely the many forms and uses of language do not in any way exhibit the regularity found where natural law is supposedly regnant and obvious. The order of events, structures, and relations, as Hobbes was well aware, may plainly be either represented or completely misrepresented by language.

Nonetheless the empiricists' claim that sensory perception is less dispensable or its objects more fundamental in veridical judgment than are linguistic symbols and concepts is at best an extremely oversimplified view of both the objects and the processes of judgment. It is not at all clear, (as almost any observant parent or teacher knows) that linguistic functions are more dependent on sensory perceptions than perceptual discriminations are on linguistic distinctions and habits. Although it is true that a person sees or hears what he sees or hears, and that from one point of view he can hardly be at all mistaken in such matters, it is also true that experience repeatedly confirms the fact that men see and hear erroneously as well as speak falsely. Sensory perception, in other words, is obviously not always and directly or necessarily more reliable than linguistic cogency. Certain linguistic claims are no doubt verified, and linguistic errors corrected, only by testing against sensory experience. But equally, if not more, significant is the evident fact that the errors which may plague any judgment are corrigible only by additional instances and very often different modes of judgment. So if linguistic claims are often verified by the senses, sensory perceptions are in turn often directed and justified (or invalidated) by the continual dialogue in the com-

munity of judgment. Also there are, plainly, dimensions of existence which no sense experiences discloses but which language—
the language of fiction, poetry, and religion as well as the language of philosophy and science—reveals, sustains, and accentu-
ates.

Each of man's powers—seeing, hearing, speaking, feeling, etc.
—is apparently unique and selective, although the specific character of each clearly depends greatly on its interactions and relations with other powers and functions. The blind man is not forbidden to hear and speak or the deaf to see and speak though no
doubt the words of each are qualified by his particular condition.
The senses as well as linguistic judgments are no doubt subject
to enormous error in regard to the conditions that sustain their
own structure and processes. Yet as Whitehead has written:

> Successful high-grade organisms are only possible, on the condi-
> tion that their symbolic functionings [which in his terms include
> sense perceptions as well as the meanings of words, icons, etc.] are
> usually justified so far as important issues are concerned.[5]

And surely it is true that poetry, mathematics, and philosophy,
which in many instances depend almost wholly on the qualities
and powers of language, are prima facie neither more nor less necessary and effective in determining, describing, and guiding characteristically human activities than are the powers of sense. But
linguistic powers and functions are apparently neither more nor
less subject to ultimate control and direction, to improvement and
impairment, than are the powers and functions of sight and hearing. There is indeed little reason to suppose that the many forms
and functions of language are other than part and parcel of the
seamless cloth of nature, which, though composed of many and
distinct threads, cannot be wholly separated without violence.

Consequently the current claim that language is simply an invention of man or that logical and semantical rules are altogether
as conventional as the rules of a game such as chess is an egregious
error. A. J. Ayer has said, "It is not self-contradictory to suppose
that someone, uninstructed in the use of any existing language,

5 A. N. Whitehead, *Symbolism*, New York, Putnam, Capricorn Books,
1959, p. 5.

makes up a language for himself. After all, some human being must have been the first to use a symbol."[6] But he also notes certain limitations of those "who have not acquired the use of language. Animals and children have feelings and images . . . but . . . they do not know that they have them."[7] The comment of Virgil C. Aldrich seems altogether correct and in agreement with the view I have expressed above: "Presumably," says Aldrich, "this is to say that only with the help of language can one identify anything, i.e., have a concept of it, even in the case of one's own 'inner life.' And if the creature that has no language cannot have such concepts, I wonder what would prompt him to invent a language. . . . My difficulty therefore with the fanciful image of a creature inventing a language wholesale is that I *do* find it unintelligible, not just 'probably false,' if the instruction is either to consider such a creature a man, or to consider the invention of a language, or to do both of these. There are latent, subtle contradictions here. . . ."[8] The power of men to communicate with one another is no less a fact of which language takes advantage than a fact itself due to language. And language is clearly supported by and intimately related to both the most ephemeral and the most permanent aspects of existence. Man cooperates or interacts with the most massive and the most fragile and intricate structures, relations, and processes to generate his linguistic habits and decisions. So even if a person may on occasion deliberately invent a language, such invention is due ultimately to the fact that language is a possible form of cooperation not only among men themselves but also between the human and nonhuman dimensions of existence and more immediately to an actual and particular language which was not itself deliberately created. In fact it is impossible even to imagine the deliberate invention of linguistic rules or semantical decisions except on the foundations of an already existing language. And the only language that does not presuppose another as its point of departure is one that develops spontaneously out of the interrelations of man and the intelligible

[6] A. J. Ayer, *Concept of a Person and Other Essays*, London, Macmillan, 1963, p. 44.
[7] *Ibid.*, p. 63.
[8] Virgil C. Aldrich, "Reflections on Ayer's *Concept of a Person*," *The Journal of Philosophy*, Vol. LXII, March 4, 1965, pp. 116-117.

power and order of objective being. Language certainly does not create—though it no doubt increases as well as bears witness to —this intelligibility. That arbitrary rules, conventions, or capricious decisions about meanings constitute the foundations of language is inconceivable simply because the intelligible order of existence is in no sense a product of man-made rules or conventions.

Yet such conclusions about the relation of language and nature in no way or measure deny or put into question the free and deliberate use of language. Instead such conclusions simply and properly emphasize that freedom and significant decision are possible only in the context of intelligence supported by more or less orderly structures and processes. Free—even arbitrary and capricious—decisions are indeed made in regard to linguistic signs and symbols. But such decisions are plainly not made in a vacuum. Ultimately they must be squared with the various modes of judging, coherently and effectively, a perplexing and manifold world which is composed at least in part of intelligible structures and processes. Decisions concerning language, like any other complex and important decision, may have unexpected and critical results. Such decisions must therefore be made with equal prudence and care as must any choice that may radically affect the affairs of men. For although language is not so much the result as the instrument of free and deliberate decision, it is nonetheless man's most spontaneous and effective avenue to the intelligibility of nature (including many important facets of himself) and the chief support of his radical and indispensable freedom.

It is of course not only through language that man knows and judges. Ludwig Wittgenstein, in spite of his emphasis on language, recognized that meaning is more basic than language when he wrote: "Can I not say: a cry, a laugh, are full of meaning? And that means roughly: much can be gathered from them."[9] And surely if much can be gathered from them, much can also be conveyed by them. In religion, for example, language is obviously only one of several significant modes of judgment, although every mode of religious judgment is profoundly influenced by concepts, distinctions, and emphases which are possible only through lan-

[9] Ludwig Wittgenstein, *Philosophical Investigations*, trans. by G. Anscombe, New York, Macmillan, 1953, p. 146e.

guage. Except for language man would apparently never know and judge many of the things he does know and judge. And if it is an exaggeration to say that the rocks and streams speak to him, it is equally indefensible to deny that language is more than mere systems of pointers which identify and record the infinite details of an independent and sensible world. As both a product of nature and the means of giving accounts of nature, language is perhaps the most suggestive paradigm of the enduring puzzle that man is to himself. For anything that can be adequately defined or described is severely limited, a species that belongs to some category or other. But language as such, as Martin Buber has said of man, is surely an irreducible category—and in one sense the ultimate one, since it is only through language that one can begin to say what anything (including man or language itself) is. Like man, who, in saying what he understands himself to be, transcends what he says and can in fact be recognized for what he is only by another person and understood in no other way, a language can be comprehended only by someone already acquainted with language. So it was not without insight that the ancients identified *the word (logos)* with *reason* and *reason* with God.

Yet poor as the understanding of language is, and will perhaps always remain, surely not much reflection is necessary to recognize its critical role in practically all of man's efforts to judge, and in judging to alter, either himself or the conditions of his existence.

ON SIGNS, CONCEPTS, AND SYMBOLS

Language fails not because thought fails but because no verbal symbols can do justice to the fullness and richness of thought.
                                            JOHN DEWEY

No problem is more difficult or important than distinguishing clearly between animal and human judgment and between the various forms and functions of linguistic and closely related activities. At least some of the fundamental differences between the judicial powers of man and animal and between the dissimilar modes of judgment peculiar to man may be suggested by careful consideration of certain primary divergencies between signs, concepts, and symbols. Though there are no clear-cut boundaries, no established definitions, and no unambiguous conventions of use in regard to these terms, distinctive traditional meanings will nonetheless guide the development here.

A *sign* is any physical object or complex which stands for or points to—as a result of frequently preceding or succeeding— another object or complex, as clouds or thunder may stand for or point to rain, as the cry of an animal may indicate hunger or pain or fright, as the ringing of a bell may mean mealtime for a child or an animal, as a track in the snow may identify an animal species to a hunter, or as certain sounds and marks on paper may stand for one another and for symbols and concepts. Signs may occur as either elements in natural and presumably causal relations or as arbitrary conventions adopted for the sake of convenience. Animals obviously respond to many signs and so achieve highly satisfactory adjustments to very changeable circumstances. In some cases the signs and the responses are extremely complicated. But the most complicated of such signs and responses are limited temporally and spatially. A sign, in the strictest sense, belongs only to a particular time and place and serves primarily as the basis of inference from one event, complex, or situation to another. But it is also conventional signs, as well as symbols and concepts, which make possible the fact and record of man's theoretical discoveries and various discursive activities. For although words, numbers, and logical operations are essentially conceptual and symbolic, signs of some kind are to all appearances necessary in order to achieve or preserve concepts or symbols and their complex relations to one another.

Signs of many kinds are then extremely important in all of man's judicial activities; but his spiritual and intellectual, and therefore his deliberate, life plainly depends principally on his capacity for using concepts and symbols. *Concepts*, unlike signs, are not predominantly physical. Although perhaps invariably physical and signlike in one respect, concepts always transcend the temporal and spatial and belong to a mode of being that is singularly unaffected by the actual processes of matter and the most critical changes in human interest and fortune. The concept of *two*, for example, is in no sense identical with the physical elements (or signs) which are used to communicate it. *Two* may be spoken or written in ways that are infinitely various: two, 2, II, deux, in ink, in chalk, in the sand. But the concept, the meaning, transcends all the physical media and is by no means commensurable with the inferences about material processes and relations which knowledge of it may facilitate. Furthermore, the near and the far, the past and the future are equally amenable to being "present" in a concept. A concept is the intelligibility of structures, relations, and functions, both substantial and ideal, reflected or generated in the mind. Concepts, again unlike signs, do not necessarily stand for or point to something other than themselves. They are meanings or organizational principles and possibilities which may be either contemplated or utilized in practical, or theoretical judgments. Concepts are achieved, manipulated, and communicated in many different systems of signs or notations. But insofar as the reality apprehended or understood is essentially structural or relational as well as functional, each concept, no matter how complex, may be translated from one notation to many others without serious loss of meaning, although some notations are obviously more burdensome and inconvenient for certain purposes than others.

The languages of mathematics, the sciences, history, and philosophy are predominantly, though certainly not exclusively, conceptual. Redundant though it is to do so, concepts can perhaps be helpfully compared to blueprints and diagrams, which may represent the purely ideal as well as the actual and genuine possibilities. Any possibility of structure and relation is presumably subject to conceptualization.

It is customary, though not etymologically appropriate (since apparently *symballein* originally implied things simply *thrown together*), to refer to certain conceptual languages—especially the languages of logic, mathematics, and the sciences—as symbolic. But *symbols*, most distinctively and properly so-called are qualitatively and functionally quite different from concepts. Existence and particularly many of the most impressive aspects of human experience plainly cannot be exhaustively apprehended or communicated in conceptual terms or in terms of structures, relations, and quantitative changes or functions. Man's existence is pervaded by qualities, moods, attitudes, feelings, and convictions of worth which cannot be articulated, sustained, or shared through the calculi of formal concepts. A symbol most distinctively so-called is then a complex of conceptual and qualitative ingredients which may, by virtue of intrinsic or relational powers and habitual use, succeed in generating, expressing, or nurturing some one or a combination of the many values, moods, attitudes, and feelings possible in a community of persons. The qualitative dimensions of existence as well as the awe-full darkness that surrounds conceptual clarity on every side can be only symbolized, articulated, and made present in constructs, words, and actions which embody, generate, or sustain identifiable forms and instances of intense experience.

Through symbols, then, man confronts and judges dimensions of existence which neither signs nor concepts can make available or even suggest. A symbol, whether mythical, iconic, poetic, or musical, like a concept and unlike a sign, does not simply stand for or point to something other than itself but *is*. A symbol is a complex that may be apprehended or assimilated, a qualitative presence which has immeasurable but nonetheless unmistakable consequences in the continuum of experience and deliberate judgment by which man limits or makes more abundant certain selected elements of the world in which he must live. Symbols may be compared to specific tools—planes, levels, squares, musical instruments, pencils, paints, and brushes—designed to achieve certain distinctive and qualitative results in products.

In John Herman Randall's terms, symbols (which he mistakenly calls "noncognitive," though he clearly has very serious doubts about the term) have at least four different functions: (1) They "provoke in man an emotional response, and . . . produce results in conduct." (2) "They stimulate joint or cooperative activity." (3) They "communicate qualitative or 'shared' experience, experience that is difficult to put into precise words or statements." (4) They "can be said to 'disclose,' or 'reveal' something about the world in which they function."[10] But symbols, especially religious symbols, in addition to being both products and the means of distinctive judgments, may also inspire the creation of elaborate conceptual frameworks, even as the clear and precise conceptual systems may suggest new symbols for (as the poets express it) the infinitely dark and "turbid ebb and flow of human misery" and the "solemn silence" of the "radiant orbs." The religions and the arts, including the literary arts, are essentially, though not in all respects, symbolic.

Through concepts and symbols, even more so than by physical signs and powers, man directs himself and shapes his world. Through religious and political symbols—icons, persons, poems, flags, temples, songs, and phrases—men are united and directed (as well as divided and misdirected) in their attempts to judge all things appropriately. Symbols as well as concepts and signs inspired, guided, and troubled Columbus across the trackless ocean. Through concepts sustained and enriched by a symbolic vision of an actual and precisely rational order, Copernicus surmised that the sun is the center of the universe and Einstein concluded that the universe has no center. Signs, concepts, and symbols are no doubt equally but nonetheless distinctly indispensable in man's judicial activity.

Some psychologists have of course insisted that the difference between signs on the one hand and concepts and symbols on the other, and therefore between animal and human judgments, is basically only a degree of abstraction. This may be so. Yet the power of language to embody and convey meanings is not at all obviously proportional to its abstractness, as this claim implies, but is evidently due also to the diversity and the specific qualities of the signs and symbols employed. The evidence that animal communication is severely limited is not that the signs employed do not abstract from or distinguish a particular feature of complex situations but rather that the signs are univocal and limited in kind, quality, and number. Apparently animals do not employ con-

10 John H. Randall, Jr., *The Role of Knowledge in Western Religion*, Boston, Starr King Press, 1958, pp. 114-115.

cepts and symbols at all, and the ways in which they respond to signs are very limited in kind as well as temporally and spatially. All this may indeed be due finally to limited powers of abstraction. However, even if signs, concepts, and symbols differ only in degree, this difference is not fundamentally any less significant. A difference in degree may in fact amount essentially to a difference in kind. So granting the claim, a high degree of abstraction would take on the characteristics and importance that are here attributed to concepts and symbols.

But it is nonetheless highly doubtful that the difference is only one of degree. There is to all appearances an incommensurable dissimilarity between reacting more or less automatically to signs— a hound following the warm and exciting scent of the fox—and the deliberate creation of elaborate symbols and concepts—the poet composing a poem or the physicist formulating a theory. The hound merely exhibits his distinctive and essentially inalterable powers; but the poet and the physicist by exercising their own judicial capacities may modify both their own powers of judgment and the world that subsequently must be judged. For example, evidently Shakespeare's earliest works not only contributed to the development and intensification of his poetic insight, symbolic vision, and linguistic powers; but his total achievement also established new standards for English usage and dramatic judgment. And Galileo not only described motion with novel and highly successful concepts but at the same time provided new criteria for distinguishing fruitful hypotheses from the unfruitful, produced a theoretical structure that had itself to be judged in various ways, and instituted modes of judgment that have radically modified the world in which men must now live and judge.

Yet ultimately in spite of all they contribute to judicial powers and processes and whether they differ in kind or degree, signs, concepts, and symbols are themselves very much a part of the mystery of being. A person may use them and comment on their functions, though such comment is itself possible only through concepts and symbols. It seems clear, however, that neither concepts nor symbols always or simply *stand for* or *point to* something beyond themselves. They function in various, complex, and interrelated ways, enriching and supporting each other. And of course different symbols and concepts function differently and are inseparable not only from systematic science, formal religion, and self-conscious art but from all deliberate judgment. Through concepts and symbols, though not only through them, man refashions the world in which he must live. Character and experience generate concepts and symbols, and these in their turn may become fundamental in the experience that inspires other concepts and symbols. The first poet had of course never read or heard a poem, and the first theorist had only experience and imagination to guide him. But wide knowledge of our rich heritage of poetry and science is now the almost indispensable condition of significant poetic or scientific achievement.

ON LANGUAGE, QUANTITY, AND QUALITY

Physical science deals with things that can be weighed and measured, but this clearly does not mean the whole of reality.
E. N. DA C. ANDRADE

What we act for, suffer, and enjoy are things in their qualitative determinations.
JOHN DEWEY

Experience, the previous section has already suggested, may be very generally divided into two distinct but not obviously or wholly independent categories: the experience of quantity and the experience of quality. An alternative way of expressing this distinction is that some aspects of existence are measurable while others, nonetheless omnipresent, are clearly immeasurable. Shape, weight, and motion are notoriously and plainly measurable. But color, taste, beauty, melancholy, delight, and hope are qualitative and immeasurable. Although modern science has by and large assumed that quantity is basic and quality a derivative, and C. S. Peirce (among others) has argued persuasively that quality, no less than quantity, is a primary, underivable element of existence or among the basic "materials" that must be given or available in any world, the question of whether one of these categories is metaphysically basic and the other merely derivative or one causally significant and the other altogether irrelevant to the causal order of nature need not be discussed at the moment. Each is, in any case, an undeniable and distinct dimension of the experienced world.

The experience of the quantitative and qualitative are principally reflected in and promoted by conceptual and symbolic languages respectively. Yet probably no language deals exclusively with either quantity or quality. The essentially conceptual languages of the sciences, however, may be very generally regarded as accounts of the quantitative and relational (or measurable) aspects of things and events as they exist or are assumed to exist independent of any experience. The sciences may be more or less adequately described as systems of interrelated concepts which logically or mathematically describe, and perhaps anticipate, the recurring relations and behavior of the quantitative features of existence. But all concepts—the scientific as well as the artistic and religious—are equally products of insight and imagination and may be called scientific only insofar as their claims and implications are validated by experiments and observations. In other words, scientific languages presumably describe the characteristics of the physical, organic, mental, and social dimensions of existence to the extent that these can be articulated in mathematical and logical formulae and unembellished prose. Science is the conceptual envisagement of the recurring structural characteristics, relations, and processes in nature. Thus, anything that enters into experience may be studied scientifically more or less successfully.

But existence is obviously not simply a matter of shape, weight, motion, size, and the relations between such structural properties. Even as every experienced quality has some structural and at least theoretically measurable attributes, if only temporal extensity and relations, so qualities of experience impinge on and are reflected in the most resolute attempts to deal only with quantity. Yet the qualitative as such is most deliberately and emphatically sought and exploited and is judicially most effective in the various arts which systematically develop the symbolic, formal, and sensuous qualities of a particular language or other medium. To judge artistically is to make available to oneself or others an unprecedented complex of qualities and symbolic meanings which reveal and increase the aesthetic and judicial possibilities within the conditions of human existence. The arts describe, intensify, extend, and communicate the immense range of experience by articulating imaginative possibilities, including the symbolic and conceptual powers of structure and order as well as the formal and sensuous qualities of a medium. The artistic judgment or the subject of a work of art cannot then be separated from its qualitative character or excellence. The artist judges only by presenting, with all the symbolic and conceptual powers that belong to his perspective, the qualities of the object which he loves or abhors. Science may speak in dull, awkward, and indifferent language, and its conceptual truth will not seriously suffer; but when art stumbles or does not speak with care and passion, art fails.

The arts are of course concerned not only with the experienced qualities of objective structures, events, and relations but also with the moods, feelings, emotions, and passions of the inward man. In Sophocles' tragedy, *Oedipus the King*, the herdsman, when he is ready to make the terrible revelation of Oedipus' identity, says, "Ah me! I stand upon the perilous edge of speech." And Oedipus responds, "And I of hearing, but I still must hear." These words reflect, in a context of dreadful but uncompromising desire to see exactly how things are, the very aim and result of the arts. The artist is the most sensitive and perilous edge of judgment where man is revealed to himself. No matter what his medium, he uses it eloquently and incisively. Whether he seeks to delight with a creation of beauty or to reveal hypocrisy and ugliness he speaks directly to and for the perplexed spirit of man. The arts are appropriately called *the humanities* because they both nurture and communicate in symbolic terms the inward and invisible worlds of passion, imagination, and care: the immense joy and the overwhelming grief, the playful fantasy and the unending struggles—worlds and perspectives as various and unique as the persons who inhabit the earth. The arts reveal man to man.

Religion also takes seriously—perhaps even more seriously

than the arts—the qualitative and symbolic modes of judgment and demands of experience. But the development of this theme must wait until the next chapter.

ON JUDGMENT AND RATIONALITY

Physics, history, and poetry are cognitive in differ-
ent respects, not in different degrees.

JUSTUS BUCHLER

Indispensable as his symbolic and conceptual powers are, the life of man may nonetheless be characterized for special purposes by any of a number of unique activities and products. It is no less singularly (even though perhaps not universally) true, for example, that man cooks his food and wears clothes than that he worships and constructs elaborate theories. And also equally as distinctive of man as any unique activity is the fact that his most generic characteristics, if they may be called such, may be expressed in many different ways. Methods of preparing food, manners of dress, languages, ways of worship, and the modes of constructing theories and works of art are so diverse that the most deliberate judgments often seem more conducive to confusion and chaos than to order and stability. This, however, is only the price exacted by the fact that man is distinguished from the animals, not by the power of judgment itself, but rather by the great variety, scope, and character of his judgments.

Man judges by asserting, acting, and making; he judges inevitably, purposively, and freely; he judges instinctively, habitually, and deliberately. He comes into the world potentially able to assimilate from culture and experience manifold powers of inventing and manipulating tools, signs, concepts, and symbols so variously and uniquely that his world will never again be wholly the same. Judgment is essentially only the exercise of individual energies and capacities, powers evidently conditioned by both original structure and the assimilation from culture and experience, but nonetheless infinitely various and indeterminate.

How does this view of judgment differ from the traditional emphasis on the rationality of man? Judgment is of course much more inclusive and multiform than rationality, particularly as rationality has been conceived by many philosophical writers in recent years. Life itself must be regarded as essentially judicial. But by and large the advocates of rationality have lately insisted on the identity of conceptual thought and judgment or on the equivalence of logical thought and cognition. Inspired by the success of the necessarily reductive claims and methods of the natural sciences, many social scientists and psychologists, particularly since the middle of the nineteenth century, have supposed that genuine intelligence and reality itself are manifest in no other forms of judgment and so have dismissed many of their most challenging problems as products of cultural failure, neurosis, and illusion. And certain so-called philosophical empiricists have joined them in promulgating, especially during the second quarter of this century, such arbitrary criteria for distinguishing the "meaningful" from the "emotive" that, according to their standards, much of philosophy, most artistic products, and practically all religious and moral judgments are altogether devoid of "intellectual" meaning or ontological significance.

Thus there has been in recent years a virtual rash of philosophical denials (sometimes in the name of science, of course) of the cognitive and judicial character of all but the strictly conceptual and empirical (or scientific) enterprises. These have all claimed in one way or another that the arts, religions, and, for the most part, morals are products of emotion and illusion and not of cognitive or judicial capacities and methods. They have also generally absolved the intellect of all responsibility for catastrophe and tragedy. For the illusions are inevitable and the emotions blind, they claim, and the intellect a powerless and therefore innocent spectator. The tendency of artists and scientists to disclaim the moral relevance of their products and activities and the prevalence of strict determinism in social and psychological theories reflect this presumption that the judicial life of man is austerely limited to certain specific methods and products.

The emphasis on judgment as more inclusive than rationality so conceived only reaffirms that man's many activities are parts

of a unified life and includes the arts and religions in a conceptual
framework which can treat them as outcomes of the same experience and judicial capacities which, on other occasions and
differently employed, result in logical and scientific judgments.
The emphasis on judgment results in the claim that, between
science on the one hand and art, religion, and morals on the other,
the difference is not in the least that the one is cognitive (or
intellectual and reliable) and the others noncognitive (or emotive
and illusory) but only that they are different forms of achieving
and utilizing the judicial powers which may be variously employed
for determinate but infinitely dissimilar ends. So the emphasis on
judgment also includes the insistence that intellectual acuity may
certainly be evident not only in assertions which are logically
coherent or empirically verifiable but also in appropriate actions
and artistic products. Theory and practice or saying, doing, and
making are, to say the least, complementary, even though they
need not be equally important or equally possible to each individual in each situation. Even Aristotle, though he considered saying
(or theory) incomparably superior to making and doing, saw nevertheless that especially in morals and politics, practice and theory
can by no means be separated.

Indeed, to claim that poetry is purely emotive, or to praise
science by calling it alone cognitive, or to regard moral principles
as intrinsically either less rational or more divine than the principles of science and mathematics, requires distinctions which critical
inquiry neither demands nor supports. For none is on the face of it
either less dispensable or more effective and appropriate than each
of the others as a way of exploring and discovering the world
and making it more fit for man's habitation.

The judgments of science, art, religion, and morals are in fact
by no means completely independent of each other. For the
claims and products of any one may, for better or worse, influence
theory and practice in any one or all the others. Yet it is also true
that each may, at one time or place or for some persons, be the
dominant, if not the only, prevailing mode of judgment. In any
case the relations of each to the others are always potentially
complex and often obscure; and it is all too easy for persons who
favor one mode of judgment to miss, ignore, or at least to under-

estimate the momentous qualities and powers of the others. The scientist may not understand the poet, the poet may declare that the scientist sees nothing but the unimportant facts, and the moralist may be convinced that neither the scientist nor the poet is sufficiently aware of his proper and awesome responsibilities. The world in which we now live is indeed, in many respects, plainly a world built by men who often could not see, in spite of extraordinary intelligence and good will, the excellence of modes of judgment other than their own because their own seemed so compelling, wonderful, and exclusive.

Consequently in the contemporary world the most talented practitioners of art, religion, and science, when not openly hostile or condescending to one another, are often and in many ways encouraged to neglect all but their own disciplines. The scientist rarely takes the poet seriously and may smile at the credulity of saints and prophets; the poet shudders at the supposed inhumanity of the scientist and may wonder at the extraordinary seriousness of religion; while the prophet concludes that neither the artist nor the scientist is aware of the profound and inescapable affinity between his own judgments and religious ideals and commitments. The possible relevance of each and every form of experience and judgment to any judicious decision, which should be a basic premise of education, is sacrificed in the training of specialists whose loyalty to their own discipline is sometimes evident chiefly in the fact that they do not speak or understand but often despise the languages of other modes of inquiry and activity. And this on a planet now altogether too small for anything but generosity, patience, and mutual understanding.

Among the current critical problems, therefore, is that of introducing and maintaining a unity, not only between the diverse languages and methods of the various sciences (as so many philosophical writers now suppose), but also between the scientific, artistic, religious, and moral forms of discourse and judgment. Such a unity cannot be envisioned of course as a single or common language, method, or content but only as a respect for—if not a cultivated sensitivity to—the many ways in which highly dissimilar forms of judgment influence each other and are jointly employed to acquire and exchange insights, to increase control over nature, and to deepen the regard of men for the lives and interests of one another. For if nature is, as it surely seems, diverse in form and action, and if it is not only by one but rather several methods that man secures his perhaps brief but mighty ascendency in nature, then his knowledge can apparently never be more profound and comprehensive than his sensitivity to the manifold powers, functions, and qualities which inspire and sustain the different forms of judgment.

Although there are in any case evidently severe limits to what any man may assimilate and manipulate or know, the aspects of the world and his own existence that may be modified by his free and deliberate decisions are nonetheless infinite. Man is then clearly neither the pitiful victim nor even the potential master of circumstances. He is instead a creature whose endowment with the powers of diverse and capacious judgment redeems him in some measure from the tyranny of what is not himself. As long as life lasts nothing can alleviate the necessity of judgment. Yet nothing in the fact that judgment is pervasive and multiform forbids it to be also, in its relevance, scope, and variety, the chief glory and the greatest delight of man.

ON JUDGMENT, MYSTERY, AND DEPENDENCE

At the basis of the whole modern view of the world lies the illusion that the so-called laws of nature are the explanations of natural phenomena.
LUDWIG WITTGENSTEIN

There is nothing which we can totally create, predestine, or dispose.
JUSTUS BUCHLER

Man judges and knows, yet his existence is surrounded and pervaded by mystery; he is dependent on complex forces and conditions, yet he is radically free in the shaping of events to come.

If there are fundamental inconsistencies in these claims, they are only the inconsistencies which have plagued man's concern, inquiry, hope, and wonder since the beginnings of his reflective history. Nothing he has discovered suggests that any of these claims can be wholly disregarded when he seeks to understand himself or the world. He obviously judges deliberately, relevantly, and effectively. His achievements in the sciences and technology, his works of art, his splendid religious visions and monuments, his relatively stable governments and moral ideals and habits are eloquent, if not altogether consistent, witnesses to both his radical freedom and his immense judicial capacity. Yet mystery and dependence, much as many seek to deny or avoid them, are also inescapable and can be denied or ignored only by the refusal or the failure to part with cherished dogmas or to think seriously about the dark origins, the precarious tenure, and the ever-imminent threats to the existence of both mankind and the individual.

Mystery and dependence are very often denied, in effect if not in word, by equating both with ignorance and proclaiming with some scientists and philosophers that by extending the methods of the sciences, man's knowledge and power will ultimately become virtually unlimited. But such enthusiastic confidence in scientific method and inquiry is sustained only by ignoring both the circumstance that the modes of existence are radically dissimilar and so must be diversely judged, and that existence itself is utterly inexplicable—even though it may be the case that the present can be significantly described or accounted for by empirically discovered laws or in terms of what is known to have existed earlier. The foundation of science, however, is the concrete fact that *what is* is in fact what it is. And the fact of existence is not by any stretch of imagination subject to explanation. As William James said, "All of us are beggars here." One can say finally only that what exists does in fact exist.

So although knowledge is in many respects the key to power, and may be infinitely extended in a universe that is unlimited in one or more directions, man's knowledge can never be exhaustive and his power can at best only protect and enhance lives and conditions which it did not create. Innumerable aspects and details of existence now completely hidden may of course be discovered, and man's control over himself and his environment may be enormously extended as his knowledge and power increase. But like life, knowledge, and freedom, which ultimately are given and not necessarily secured or illumined by their own increase, mystery and dependence are also among the radically awesome and inescapable facts of existence. And evidently man himself, insofar as he may reflect in his own being the immensity of time and space as well as the marvelous companionship of both the infinitesimal and the astronomical, is equally as mysterious as the universe. Recent achievements have indeed made increasingly clear the fact that to know the potentiality of man is to know in many, if not all, respects the vast intricacies of the universe. And so to understand man fully is surely to all appearances an incommensurably more ambitious project than the exploration of the physical universe in all its amazing vastness.

Nonetheless, another, and perhaps more widely accepted, method of denying or evading the mystery of man's own distinctive character and conduct is to claim that special revelation (such as the doctrine of original sin) or universal laws (such as the dialectics of reason and history or of sex and the subconscious) explain and prescribe his behavior in all circumstances. Although the appeal to both special revelation and universal law may be in important respects legitimate accounts, when cautiously used, of the fact and character of experience and presumed knowledge, ultimately neither, to say the least, is less mysterious than the facts it supposedly explains. Appeals to either revelation or ubiquitous law, indiscriminately employed, instead of elucidating immediate and particular problems, only conceal, in the name of either a remote and uncertain revealer or a dull abstraction, the luminous and awesome diversity of the infinite facts which surround and include man. Thus overly ambitious and highly speculative science and philosophy as well as religious movements which emphasize the certainty of their so-called revealed truths may effectively, uselessly, or even tragically hinder or destroy the sense of wonder and freedom at the heart of man's existence.

A parallel, though perhaps paradoxical, method of denying dependence is to identify one's own will or all events with supreme and universal power, whether that of God or nature, or to conceive of one's own existence and conduct as necessary elements in a thoroughly comprehensible and noncontingent universe. Such schemes in effect annul not only the freedom but also the meaning and purpose of all individual and personal judgment. For clearly the individual life can have its own meaning and purpose only to the extent that power is limited and distributed, and freedom can be other than mere appearance only if some events are radically contingent on personal choice or decision. The distribution of power and the determination of action by choice, as prerequisites of freedom, are no less sound as metaphysical than as political principles.

Still another common way of denying or ignoring the specific and extraordinary significance of both mystery and dependence is to regard them as the only pervasive and important aspects of the human condition. Both consistent theists and thoroughgoing materialists, such as Saint Augustine and George Santayana respectively, have of course agreed that ultimately and essentially nothing other than complete dependence and categorical mystery can be finally asserted with certainty. But such emphasis on the contingent and mysterious is clearly and inexcusably paradoxical insofar as it is bound to put into unresolvable question both the judicial capacity and the freedom of man. If the ways of God or the ways of nature are wholly inscrutable, and if man never directs and controls his own affairs in any measure, all explanations are equally superfluous and no existential import can be claimed for either individual intelligence or for the laudable and persistent intellectual and moral choices which apparently men must make. Furthermore, that existence is wrapped about with mystery is simply a fact; but obviously this fact implies or effectively explains nothing other than that a man may sometimes stand face to face with mystery.

Mystery itself is never present as sheer darkness and in ignorance, however, but only as the context of knowledge. Where some things are clear, there and there alone can mystery also appear. Explanation begins with particular facts and relations. And although dependence is always inseparable from specific facts and relations (as mystery is not, since ultimately no fact is any less involved in mystery than another) such facts and relations support as well as limit the effectiveness of the individual's judicial power and action. The very same circumstances that make freedom possible may also limit freedom in any particular context, even as the air not only sustains but also resists the bird in its flight. So no man is absolutely free. For dependence and independence are always relative and complementary. Each in its own way is an element of the necessary conditions (which include limits, whether definite or indefinite, temporary or permanent, as well as opportunity or openness) for the effective use of the specific instruments and processes of judgment by which a man shapes and becomes responsible for certain selected structures and qualities of the world in which he must live.

Yet ultimately of course logic does not compel one to admit that either religion, science, or metaphysics must take mystery or even man's curious combination of freedom and dependence seriously as significant ontological fact. Surely many highly successful enterprises in religion, as well as in science and philosophy, proceed as if no important matters ever escape the current complex of methods, instruments, and aims which they employ. And in any case to underestimate or deny judicial powers is by no means necessarily a lesser error than the assumption that all notable truths (or at least the methods of their attainment) have already been discovered. It may indeed be the case that the paradoxical combination of freedom and dependence which makes the life of man so problematical—so irrevocably solitary and yet no man an island—is only apparent and that both freedom and dependence belong ultimately to a single rational order which, when properly understood, renders both terms either meaningless or else wholly compatible with one another.

Yet the acknowledgment that mystery and dependence are apparently inescapable, although perhaps logically irreconcilable with each other and with freedom, is at least for the time being a partial, if not invulnerable, defense against the dangers of the blind and presumptuous enthusiasms which so often accompany not only the belief that truth and justice are now finally attained but also the claim that they are only fictions. It can hardly be denied at all, however, that to many intelligent men—even to some who have elaborated theories which ultimately imply the contrary

—man's life has appeared both profoundly mysterious and yet subject to effective, though limited, direction by judgment; and his ultimate dependence has seemingly been mitigated by genuine, if not absolute, freedom.

The Mystery of Existence by Milton Munitz appeared after the present work was essentially complete. His conclusion, however, is strikingly similar to the theme of this section:

> The mystery of existence occupies a position in our efforts to come to terms, philosophically, with the world at large, that is, in some respects, similar to the fact of death, in our efforts to come to terms with the conditions of our own individual life. Each, in its own way, marks the impenetrable boundary that defeats our deepest longings: the one marks the limit to any hope of understanding the existence of the world; the other marks the limit to our hope of finding endless satisfaction in all that we achieve in life. Out of the refusal to acknowledge the first type of limit are born on the one hand those metaphysical schemes that would—in one way or another—penetrate the abysmal mystery of existence and solve it. Out of the other, are born all those religious schemes that promise eternal salvation or immortality to the person. Such systems of thought betray, all too clearly, the attempt to circumvent the genuine limits to human knowledge and aspiration, by indulging in what is, after all, only a fancied perfection and a false idealism. They cannot inspire confidence in their solutions.
>
> A more responsible and candid philosophy would start by acknowledging the facts of the mystery of existence and the final defeat that awaits us in our personal death.[11]

I do not myself think that enough is known about the complex and mysterious relations between mind and body to argue, contrary to the hopes and convictions of so many, that death is certainly "the final defeat that awaits us." Indeed, the categorical assertion that death is the final defeat of the individual, no less than dogmatic doctrines of immortality, must deny or ignore the mystery of existence. This seems to me much sounder philosophy nonetheless than *any* dogmatic defense of particular forms and means of survival. As Socrates recognized, we cannot guide our

---

[11] Milton Munitz, *The Mystery of Existence*, New York, Appleton-Century-Crofts, 1965, pp. 262-263.

lives or defend our actions in terms of the possibilities we confront in death; yet the mind, when it regards itself candidly, appears to itself, as he also thought, independent and capable of surviving the separation (or death) of the body.

But tragedy apparently haunts and ennobles the very best of man's days only because man is presumably both free and mortal; for tragedy occurs when freedom is crushed by its very own hand in the terribly complex circumstances in which judicial powers and instruments must seek their own extension. If the actual life and death of Socrates, for example, or the dramatic life of Antigone as presented by Sophocles, must be called tragic, it is primarily because to all appearances the situation required each, in passing judgment *freely* and *rightly*, to choose death—a final defeat—in order that greater freedom and justice might eventually become the judges of men. And Galileo was tragically imprisoned for teaching a more comprehensive version of the truth about the physical world, not principally, if at all, because men are basically perverse, but because the freedom to judge is always so much greater than the understanding of the proper uses and consequences of the various modes of judgment. Tragedy must be endured and even admired because freedom and judgment bounded by dependence and mystery, and perhaps ultimate defeat, are the generic, if infinitely mutable, aspects of man's career in the world. But only through freedom and judgment, which must sometimes run the risk of overwhelming and irreparable tragedy, can the life of man be guided into ways more rewarding than the splendid ways already found.

2

On Philosophy and Religion

Seeing there are no signs, nor fruit of religion,
but in man only; there is no cause to doubt,
but that the seed of religion, is also only in
man; and consisteth in some peculiar quality,
or at least in some eminent degree thereof,
not to be found in any other living creature.
                                    THOMAS HOBBES

ON PHILOSOPHICAL JUDGMENT

In the beginning, the Gods did not show to man
all he was wanting; but in the course of time, he
may search for the better and find it.
                                    XENOPHANES

Philosophy is primarily the attempt to discover judicial premises or to formulate basic principles, which are both conceptually
and symbolically adequate, or to judge in terms that take proper
account not only of pervasive structural and relational properties
but also of the intense qualitative character and demands of experience.

In the most general terms, philosophy asks fundamental questions and attempts to give at least tentative answers to them. And
fundamental questions are presumably those which ask about the
basis and character of all existence, knowledge, and choice. Philosophical questions are then the most inevitable, the simplest, and
the most radical, even though most men do perhaps succeed in not

thinking at all philosophically. For basically philosophy demands only clear and candid examination and decision concerning the difference between appearance and reality, knowledge and opinion, good and evil, right and wrong. And perhaps nothing is easier than to assume that common sense opinions in these matters—opinions inherited from parents, church, and intellectual traditions—are sound and do not need to be critically examined. Yet the entire history of human progress—if we may speak of progress at all— in religion and politics no less than in science and technology, is largely the result of changes which originated at least in part in the deliberate examination and rejection of long-established opinions about the way the world is.

In slightly different terms, philosophy as the pursuit of wisdom may be called the search for the proper combination of love and knowledge in the life of man, individually and collectively. The history of philosophy, though surely it includes much else, is essentially a record of the discoveries and recommendations of extraordinary men concerning the fundamental principles of knowledge and the proper objects of love. All else in philosophy flows from the discoveries or convictions about these two fundamental matters. Thus, in its many highly dissimilar and historically most distinctive forms, philosophy is systematic inquiry and creative argument which seek, first, to discover and articulate the basic conceptual premises in accordance with which such activities as social and political life, the economy, religion, art, and science do and can proceed; and secondly, to promote, protect, and enhance certain qualities that are always in danger of being overlooked or sacrificed in the pursuit of specific ends such as political harmony, economic abundance, or the accuracy and clarity of abstract principles.

Philosophy attempts, it may be said, to embody in judgment the rigor and accuracy of the sciences, the qualitative vision of the arts, and the intense concern for the quality of life itself which has often characterized religious commitments. So philosophy may perhaps best be described as an inconclusive, if not endless, dialogue (as it was in Plato) between the manifold claims of experience: the dialogue of the self as scientist (biologist, physicist, or psychologist) with the self as artist (poet, painter, or musician); the dialogue of the self as a citizen of a particular state with the self as a member of mankind; the dialogue of the self conditioned by the particularities of time and place with the self aware of other times and places and eternity; the dialogue of the self that observes, reasons, and doubts with the self that believes and acts.

Thus philosophy is always criticism or interpretation of one aspect of experience in the light of another: the criticism of science in the light of religious and artistic experience, and the criticism of religion and art in the light of scientific discoveries and social needs. It is surely true, as Whitehead claimed, that "One aim of philosophy is to challenge the half-truths constituting the scientific first principles."[1] But it is equally true and no less important that philosophy may also challenge all the half-truths generated when it is supposed that one form of experience—whether sensory, rational, aesthetic, mystical, religious, scientific, or artistic—is an altogether privileged or extraordinary avenue to the character of all that is *real*. In the pursuit of adequacy in conceptual and symbolic judgment, philosophy is potentially the critic of all ideas and all institutions, including especially those that philosophy itself produces and defends.

It is often said that philosophy begins in wonder. No doubt it does, but not more so than poetry or science. And wonder results in specifically philosophical activities and products only when men discover or create more or less elaborate conceptual and symbolic systems to describe, interpret, originate, or enhance experiences which in some measure satisfy both logical and qualitative needs, or the demands of both knowledge and love. As some have noted, philosophy also ends in wonder no less than the wonder with which it begins. For man's conceptual and symbolic needs and demands, in spite of amazing achievements and ever-increasing powers, seem always to outrun or extend beyond his accomplishments.

[1] A. N. Whitehead, *Process and Reality*, New York, Macmillan, 1929, p. 15.

ON PHILOSOPHY AND RELIGION

Beware when God lets loose a thinker on the world . . . for all things then have to rearrange themselves.

WILLIAM JAMES

Although they are not always entirely distinct, *philosophy of religion* may and should be carefully distinguished from *religious philosophy.*

Much important and purely philosophical inquiry has of course begun as the attempt of individuals to account for their religious experience or to justify the claims and practices of a particular religious tradition. This, however, is evidence, not of any special relation between philosophy and religion, but simply of the fact that the religious experience is often dominant and highly valued among men. Nevertheless many contemporary philosophers regard religion as philosophically irrelevant, if not the very antithesis of genuine philosophical activity; and much religion remains altogether innocent, if not contemptuous, of philosophy. Even the philosopher who takes religion most seriously often does not and need not consider the fundamental principles of religion philosophically basic or indispensable; and the religionist who employs philosophical methods in the defense of religion may still insist, and quite rightfully, that religious principles are in certain basic respects prior to and independent of their philosophical justification.

Thus the interpretation or criticism of religion from a conceptual and nonreligious perspective or the attempt to discover the generic traits of religion and its place in the total pattern of value and culture may be most appropriately called *a philosophy of religion.* And the interpretation or criticism of conduct, inquiry, belief, and value—whether social, scientific, philosophical, or artistic —in terms and categories derived from a religious perspective or tradition is *a religious philosophy.* There are of course many varieties of both the philosophy of religion and religious philosophy.

Yet the philosophy of religion, compared with either religion itself or even philosophy, is a relatively recent development. Among the Greek philosophers there was little that may be accurately called philosophy of religion, although there were many significant speculations and arguments concerning the nature of piety, the immortality of the soul, and the existence and nature of the divine, themes that are now regarded, more or less correctly, as essentially problems for the philosophy of religion. Much of philosophy, however, was pervaded by religious qualities, and many philosophers rejected "mysteries" and "myth" in the name of philosophic reason. Yet the Greek philosophers regarded religion largely as a matter of ritual, not of doctrine or belief, and so made no sharp distinctions between what are now called religious themes or questions and other philosophic issues. Questions of the existence and nature of the divine and the immortality of the soul, for example, took their place alongside questions about the nature of knowledge, justice, and beauty; all these questions were approached with equal confidence that extended inquiry would bring unambiguous answers.

In the medieval world, where philosophy was clearly subordinate to religion, religious philosophy rather than philosophy of religion was the concern of the more speculative and profound minds. Although the idea was nurtured that certain problems are exclusively religious and others predominantly philosophical, it was also thought that outside the religious perspective no question is fully intelligible or answerable. If philosophy is to achieve its primary aim of giving a comprehensive and judicious interpretation of all experience and existence, said the medieval philosophers, it can do so only from the vantage point of a religious perspective.

But the Renaissance and the subsequent intellectual developments which brought about the success of seventeenth- and eighteenth-century science and made the problem of knowledge the dominant and a critical issue in philosophy also brought religious claims into serious question. By the end of the seventeenth century, it was no longer unquestionably sufficient among the intel-

lectually inquisitive to have a religion or a religious philosophy
or to construct a philosophy on the explicit but unsubstantiated
premise that any comprehensive view of existence must be religious. Increasingly it appeared necessary either to reconcile religion with the new scientific methods and discoveries or to confine
religion to the claims and principles presumably discovered by
"unaided natural reason." In the eighteenth century David Hume
suggested, more forcefully than anyone else perhaps, that religious
doctrines and especially the claims of the so-called "rational religion" are not less dubious—even if no less inevitable—than other
fantastic and unproved claims. The sceptical but nonetheless
sensitive and sensible Hume observed that although men without
any religion are little better than brutes[2] there can be no reasonable confidence concerning the truth of religious claims in regard
to such nonempirical matters as miracles, the existence and nature
of God, the immortality of the soul, and the origin of the world.
Hume's sceptical reasoning, if not wholly impeccable, was surely
rigorous and uncompromising, though he was himself gentle and
profoundly tolerant towards the different religious claims generated,
he thought, by imagination and desperate need.

In a world in which science was inspiring the confidence, no
matter how unjustified, that with time and the extended use of
methods and principles already discovered all questions would
be answered from the scientific perspective and in the precise
language of science, religious philosophies were no longer the
fashion, even though there were many whose religious faith was
essentially unaltered. But religion was intellectually on the defensive, where by and large it still remains. And the philosophy of
religion, as a critical attempt to fit the religious experience and
claims into broader contexts, soon became largely an effort to
conceive religion in such a manner that its claims would not
conflict with the principles and facts discovered by the sciences.
This effort, apart from new and elaborate attempts to discover
the "reason" in religion itself, took two extreme forms. On the

[2] "A maxim that is proverbial and confirmed by general experience: Look
out for a people, entirely destitute of religion: If you find them at all, be
assured that they are but few degrees removed from brutes." David Hume,
The Natural History of Religion, Sec. XI. There are several good editions of
this work, first published in 1757.

one hand was the thesis of the religious philosophers (inspired primarily by Descartes but also by certain aspects of the writings of St. Thomas Aquinas) that science and religion are concerned with two utterly different realms of existence and cannot possibly conflict with each other. On the other hand (inspired by the exciting theoretical achievements of the sciences) was the attempt by both philosophers and scientists to explain or to explain away the many forms of religion as products of ignorance, fear, and superstition, or the symptoms of unhealthy economic, cultural, or neural conditions. Holbach, Comte, Marx, and Freud are only the most notorious names in this tradition.

Such approaches to religion are of course still current; but they will not receive direct attention here. Instead, the presumption of the present context is that both science and religion are essentially and equally obvious and irreducible forms of man's possible and enduring judgments of both the objective world and his own experience; and that any aspect of pluralistic existence may, though it does not necessarily, influence any other. Consequently it would be incongruous to insist either that religion is altogether independent of the principles and facts disclosed by the sciences or that science can explain religion away as a product of noncognitive emotions or undesirable cultural conditions. Both science and religion are in a sense products of culture. But this by no means implies that either is reducible to something else, is other than a way of judging and modifying certain aspects of existence, or is devoid of either cognitive or emotional elements. And it is not clear, to say the least, that religious claims and values are either more or less permanent or more or less important than scientific claims and values.

Historically considered, science and religion alike are always obviously subject to critical examination and revision. The claims and values of both, at least in their particular manifestations, are constantly changing. At the heart of both, unrealistic hopes and proposals aside, is plainly, not the revelation of complete and eternal truth, but success in the continuous processes of exploration and judgment. And although in the final analysis religion and science are perhaps each its own best critic, it is also evidently the case that independent criticism—including not only scientific and philosophical study of religion but also religious and philosophical speculation, critically employed, in regard to the basic character and implications of scientific claims and possibilities —may help to discover the relations of each to all the other aspects of existence and to clarify values or identify dangers which the most zealous practitioners of each may otherwise miss altogether.

But even though neither science nor philosophy can ever wholly explain religion or even altogether adequately describe its characteristic forms, functions, and values, religion can hardly expect to escape the profound effects of modern scientific and philosophic inquiries, even as it also cannot escape the general increase of knowledge or the influence of particular social and economic factors. But this need not imply at all that religion is not now fundamentally important as a mode of judgment. It means only that the context within which religion now exists, and therefore its specific manifestations and functions, will be in important respects different from the context and specific character of ancient Jewish, Greek, Medieval, or Reformation religion. No matter how deeply relevant the recorded experience of the past may be to the problems faced by contemporary man, his world is now immensely complicated by conceptual schemes, methods of inquiry, knowledge of facts, and modes of action which were not only unknown but impossible and even unimaginable in earlier cultures. Consequently any attempt to understand or reconstruct religion solely in terms of its great historical forms and symbols must not only repudiate the faults and limits but also the values which belong to man's increased knowledge and success in dealing with himself and his environment.

Why indeed should any human interest or enterprise stand or fail solely on the merits of its historical record? Both the successes and the failures of the past have obviously been much too varied and ambiguous to be wholly reliable guides for the present. A religious heritage may of course be of extraordinary importance, in spite of the fact that nothing is genuinely valuable simply because it has been inherited from the past. For no one actually shares and understands his heritage except as he also shares and comprehends the immensely complex problems of his contemporaries, and finds in the artifacts and documents of the past signs, symbols, and concepts in terms of which he can pass discriminating and effective judgment on the present. Unless we perceive that there are religious needs in our own times, and that these are somehow continuous with the past, the religious commitments or judgments of historical persons and cultures are bound to seem only the symptoms of disorder or the products of ignorance, fear, and superstition.

Therefore the philosophy of religion must seek, not simply to grasp or elucidate the meanings of certain ancient and esoteric scriptures or to offer arguments for the basic premises of particular religious traditions and claims, but to examine the various forms and functions of religious judgment in order to discover its generic characteristics and most important powers or to describe the most significant ways in which religion may in fact further or, as the case may be, hinder the judicial life of man. The varieties of religion and religious judgments should then prove no stumbling block to—though they may surely complicate—philosophical inquiry into religion. For the fact that religious judgments have generic characteristics is by no means contradicted by the variety of particular forms and functions, which are apparently due in part at least to the infinitely mutable circumstances, needs, and powers of individual persons and communities. Though all men share, as George Santayana said, the same sky, they do not share the same soil, speak the same language, suffer the same ills, cherish the same ends, or understand equally the many forces which sustain and destroy the life of man. And if religion speaks, as it seems to do, to and about the problems and values of man's complex qualitative needs and circumstances, there need be no labored attempt to account for the fact that *una est religio in rituum varietate* or that the perspectives, symbols, concepts, and actions which are religiously appropriate and effective at one place and time are not necessarily so in another.

The philosophy of religion as an attempt to discover and articulate the generic forms and functions of religion and the relation of religion to other forms of experience, judgment, and

value must not be blinded or misled by the unique appeal of
any particular age or tradition. Religion in its many forms, at
its worst as well as at its best, must be included in the phenomena
described.

ON THE PROBLEMS IN DEFINING RELIGION

In the garden of Eden Adam saw the animals be-
fore he named them.
                                              A. N. WHITEHEAD

The problems in defining religion are notorious and have
been notably increased by the failure to distinguish the generic
or universal characteristics of religion from the particular claims
and activities of specific religions. Most religious philosophies and
many philosophies of religion have indeed suffered greatly from
the failure to define religion unequivocally or without seeking by
the definition itself to influence all subsequent judgments of the
nature and value of religion. Of course completeness and strict
objectivity are both evidently impossible. But definitions of religion tend to be either altogether unnecessarily honorific or highly
derogatory.

Men who are deeply religious or sensitive and sympathetic
only to a particular form of religion generally define religion in
such a way that to call a person *religious* is the epitome of praise.
Even John Stuart Mill, though he was unusually circumspect and
critical of the various forms of question begging, as well as of
traditional forms of religion, claimed that "The essence of religion
is the strong and earnest direction of the emotions and desires
toward an ideal object, recognized as of the highest excellence and
as rightfully paramount over all selfish objects of desire."[3] This
definition, besides being so vague that it might be taken as an
equally good definition of either moral character or romantic

[3] J. S. Mill, *Nature and Utility of Religion*, New York, Liberal Arts, 1958,
pp. 71-72.

love, suffers most gravely from what A. N. Whitehead has called
the "dangerous delusion" that religion is beneficent[4] or "the uncritical association of religion with goodness."[5] Such definitions
are always unempirical, idealistic, and normative; instead of increasing the understanding of the varieties and powers of religious
values and judgments, they exclude from the category of religion
all activities, beliefs, and values which do not conform to specific
ideal requirements. Other examples obviously of this type include
F. H. Bradley's claim that "Religion is . . . the attempt to express
the complete reality of goodness through every aspect of our
being,"[6] and E. S. Ames' description of religion as the "conserva-
tion of the highest values" or the "consciousness of the highest
social values."[7] Although such judgments do not miss their mark
entirely, they clearly do not take account of the many forms
and facets of religion objectively regarded.

On the other hand are those who, completely disenchanted
with both the actual and the ideal in religion, offer definitions
which, if accepted, would persuade everyone of its nonjudicial
or even malicious character. "Religion is the opiate of the people"
and religion is a "delusional transformation of reality" are perhaps
the best known examples, endorsed by Marx and Freud respectively, of disparaging descriptions which, though not necessarily
any more inaccurate than the laudatory, are in some respects
even less reliable as guides to the actual character and functions
of religion. For in spite of the obvious and pernicious effects of
even the most idealistic credulity, the course of history, intellectual
as well as social and political, makes it fairly clear that it is
better—more conducive to discovery and peace—to err, since err
we must, on the side of charity rather than on the side of a
stringent lack of sympathy and imagination. Even the most

[4] A. N. Whitehead, *Religion in the Making*, New York, Meridian Books,
Living Age Books, 1960, p. 17.
[5] *Ibid.*, p. 36.
[6] F. H. Bradley, *Appearance and Reality*, New York, Macmillan, 1899, p.
453. Bradley is even more specific on the essentially moral character of religion
in *Essays on Truth and Reality*, Oxford, Oxford University Press, 1914, p. 442,
where he says, "everywhere religion must be taken as the completion and
fulfillment of what is moral."
[7] E. S. Ames, *The Psychology of Religious Experience*, Boston, Houghton
Mifflin, 1910, pp. vii-viii.

derogatory of definitions may of course have some value; but fortunately such definitions generally, as C. D. Broad has said, "wear too jaundiced a complexion to inspire complete confidence."

The first requirement of a philosophical definition of religion is, then, that it should be neutral or in itself neither religious nor irreligious and neither praising nor blaming an undeniable and persistent feature of culture and experience. It may be that religion, properly regarded, is altogether praiseworthy or wholly execrable, though more probably it includes both much to acclaim and much to damn. But the facts, whatever they are, must surely not be accepted in the light of uncircumspect and premature definition.

Almost as frequent as the laudatory and disparaging forms of definition, and not often independent of the one or the other, is the practice of defining religion either so narrowly that it includes only the members of a particular group, creedal or ritualistic, or so broadly that religion is held to be an attribute of every person, no matter what his beliefs and activities. For example, the popular conception of religion (among both its friends and foes) as "belief in the existence and providence of God," implying as it usually does a particular concept and image of the divine, is so narrow that it excludes certain high and established religions such as Hinayana Buddhism, many primitive practices almost invariably called religious, and the professed religion of many contemporary humanists who explicitly deny that religion or the religious experience is in any sense equivalent to or demanding of belief in the existence of God. The claim that religion is inseparable from belief in the existence of God must be examined more carefully later. But for the moment at least it must be included among the too narrow concepts which commit what has been called the "nothing but" fallacy and are equally vulnerable whether they identify religion with opiates, superstition, delusion, fear, feeling of dependence, morality, or any other single emotion or conviction about or attitude towards existence. For religions, as the most cursory critical survey should make clear, are at least among the most complex and various of phenomena.

On the other hand, sophisticated definitions in particular are frequently so broad that they identify religion with the deliberate and honest pursuit of any value in any manner and make it virtually impossible for any person to claim truly that he is not religious. Peter A. Bertocci's claim, for example, that religion is "the personal belief that one's most important values are sponsored by, or in harmony with, the enduring structure of the universe. . . ."[8] would include practically everyone, excepting only those too young or too stupid to have any beliefs about values; for even those who deny the universal relevance of their own values do not deny that such values, in their particular context and whatever their ultimate ontological status, are in harmony with the universe. The Marxist no less than the Christian claims that his values are supported by and in harmony with the enduring structure of the universe, though he dismisses religion as the opiate of the people. And the scientists and philosophers who regard religion as the product of illusion, fear, or neurosis would certainly insist that their own values are nonetheless fundamentally important and grounded in the actual and perennial character of the universe. Nor will it do to say that the Marxist, or the scientist and the philosopher, have altogether inadequate concepts of religion and are consequently religious without knowing it. For although there may be some noteworthy truth in this claim, the person who rejects religion may surely know what he denies as well as the most candid religionist knows what he affirms.

Religion, in spite of the claims of intelligent men to the contrary, is clearly not simply identical with the pursuit of value or with certain convictions about the nature of value. For value is obviously in many respects a much broader category than religion, and it is necessary at least to distinguish religious values from artistic, ethical, scientific, and economic values, even though it must be admitted that none of these is ever completely free of the influence of the others. All values are presumably products, in some sense, of universal forces and circumstances or of the enduring character of the universe. Surely then one may believe that his values, whatever they are, are in harmony with the universe without being religious in any traditional or concrete manner. And one may also deny that the highest values have

8 Peter Bertocci, *Introduction to the Philosophy of Religion*, New York, Prentice-Hall, 1951, p. 9.

anything in common with the enduring structure of the universe as a whole and yet be religious in the sense that he participates, honestly and enthusiastically, in practices that are clearly religious but seek only some local and immediate good.

Those who define religion in terms which are either too narrow or too broad contribute very little, if at all, to a philosophical understanding of it. At best they only bear witness to the character, the values, or the faults of a particular form or function of religion; and at worst they may cause others to miss its most characteristic and commendatory powers and values. So the second requirement of a definition of religion is that it must be broad enough to include all actions, assertions, products, and situations commonly and historically called *religious* but yet narrow enough to recognize the meaning of both *irreligious* and *nonreligious* as terms which may accurately describe certain persons, claims, objects, and situations. A definition of religion which is neither eulogistic nor derogatory, and neither too broad nor too narrow, will not beg the question of its value but will acknowledge that religion per se is neither high and noble nor perverse and dogmatic, neither the greatest good nor simply a fanciful panacea for the desperate ills of mankind.

ON FAITH AND RELIGION

Now faith is the substance of things hoped for, the evidence of things not seen.

SAINT PAUL

. . . without some credulity science itself would crumble and collapse.

BERTRAND RUSSELL

Faith, no matter what its object or how it is expressed, is often said to be the defining characteristic of religion. And because faith is sometimes almost totally blind and absolutely tenacious, religion is often equated (by its critics) with any form of credulity or fanaticism or (and even by its defenders) with conscientious loyalty or devotion to any cause.

Yet religion obviously has no monopoly on either faith or devotion or on tenacity, credulity, and fanaticism whether in the service of extraordinary hopes and expectations or in the name of necessity. As Justus Buchler has observed:

> Faith, in some minimal sense, is part of all query and all validation, even the surest and most advanced like pure mathematics. Faith, whatever its species, is relative confidence in what is unknown or unavailable—belief that a judgment beyond the pale of present validation, at best escaping from us Tantalus-fashion, is valid.[9]

To have faith is then to rest in, or proceed on, the premise, whether implicit or explicit, that at least for the time being and in regard to a particular and important situation, claim, or action, further doubt or inquiry is either not necessary or not possible.

Consequently it may be said that a life of deliberate judgment, in every feature and moment, involves an elemental and inevitable residue of faith. This faith may be enlightened—the luminous climax of penetrating inquiry and criticism—or simply credulous and unexamined. Scientist, artist, businessman, poet, and prophet are one and all committed to first principles or axioms which are beyond the immediate reach of proof. Such principles are not necessarily self-evident, even as they are not the direct result of inquiry or reason. The fact that the moment or situation requires them guarantees neither their truth nor their permanence. Yet they are inescapable in the sense that thorough and perpetual doubt is catastrophic for thought, action, and life itself.

The late P. W. Bridgman, physicist and philosopher of science, wrote about the first principles and methods of scientific inquiry that:

> In the end, when we come to the place where human weariness and shortness of life force us to stop analyzing our operations, we are pretty much driven to accept our primitive operations on the basis of a feeling in our bones that we know what we are doing.[10]

[9] Justus Buchler, *Towards a General Theory of Human Judgment*, New York, Columbia, 1951, pp. 164-165.

[10] P. W. Bridgman, *The Way Things Are*, Cambridge, Harvard, 1959, p. 44.

If it is possible to quarrel at all with this candid admission, it is chiefly with the assumption that if life were only more energetic and longer we might then escape, through more thorough analysis, the necessity of accepting or trusting our "primitive operations." To all appearances, however, it is not only "human weariness and shortness of life" but the very structure of existence and judgment that requires such faith. If it is fair to say that all claims neither deductively demonstrable nor verifiable by the senses must be in some measure accepted on faith, then much of science as well as much of religion, philosophy, and politics is a matter of some degree of faith. The most careful analysis is itself made possible only, though surely not wholly, by *faith* in the methods and products of analysis. Some men may succeed in not being religious or scientific, as the case may be, but none can avoid faith. Yet in terms of their distinctive features, neither religion nor science can be described simply as a faith. Both appeal finally and fundamentally to *theoria* (to a characteristic vision of the way the world is) but inevitably include the faith that the vision is not simply an ephemeral appearance.

Religious persons often insist, however, that religious faith is unique, or that the most critical matters are ignored when religious faith is compared to the various forms of trust or confidence which, they admit, characterize the sciences, the arts, and common sense. Religious faith, they insist, is inseparable from the structure and content of the faith. This argument, though surely not irrelevant, in effect only reaffirms faith in the supremacy of the religious modes of judgment. For if religious judgment necessarily involves distinctive forms and combinations of belief and hope, or extraordinary trust in the qualities of vision, character, and action demanded by the prophet, or perhaps in the presumably beneficent but unfathomable order of the cosmos, the scientist exhibits a no less necessary and distinctive faith in the perceptive and logical powers he and his peers possess, or in the relevance of his methods and judgments to the enduring and intelligible order of certain facts, processes, and relations. The fact and uniqueness of religious faith are neither more evident nor judicially more important, prima facie, than the fact and uniqueness of the faith involved in common sense, moral action, artistic creation, or scientific inquiry.

Yet the philosopher or the scientist in his turn also often insists on crucial and incommensurable differences between scientific judgments and religious judgments in respect to faith. The former, he claims, is always tentative and open to revision while the latter is characteristically authoritative and tenacious or dogmatic. The latter, he frequently asserts, exemplifies *faith* and the former *reason*. Again, this distinction, though no doubt justified in many instances, also often ignores the great variety of scientific attitudes and suggests, without any genuine or valid reason at all, that the person who admits that every judgment is tentative, or subject to revision, cannot be religious. The faith of an individual scientist may of course be in sharp contrast with the religious faith of a particular person. But in fact it is not unusual, no matter how unscientific it may be, for a scientist to be altogether as uncompromising and dogmatic about the current methods and conclusions of science as the most authoritarian religionist is about his creed.

Logically and empirically considered there is of course little doubt that the sciences can produce evidence for specific methods and judgments with great facility and persuasion which cannot be matched by the religions. Yet unless the historical changes in religion are denied altogether or unless it is denied that religious changes ever result from critical inquiry and insight, the claim that science is intrinsically more tentative and open-minded than religion is largely indefensible. For although as a judicial form religion principally neither seeks nor demands evidence, the histories of the religions clearly include, not only the record of the impact of dogmatically accepted doctrines and practices on persons and cultures, but also accounts of rigorous critical inquiry, insight, revision, and revolution. The claim that science is essentially open-minded and religion dogmatic almost invariably oversimplifies the facts in both cases and evidently seeks primarily to honor in one instance and to castigate in the other.

It does not follow, however, that the widespread notion that religious faith is characteristically dogmatic and tenacious is simply and obstinately arbitrary. Nothing great, Sophocles observed long

ago, enters into the life of man without a curse. And rarely at
least do men face greatness, whether great good fortune or great
catastrophe, with composure and reason. Religious faith and vision,
involving as they so often do the most profound sense of present
worth and future hope, are particularly apt to inspire extreme confidence and excessive enthusiasm and all the dangers to deliberation,
generosity, and patience which these imply. The greatness of
Christianity, for example, plainly brought with it a curse when
Christians, inspired by the radiance and promise of the Christian
view of man and the world, were not able to see the importance of
other religions, economics, politics, science, and philosophy except
as these could be turned directly and immediately to the cause of
the church. Christians, presumably in honest and courageous commitment to one of the most luminous forms of religious judgment,
have repeatedly become a party to intolerance, persecution, war,
and almost every imaginable form of man's inhumanity, in spite
of professed doctrines utterly incompatible with their acts.

Yet the apologists who claim that the evils and inconsistencies
which so often accompany religious enthusiasm are not integral
parts of religion or occur in spite of religion are nonetheless partly
right. The fault is surely not altogether in religious faith and judgment but in the fact that in the grip of enthusiasm men so often
disregard their power, and the necessity, of judging in many ways.
R. G. Collingwood is then probably right in claiming:

> The dreadful history of witchcraft is no cruel freak of the world
> spirit; it is a necessary manifestation of the religious consciousness,
> and every religious age, every religious revival, will always produce
> similar fruits.[11]

But he is right only in so far as the "necessary manifestation of . . .
similar fruits" can be reconciled with the free but enthusiastic and
ill-considered choices of men.

Not only religion, however, generates excessive enthusiasm
or inspires faith that is blind and tenacious. Obviously it is difficult
for many kinds of greatness to exist side by side or to admit that
one's own favorite forms of the great and the beautiful must

[11] R. G. Collingwood, *Speculum Mentis*, Oxford, Oxford University Press,
1936, p. 117.

sometimes be sacrificed; so the great achievements by great men often breed fanaticism, especially in the lives of the less imaginative. But greatness can never really redeem or justify the evil which it may inspire. And any argument or logic, whether in the name of the dialectics of history or the omnipotence of God, which excuses religious greatness from the evil done in its name also implies the innocence of all judgments characterized by sincerity and good intentions, no matter what their methods and results. This, to say the least, is a terrible price to pay for the claim that religious judgments are somehow immune to the severe demands of moral and logical criticism.

When the exclusive right of any vision of the world is dogmatically defended—when Newton will not tolerate Shakespeare, when Marx discredits all religion, when Mohammed will not sit down with Moses, when Christ seeks to displace Buddha, when faith abandons reason or religion suggests that science is bankrupt, and philosophy declares that religion is nonsense or nothing but the expression of emotion—then, to be sure, greatness enters, if it enters at all, into the life of man accompanied by a curse. And it was not without insight into such matters that Denis Diderot said of his brother, the Abbe Diderot, "He is a good Christian, which proves to me every moment that it would be better to be a good man."[12] It may of course also be said, with much the same, if equally equivocal, meaning, that it is also better to be a good man than to be a good scientist, teacher, poet, or painter.

Yet much must still be said also, even if somewhat paradoxically, for uncompromising devotion to an ideal or object of faith and commitment. Indeed, it is so obviously true as to hardly deserve mention that artists devoted to their art, scientists to the principles and aims of their inquiry, and religious persons to the demands of their vision of the divine—in spite of threats to personal happiness and life itself—have often made the most notable and beneficent contributions to whatever slow progress mankind has made. So apparently the gulf between irrational fanaticism and necessary commitment is at least sometimes as narrow as it is deep, and the person who can always distinguish clearly between them must

---

[12] Quoted in Ernst Cassirer, *The Philosophy of the Enlightenment*, Boston, Beacon Press, 1955, p. 247.

observe the landfall of events only in the light of his own ideals and commitments. Perhaps such forms of good and evil, in spite of all the visions and hopes to the contrary, are always sadly if not tragically intertwined; and it is impossible to possess the wisdom and courage of a Socrates without also the impatience and arrogance and ultimately the hemlock.

But whatever the word on the ultimate relation of good and evil in their various forms the religions clearly have no monopoly on inordinate faith or fanaticism and the resulting catastrophes. Those who emphasize reason and objectivity as the exclusive method and prerogative of science and philosophy and tenacity as the necessary condition of religion have evidently not examined critically the character of either. The faith that sustains and informs—and surely in some sense is—religious vision and judgment differs radically of course, in instruments, methods, and functions from the faith which sustains or the instruments, methods, and functions which guide and support scientific theory and judgment. And indeed it may be the case that, relatively speaking, faith is subordinate in the sciences and reason of only minor importance in religion. But that this is in fact the case seems altogether dubious. For questioning and answering, seeking and claiming, accepting and rejecting—to all appearances the essential elements of reason— are clearly neither absent nor unimportant in religious persons and the records of their activities. Taken almost at random, the following are not wholly unrepresentative of the religions' own estimate of reason:

Come now, and let us reason together saith the Lord.

Isaiah

Who hath put wisdom in the inward parts?
or who hath given understanding to the heart?

The Book of Job

Do not believe anything on the mere authority of your teachers or of the priests. After scrutiny, believe what you have yourself experienced and perceived as reasonable, that accords with the good of yourself and of others.

Kalama Sutta

All that we are is the result of what we have thought: it is founded on our thoughts, it is made up of our thoughts.

The Dhammapada

The deliberate use of reason is no doubt often absent in religion, and even in science; and reason as employed in religion may perchance always be employed in vain, but it is nonetheless employed. Also, faith may perchance mark, not the perennial character, but the temporary limits of science. Apparently, however, every mode and instance of deliberate judgment involves some measure of reason and is at the same time an object—though perhaps not the ultimate object—of faith.

The practice of identifying religion with faith no doubt often promotes the failure to distinguish more clearly between the specifically religious and the moral modes of judgment and encourages the view (which should be anathema to those concerned about religious values) that no unique problems or dimensions of existence are revealed or introduced by religious experience and activity. But more important for the moment is the fact that equating religion with faith and science with reason also suggests that the problem of reconciling religion and science is simply a matter of clarifying the relation of faith and reason. Accordingly, some appear to believe that if faith is inevitably a part of scientific inquiry and reason indispensable in religion, there can be no serious difference or conflict between them. But in fact the difference and the conflict are not necessarily any less when the place of faith in science and the role of reason in religion are admitted. For the conflict is not totally different from the conflict between the various religions, or between fundamentally different orientations such as rationalism and pragmatism in science and philosophy, and is neither more nor less amenable to resolution by inquiry and argument than the conflicts between and within various groups whose methods and aims oppose each other. The radical difference between the instruments, methods, and functions of science and religion is no doubt sufficient to account for the serious personal and psychological conflicts between the practitioners of these diverse forms of judgment. But the crucial conflict is of course deeper and metaphysical and is reflected in the fact that religious judgment, which is always in terms of specific symbols and derives only a part of its meaning from a conceptual framework, functions only for certain persons making decisions in a given cultural context, while scientific judgment apparently demands conceptual universality. Religion in other words must evidently sacrifice universality in order to speak to the intensely personal needs and unique perspectives; and its judicial relevance is inseparable from the actual capacity of individual persons to choose either the one or the other from among alternatives of action. The sciences, however, must ignore the needs, commitments, and unique capacities of the individual in order to attain universality. Indeed, if the goal of science, to describe all phenomena in terms of general laws, can be achieved, then religious claims and symbols are radically illusory. Or alternatively, if the religions correctly assume that the judicious life is significantly, though even only partly, dependent on choice guided by symbolic expression, the descriptive powers of science are limited, at least insofar as scientific description involves regularity and prediction. But of course the judicial relevance of neither, when each admits its special functions and limits, can be placed in question by the other.

Thus Julian Huxley is obviously more wrong than right when he claims:

> The only possible solution, save an indefinite prolongation of the conflict, is for religion to admit the intellectual methods of science to be as valid in theology as everywhere else, while science admits the psychological basis of religion as an ultimate fact.[13]

First of all, theology is not necessarily any more closely related to religious judgment than the philosophy of science is to scientific inquiry or than aesthetics is to creating works of art. Theology is religion philosophically interpreted or philosophy attempting to come to grips with the metaphysical assumptions and implications involved in certain conceptual interpretations of the experience of the divine or sacred. And though philosophy may render

---

[13] Julian Huxley, *Religion Without Revelation*, New York, Mentor Books, 1958, p. 108.

religion or science and art more circumspect, the judicial functions of religious acts and symbols are not determined, though they may surely be influenced, by their theological interpretation. Religion must not aim to be—and indeed cannot be—any more scientific than art or love. Consequently to admit that theology should be scientific would not resolve any of the basic conflicts between science and religion. Theology may be as scientific as you please, but in being so it will be an altogether different form of judgment from religion itself.

But more significantly, the admission that "The psychological basis of religion is an ultimate fact," unless a great deal more is said, in effect denies everything that any genuine religion claims about itself or the nature of its judgments. Religion, like science, morals, and sexual perversion, no doubt has a psychological basis which is a legitimate object of inquiry. But the cardinal question about religion, even as the principal question about science, is not its psychological basis or origin but its reliability as a judicial method or approach to existential questions. To suggest that the value and future of religion rests on the recognition of its "psychological basis," rather than on its judicial powers and functions, is to accept the claim that science can explain religion and perhaps explain it away. But to take religion seriously, in the manner in which its most notable advocates have always taken it, requires that it have not simply a psychological basis or a factual character discoverable by science, but an ontological meaning and a judicial validity. Religion must be included not only among the "facts to be understood," but also as a significant form of both existence and judgment.

The conflict between religion and science is then finally due very little if at all to the respective roles of faith and reason in each. The conflict is obviously above all a product of dogmatism—but of a dogmatism generated apparently by the fact that both are, to say the least, tremendously important. The religious dogmatists maintain that truth—or at least the highest truth—is attained only in the religious experience and communicated only in religious language or symbols. The scientific dogmatists (and they are not as rare as some seem to think) claim that the whole of truth—or at least the only truth that can be reliably affirmed—is gained through the scientific methods of inquiry and expressed in mathematical formulae or logical prose. The conflict between the two can end only if each recognizes the other as a necessary and effective, though limited, form of discovery and judgment. The crucial problems are how to determine when each form of judgment is most appropriate and how the methods, values, and results of each can be most honestly and effectively reflected in the other. "Once and forever," as A. N. Whitehead has written, "[their] duty of [mutual] toleration has been summed up in the words, 'Let both grow together until the harvest.' "[14]

ON GOD AND RELIGION

It is one thing to destroy the 'presumed' evidence for the existence of God; it is quite another to destroy religion.

JOHN HERMAN RANDALL, JR.

See ye make it very plain. Give no poor fool the pretext to think ye are claiming knowledge of what no mortal knows.

C. S. LEWIS

In the Western world, religion is most often regarded as belief in the existence and providence of God. But if faith alone is not the distinguishing feature of religion, neither is belief in the existence and providence of God. For although many religions have made the worship of "God" or "gods" the central and crucial religious fact, it is nonetheless clearly the case that many other religions have flourished when centered around objects which no informed or critical intelligence could regard as a god or God. The sun, rivers, mountains, trees, and men themselves have in some cultures been the chief symbols and inspiration of significant reli-

[14] A. N. Whitehead, *Science and the Modern World*, New York, Mentor Books, 1948, p. 186.

gious activity. Hinayana Buddhism is notoriously nontheistic, and many contemporary Unitarians, members of the Ethical Culture movement, and Humanists insist that religion can best serve mankind without any claims, implicit or explicit, concerning the existence and providence of God.

These groups, no matter how little sympathy one has for their claims, can hardly be dismissed as either completely nonreligious or simply the products of religious ignorance. Unless "God" may be defined as any ostensible focus of religious activity or object of devotion and worship, there is surely no reason to insist on a necessary relation between religion generally so-called and belief in the existence of God. That men engage in various activities generally called *religious* is clearly a fact, if any facts are clearly so. But the belief in the existence of God as a personal and necessary source of religious symbols and concepts or the justification of religious activities is an interpretation of the fact. The fact may be and has been interpreted in other ways without doing violence to its ontological and judicial validity. Of course those who are committed to the idea that religion is impossible apart from faith in the existence of God have sometimes sought to save this principle by suggesting that any act of worship, no matter what its form or apparent object, is at least an implicit recognition of the existence of God. This, though certainly more generous than the more frequent practice of simply identifying the truly religious with one's own beliefs and activities, begs the question of the actual relation of religion per se to belief in the existence of God. It begs the question by an obvious circularity: Religion is belief in the existence of God, and belief in God's existence is evident in any religious act. Such arguments are not only circular but also useless and often vicious.

It may be admitted, however, that it is not altogether inappropriate to define any apparent object of worship as a 'god,' since the term does obviously function symbolically as well as conceptually, whether the ostensible denotation is the sun, a river, one's own country, a moral ideal, or the supposed actuality corresponding to the concept of omniscient and omnipotent personality. In the strictly symbolic use of the word, all religion may indeed be said to begin with the experience that finds some object godlike, or of supreme worth, holy, or divine. And in the most fundamental meaning, apparently, the nonreligious person is simply one who denies or fails completely to recognize that anything is ultimately sacred or divine or that devotion or worship in any form is either necessary or appropriate as a way of discovering, apprehending, or passing judgment on any aspect of existence, whether actual or ideal.

Hence, to identify the religious person as one who does and the nonreligious person as one who does not believe in the existence of God or gods has at least a specious logic, though such a definition cannot avoid very serious ambiguity or equivocation. For it is also clear that many of the most notorious and self-identified atheists, far from claiming that nothing is of supreme worth or ultimately inviolable, have often justified their posture precisely by insisting (and often in the circumstances, quite rightly) that only the atheist is able to see without illusion, and is therefore able to recognize, the actual objects and dimensions of worth in existence. In other words, some are, with persuasive reasons, convinced that belief in the existence and providence of God or gods is a perspective from which the only objects of genuine worth are bound to be obscure or completely hidden. Thus, if we persist in speaking a language which identifies any object of extraordinary devotion or profound symbolic significance as a god, we shall inevitably be in the peculiar position of claiming that the atheist is also a theist—and even sometimes a better theist than the theist himself. Attractive and popular as Paul Tillich has made this sort of apparently paradoxical language, and effective as it may be religiously, it is still bad logic and incoherent philosophy.

That God (conceived as an omnipotent and omniscient being with every perfection, including personal character and attributes and thus also ultimately inconceivable) exists and cares for mankind is primarily a Judeo-Christian symbol and concept. Historically regarded it seems highly plausible, as Sigmund Freud suggested, that the concept—though surely not the symbol—originated by transferring to the cosmos as a whole an infantile view of the household dominated by the father. But in admitting the plausibility of this so-called explanation of the origin of the concept, we must be very careful not to take for granted (as Freud apparently did) the imaginative and conceptual powers by which the feat was accomplished. Whatever the analogies in everyday experience, the concept of God was still an extraordinary achievement which in many respects reflected and intensified, though in others it may have cast into shadows, man's unparalleled capacities for knowing and loving, for responsibility and suffering. In any case, origins bear no relation to significance and truth; and certainly Western civilization is, from any comprehensive point of view, highly indebted to this concept for its beneficent influence on the most commendable ideas and practices. And indeed one cannot be an orthodox Jew, Christian, or Moslem without faith in the providence of God.

Yet within any of the theistic traditions the meanings of the claim that God exists, if we judge by either the ways in which the belief is supposedly manifest or by its presumed basis and implications, are so various that the most plausible conclusion seems to be that there are many gods who demand or inspire very different and even conflicting beliefs and actions. This, combined with the fact that other religions make no claims about God or gods or even deny that such claims are necessary, suggests that any particular belief is as irrelevant to the defense of religion as a generic form of judgment as any specific claim (such as that matter or atoms or the ether or indeterminacy exists) is to the defense of scientific methods of inquiry and judgment. It may nonetheless be the case that no nontheistic view can ever satisfactorily account for the world and man's peculiar status in it. But this fact, if it is a fact, by no means proves the existence of God; and among the partial accounts, since no other seems to be possible, there may surely be intelligent use and defense of religious judgment without the faith that God exists and cares for mankind.

And conversely, one might believe in the existence of God without being religious in any specific or significant sense. That is, one might be thoroughly convinced by either rational or empirical arguments (the arguments of Anselm or Thomas Aquinas, for example) that the existence of God cannot be reasonably denied but find nothing in this conclusion to suggest that religious judgments (as distinct from practical, scientific, and artistic judgments) are necessary or appropriate in discovering, articulating, or altering any important feature of the world, including human thought and behavior. Proof of God's existence, if such proof is at all possible or relevant, is clearly a philosophical (or theological) task. And although a theology may influence religious judgments, there is no certainty or a priori necessity that it will do so. Symbolic expression rather than conceptual justification (or theology) is the basic characteristic and the indispensable instrument of religion. If a person finds religious symbols utterly meaningless, there is little likelihood that the study of theology will bring him to see their relevance. Yet within a framework of religious activity and conviction, a theology may of course increase and sometimes decrease the scope, intensity, and relevance of religious judgment.

No doubt many who believe and the majority of Occidentals who disbelieve in the existence and providence of God are convinced that the ultimate meaning and the total value of religion are inseparable from this belief or that if God does not exist religious judgments and activities are indeed altogether in vain. However, if the nonexistence of God implies the vanity of religion, it must imply equally the vanity of science and art and the concern of men for one another. For the basic question concerning the justification of religion is not whether there is some supreme and personal being, designated by the word *God*, that sustains or directs natural and human events but whether or not it is the case that the cosmos, or man's most luminous and rewarding moments in this particular corner of it, are such that religious symbols, concepts, and activities are indispensable in the total judicial enterprise by which man ascertains and secures the optimum conditions of his existence. The existence of a personal God as the creator of the universe and the source of human destiny, if it is in fact the case, is of course not irrelevant to religion or to philosophy, science, and art, for that matter, though none of them can presently relieve our profound ignorance on the subject. But religion, like the arts and sciences, apparently can and will survive the conclusion that dark impersonal forces, organized matter, "an accidental collocation of atoms," or what you will, and not a personal God, is the source of whatever good man can hope for and the ills which he fears and suffers.

Are religious symbols and concepts necessary and effective in the attempts of man to discover the various and complex dimensions of existence and to fashion a world that will sustain his highest powers and values? If a positive answer to this question implies the existence of God, it implies it only in the sense that the order or complex which requires and supports religious judgment is called "God." It does not in the least imply the existence of God or any other personal being as conceived in any particular religious tradition. God, as the symbolic expression of the profound mystery and awe-fullness of the splendid and intelligible order of being, has without question functioned as an exceptionally effective symbol—often if not always inadequately conceptualized —in religious judgment. But surely we cannot conclude, since all recorded history bears witness to the contrary, that long and effective use proves the unqualified truth of a symbol or concept. Neither does its effectiveness mean that other religions which have no symbol or concept corresponding to the Judeo-Christian God are in every respect inadequate or inferior.

All that is needed to defend the validity of religious judgment is *some evidence* that religious symbols and concepts are required to judge relevantly and effectively some important aspect of the existential order, including man's own possibilities and needs and the relation of these to the general structure of the world he builds and in which he must live. If there is *any* such evidence, the religions must receive sympathetic but critical care. If there is *no* such evidence, the religions may be, in spite of deep and abiding convictions to the contrary, at best innocent though congenial illusions and at worst fatal distractions from the methods of judgment, action, and inquiry on which man's welfare may now depend. In any case, to deny the existence of God is not, necessarily, to deny that existence must be judged religiously. For with or without the concept of God, the power of religious judgment may wax or wane.

The denial of the existence of God essentially only calls into question the religious and judicial relevance of a particular concept and symbol and may be as appropriate or inappropriate as any other critical effort to alter the basic presuppositions of judgment. And in fact the terms *religion* and *religious* are applied apparently with very similar meanings, to those who follow Buddha and to those who worship Jehovah, to those who pray to the sun, and to those who seek through any ritual or symbolic action to change their lives or to alter some aspect of the world in which they must live. The Western scientist or philosopher who denies the existence of God is of course apt to be affirming the supremacy of scientific or philosophic methods of inquiry or the irrelevance of religious judgment. But the Buddhist who denies that questions concerning the existence of God are religiously significant may be only reaffirming his faith in his own long and distinguished religious tradition.

ON INSTITUTIONS, MORALITY, AND RELIGION

Society is like the air, necessary to breathe but insufficient to live on.

GEORGE SANTAYANA

Religion, even when presumably inseparable from faith in the existence and providence of God, has also often been identified, more or less, with the institutionalized promotion of specific rituals, beliefs, and activities. This view is of course profoundly erroneous. Yet contrary to what so many critics of religion seem to think, this suggests no indictment of either institutions in general or organized religion in particular. Religion is neither an institution nor, like other elements of culture, altogether separable from institutions. Religion is of course protected and nurtured, for better or worse, by various kinds of institutions. But so are children and domestic plants and animals. Institutions are relatively permanent arrangements for the judicious and systematic care of valuables of many sorts.

But institutions are not identical with the values they nurture and protect, although their character is no doubt in part determined by what they seek to do, even as what they are able to promote depends on their specific resources, instruments, and methods. Science, art, politics, and health are all supported more or less directly by institutions and are accordingly influenced by the forms and fortunes of institutions; but not a single one is identical in its fundamental respects with the particular organization on which its existence may very well depend. No one becomes a scientist, artist, statesman, or biologically healthy simply by identifying himself with the institutions that promote specific disciplines, ideas, and activities. A person may support scientific inquiry or medical research without increasing his own knowledge of science or affecting his own health. Likewise, identifying oneself with religious institutions, no matter what the incidental results, cannot of itself make one religious. Indeed, rebellion against current forms of institutionalized religion, far from always being irreligious, frequently proves to be the most profound religion.

A religion, like other interests and values, is institutionalized through the very processes by which it proves itself precious or apparently precious, not only to individuals, but to the entire community. So although there is a sense in which religious experience and judgment are invariably and intensely personal, religious institutions are not any less inevitable or more superfluous than other communal projects, such as homes, schools, and hospitals. Many, if not all, of the most personal aspects of man's life—and especially the symbols and concepts which constitute significant religious judgment—are apparently possible only through the combined resources of the community. Consequently the question so often posed concerning the justification of organized religion is either ambiguous or specious. The question is ambiguous if it means to call religion itself rather than particular institutions of religion into question; and it is specious if it assumes that a religion or any characteristically human activity could arise or survive without any institutional support whatever. If a religion is worth having at all, it is also worth caring for with whatever arrangements are necessary. Of course, the communal support of religion need not be by means of institutions designed specifically or only for that purpose. But surely a religion will not affect many lives or contribute greatly to intellectual and moral concerns unless there is

some customary and effective way in which religious judgments
influence and are responsive to the complex affairs of the community.

Religion must nonetheless not be identified with the institutions that support and nurture it. Great, if not unusual, care must
indeed be taken to insure that religion is not tragically victimized
by the nonreligious requirements of institutional organization and
adminstration. The same might also be said of course about education, science, and the arts. But precisely because the problems of
religion are transcendent (problems which do not grow directly
out of, but may nonetheless radically transform, the practical
affairs of men) no aspect of life is more susceptible to being warped
or completely marred by institutional interests and demands. Religion, to a greater extent than either science or art, must be both
a consuming interest in the community and an uncompromising
critic of prevailing ideas and practices. When a religion becomes
simply another institution among a host of institutions and pro-
fessions designed to make life more comfortable and easy—rather
than the insistent and passionate voice of insight, care, and concern inspired by a compelling vision of the divine—its judicial
function is reduced to an ineffective apology for traditions that
are already dead or dying.

Another common practice is to identify religion with morality
or with the acceptance of a particular moral standard or ethical
code. Since the next chapter will deal at length with the issues
raised by the complex and controversial relations of religion and
morality, it is sufficient to note here that the widespread habit
of identifying the good man and the religious man blatantly ignores
the fact that, judged by any consistent code of ethics, all historical
cultures and many devout individuals have engaged in grossly immoral activities in the name and with the support of religion.
Also many men of indisputable moral stature and integrity are
antireligious, while persons who sincerely proclaim that religion
is the hope of the world cannot always be trusted, especially
when dilemmas and conflicts arise, to act morally or even to speak
candidly and critically on moral issues. There is no self-contradiction involved in speaking of goodness without religion or of the
immorality of a religious person unless the issue is uncritically

begged by identifying the one with the other. At least a religion is something other than, though it may invariably include, a moral code.

Of course no form of cooperative activity and no interest which contributes to the path and character of man's judicial life can avoid moral questions and decisions. And the relation of religion to moral concepts and actions has been almost universally regarded as momentous and intimate, if not altogether inevitable and beneficent. Nonetheless religion cannot be defined simply in terms of its close and perhaps singular relation to morality. Rather, the great and mutual influence of religion and morals on each other must apparently be accounted for in terms of both the specific character and function of religion and the basic features of moral insight and decision. Most, if not all, religions have attempted to locate all moral principles and actions within the jurisdiction of religion or to buttress moral doctrines by religious sanctions. Many philosophers have construed moral experience as one of the chief evidences for the validity of important religious doctrines; and some have reasoned that since religious claims cannot be logically or empirically validated, moral nihilism is justified. However, there is still much to be said in defense of the view that, though they may influence each other profoundly, morality and religion are logically quite independent of each other. At the very least, certain individuals and some religious traditions have sometimes emphasized the one or failed to emphasize the other. Therefore, it seems necessary to treat them as essentially different, though surely mutually influential, modes of experience and judgment.

Religion cannot be identified with any particular belief, feeling, or attitude because religious beliefs, feelings, and attitudes are multitudinous. Even as the body of scientific conclusions is not the distinctive element of science but the result of inquiries conducted scientifically, so the specific beliefs, feelings, and attitudes characteristic of any single religious tradition are not the essence of religion as such but only the products of religious methods employed in particular circumstances and at a certain stage of development. Apparently any aspect of life, whether intellectual, moral, or physical, may influence or be influenced by religious judgments. A religion may honor or despise the body and encourage either a sense of total dependence or a sense of personal power and responsibility. A religion may advise and nurture humility or provoke boldness, praise the power of love or defend the righteousness of hatred. The prophet—the voice of intense religious judgment—speaks in a context and modulates his mood and words to the supposed requirements of the particular situation. He speaks now of God's mercy and again of his anger and jealousy. He rejoices in the many gifts bestowed on man and weeps bitterly at his limits and the briefness of his days. He must speak appropriately to both the joy and the sorrow of man's life. There is consequently no specific belief, feeling, or attitude that is invariably and unequivocally religious or irreligious.

A DEFINITION OF RELIGION

Religion, like science, is grounded in the need of doing the right thing under the given circumstances.

RALPH BARTON PERRY

It was suggested earlier that existence as given may be very generally divided into the quantitative and the qualitative and that the sciences may be said principally to describe or reconstruct in conceptual terms the quantitative or measurable aspects of the world which presumably exist independent of experience, while the arts originate, convey, and intensify, in sensuous and symbolic forms, the qualitative features of both objective and subjective existence. These distinctions, however, though certainly justified in many respects, are not intended to be sharp or exhaustive; for science, the objectivity of which is always in question, can by no means ignore qualities altogether, and concepts are quite indispensable in most, if not all, that may be appropriately called art.

But also, when the quantitative features and relations of

things, their qualities, and man's own qualities of perceiving, thinking, and feeling have been noted or when all has been judged that can be judged in strictly scientific and artistic modes and in the philosophical languages which may occasionally combine significant powers and functions of both, there remains, at least for many persons, one other distinctive experience which may be expressed and communicated. This is the twofold conviction, sustained primarily by love and awe, that existence or some dimension of it is sacred or holy or of ultimate and inviolable worth, and that the judicial and judicious life can and must be supported and guided by symbolic acts and objects which disclose, or bear witness to or are constant reminders of this fact.

Religion is the articulation through the various arts and symbolic forms or in moral reflection and action which also have symbolic significance of that which is presumably *sacred* or *holy*. Such articulation includes of course the faith that the symbolic acts are necessary and effective modes of disclosing and pursuing things of inestimable worth. In slightly different terms, then, religion is the performance of symbolic acts which identify, directly or indirectly, the inviolable, the divine, the sacred, the holy, and the faith that the character and destiny of persons will be somehow, and more or less radically, altered by the relations and qualities which such acts signify or achieve.

The *holy* or *divine* need not imply, however, the existence of purposive and supernatural powers which impose a priori conditions upon man, but only the extraordinary and partially attainable qualities and complexes without which his life lacks the ultimate meaning and joy which he seeks. Unless the divine is in fact a matter of experience, no amount of theoretical superstructure involving such dubious matters as the existence of a personal God or the immortality of the soul can make a man religious or bring to his life the faith that by seeking, through the religious arts of saying, acting, and producing, he can understand and embody in his own life the excellence which this apparently far from perfect—but nonetheless splendid and amazing—world makes possible.

The roots of religion are then equally grounded both in the impulse to and the objects of worship, though ultimately religion includes not only worship, but also many tasks or duties required to keep the world worshipful or man sensitive to the presence and the demands of the holy.

What is worship? Do the many forms of worship have any common or defining characteristics? Because worship is primarily symbolic, no conceptual answer to such questions can be direct or wholly satisfactory. Yet few would fail to recognize that the history of man is shot through with confrontations of the presumably holy or worshipful or informed by instances of experience which embody or convey a sense of extraordinary worth and thus become paradigmatic of the total meaning and value of existence. Essentially then worship only bears witness to something presumably objective which is neither simply order nor beauty, which inspires neither the desire to analyze nor to possess, but is simply recognized and praised with whatever eloquence stammering lips can manage. Worship is often, if not always, a notable element in the accents of greatness and wisdom—in the accents of an Aristotle, an Augustine, a Spinoza, a Newton, a Schweitzer, an Einstein, and a Camus. Although there is in such diverse accents no common substance, the common quality suggests that each might perhaps have said with the poet, Rupert Brooke:

> I have been so great a lover: filled my days
> So proudly with the splendor of Love's praise,
> The pain, the calm, and the astonishment,
> Desire illimitable, and still content,
> And all dear names men use, to cheat despair,
> For the perplexed and viewless streams that bear
> Our hearts at random down the dark of life . . .
> Shall I not crown them with immortal praise
> Whom I have loved . . .
> And set them as a banner, that men may know . . .
> These I loved.

The highest forms of religion—the sense of the holy when purest and most beneficent—are primarily inspired by and inspire love. And protests to the contrary not withstanding—the basic problems of philosophy and science, of political justice and cosmology—are not necessarily far removed from the fundamentals of religion; for such problems are neither forced upon 'is by the necessities of life nor merely the products of idle curiosity. Instead, we are led into them, we explore them, in order to see more clearly the exquisite patterns of splendor that are in the world. We explore the world in order to discover it, to see it; and we desire to see it because we love it. All our action, inquiry, and creativity, insofar as they are informed by love rather than by need or greed, may be modes of worship or of recognizing what is beyond all price.

Yet it is nonetheless necessary and significant that, like the other dimensions of experience, the sense of the presence of the sacred, though it may pervade life, also inspires the development of its own instruments, methods, and institutions and becomes formalized in particular religions. Consequently the methods and aims of religion are often as specific and well defined and its particular claims as mutable as the corresponding elements of the sciences or the arts, though its ultimate results are perhaps often more difficult to identify or evaluate. Worship, no less than analysis or creativity, apparently seeks to discover or disclose and in some degree modify, aspects of both the self and its environment. There is indeed a sense in which religion frankly attempts to achieve the miraculous through mysterious and apocalyptic concepts and symbols. As Ludwig Feuerbach has said, "Man truly prays when he regards prayer as in itself a sacred power, a divine force."[15] Yet no one who has considered Hume's critique of the foundations of modern science or reflected briefly on the wonder that any, even the least, of man's enterprises achieve their aim should be led to exaggerate the differences in this respect between the arts and sciences on the one hand and the religions on the other. No method of judgment demonstrates its own cogency or is ever altogether self-justifying, and the immense success of science is surely more a gratuity than a recompense.

In the beginning, then, the honest and unprejudiced seeker must regard religion as neither a nonintellectual (or emotional) nor an extraintellectual (or wholly transcendent) response to existence. Rather, he must admit that religion is one of the modes in which man, conditioned by time and place, attempts to

[15] Ludwig Feuerbach, *The Essence of Christianity*, New York, Harper & Row, Harper Torchbooks, 1957, p. 194.

pass appropriate and reliable judgment on himself and his world. And if this effort is not wholly illusory, particular religious judgments may turn out to be either appropriate or inappropriate, effective or ineffective, the result of either insight or illusion. Also religious aims, though all religions are probably similar in form and function, may be as diverse as the momentous occasions and situations in which symbolic acts are regarded as either necessary or effective ways of disclosing or apprehending things of inviolable worth and altering accordingly the character or the course of events. War dances, fertility rites, hymn singing, dependence on prayer in crisis, sit-ins and peace walks, and the rendering of moral judgments in parables and fables may be equally religious, though perhaps not equally effective or equally cognizant of the actual circumstances, powers, and consequences involved. A religion may be as badly mistaken about the truly sacred as science sometimes is about causes and consequences. Also the resources of religion, like the resources of science and rhetoric, may be either misunderstood or deliberately misused. But presumably, insofar as truth is the perception or presence of aspects of being in forms which sustain or guide judgment, religion, even as science and philosophy, may either reveal or obscure the truth.

Having now defined religion, the nonreligious person may be said to be one who is convinced either that nothing is sacred or that the attitudes, concepts, and symbols of the sciences, the arts, common sense, or some combination of these are sufficient to discover and express all truth and guide all enterprises. The religious person, in contrast, employs concepts and symbols of the holy with the conviction that these are singular and indispensable modes of grappling with existential truth or the only effective means of securing certain things of intrinsic and ultimate worth. And the moral person who is not religious is convinced, whether correctly or not, that it is only through observation and logic or decision guided by social and economic circumstances and never through the symbolic recognition of the sacred that all things of worth are attained. He regards worship as either altogether superfluous or perhaps a symptomatic result, but certainly not a cause, of character and destiny. And the person who is religious but not moral is convinced that conduct in conformity with current ethical concepts and practices is far less important than the symbolic acts required by the vision of the sacred. Abraham's willingness to present Isaac as "a burnt offering" to God, Agamemnon's sacrifice of Iphigenia at Aulis, the self-sacrifice of the Christian martyrs who defied Roman custom and law, and Calvin's determination to have Servetus burned at the stake were clearly religious rather than moral acts. And although it may exaggerate the importance of faith in religion, the idea that what is required above all is faith and symbolic, if not sacrificial, evidence of faith, rather than moral excellence or beneficent deeds, is essentially sound as a recognition of the fact that religion is profoundly distinct from morality. As *theoria*—or a vision of the wonderful and awe-full—religion transcends, though it may in some instances transform, morality.

In summary, religion, in terms of its origin, is the experience of presumably intrinsic and ultimate worth—the inviolable, the sacred, the holy, the divine. Depending on circumstances, including the character and scope of human sensitivities and powers, a religion may emphasize the splendor or the tragedy, the beauty or the vanity, the joy or the terrible sorrows of existence. A religion may praise man for his noble works or heap curses on his head because of his perversity. Thus, many radically different qualities and objects may become religiously dominant or serve as the symbolic matrix of either divine power or worth. For whatever the highest in value, it may presumably be achieved only insofar as men come to grips with the preeminent qualities and characteristics of their concrete existence, which may of course vary greatly with circumstances. So in terms of its form and function, religion is the attempt to qualify (to inform or alter) personal character and possibilities by the use of symbols which recognize the sacred, whether as basically goodness or power, as the source of much, if not indeed all, that is worth being, doing, or having.

To have said, however, as best one can what religion is, should take from it none of its mystery, beauty, and significance. To define religion is not to explain it or to offer a substitute for it. Religion at its best remains, after it has been defined, a luminous though mysterious way of accomodating ourselves to the infinitely complex world within which we live. At best a definition—even a philosophy—of religion can only aid us in being more provident and prudent in relating it and ourselves to the total and awesome pattern of our existence. Much more than has been touched by our plainest words is still shrouded in darkness.

ON RELIGIOUS AND NONRELIGIOUS LANGUAGES

My words must maintain a certain relation to
other words which I use and to the things I do.
                                                    C. I. LEWIS

The claim that religion is essentially a symbolic form of judgment or a special way of dealing with distinctive aspects of experience must not suggest that religion fails to come to grips with the actual and objective character of existence. Each form of judgment, conceptual or symbolic, and whether poetic, scientific, dramatic, or musical is presumably rooted in, though not limited to, the unique conditions of an individual's existence. Not only the subjective conditions of the psyche apparently, but even the totality of nature's dynamic order, as well as the infinite realm of ideal possibilities, including the formal structures of mathematics and logic, may deeply affect and be reflected in conceptual and symbolic judgment. Of course linguistic usage probably always reflects in some measure (and in some respects alters) the temporal and local circumstances in which it occurs or the specific character and involvement of individual persons. But evidently a language also bears witness to universal and unalterable characteristics of being which support objective and unlimited communication. The actual, the potential, the possible, and the purely ideal are all, if not all equally, in the province of conceptual and symbolic judgment.

Consequently, to conceive religion as primarily a distinctive form of symbolic judgment and highly dependent on linguistic powers puts no specific limits on its judicial functions or ontological truth. A religious language, even as any other language, is based ultimately on the conviction that both subjective and objective conditions require and support its use. And since all the different forms and features of experience and being may overlap and interact, the distinctions between the various uses of language (objective, subjective, scientific, poetic, religious, etc.) cannot be hard and fast. Science, however, is rarely mistaken for religion or religion for science or the arts for either science or religion. Each form of language is at least sufficiently distinctive that only minor difficulties stand in the way of characterizing particular cultures, events, or persons as predominantly religious, artistic, scientific, or philosophical.

Yet the differences between religious and nonreligious judgments are often unnecessarily obscured by the claims of individuals and traditions. In the Judeo-Christian tradition, for example, essentially artistic literature (such as *Esther* and the *Song of Songs*) and various historical and legal documents have found their way into the sacred canon. Yet much literature that has all the earmarks of the religious is nonetheless frequently classified as primarily artistic or poetic. Such facts, although perhaps often due to obvious religious needs or aims, can be generally accounted for only in terms of the quirks and accidents of history. Even the languages of philosophy and religion, in spite of great dissimilarity in fundamental assumptions, methods, and aims, are not always easily distinguished. Though no one would mistake a technical treatise in logic for a religious document or a hymn for a philosophical appraisal there are many instances, including some of the most influential works and not only those in the obviously religious philosophies, in which it is virtually impossible to distinguish the religious commitments and symbols from the purely philosophical judgments.

Should Benedict De Spinoza, for example, be called a religious philosopher? Certainly in terms of the particular symbols and concepts of the Judeo-Christian tradition, he cannot. Yet he was deeply concerned about the qualities which are possible in human existence and was clearly convinced that the rigorous use of language to promote understanding could also result in a state of supreme blessedness or in the intellectual love of God when God is conceived as the dynamic and eternally necessary order of nature. His passion for worship or for a combination of conceptual and symbolic judgments that would directly affect the quality of man's life was apparently profound and effective. So we may say that his life and vision were unmistakably religious in spite of the fact that he supposed all things, except perhaps the exercise of wisdom in the control of the passions, to be completely determined by nature and repudiated traditional religious beliefs and language. And if there is any sense at all in which it must be said that he was not religious, it is surely related only to the fact that his symbolic concerns and commitments were consummated in essentially solitary vision and contemplation rather than in the public acts and values shared by the larger community of persons and so often identified with religion. For Spinoza the individual and not the community must be primarily responsible for a vision of the splendid order which will inspire worship and redeem the "exceedingly hard" way of the wise man from vanity.

What about Bertrand Russell? It would be utterly unfair (in the face of his own objections) to call Russell religious in any ordinary sense of the term. Yet few men have been more deeply concerned about the relation of belief to action and thus ultimately to the quality of man's life; few have spoken a more obviously symbolic language in the attempt to disclose and perhaps modify the relation of man's life to the qualities of its cosmic setting:

> Brief and powerless is Man's life; on him and all his race the slow, sure doom falls pitiless and dark. Blind to good and evil, reckless of destruction, omnipotent matter rolls on its relentless way; for Man, condemned to-day to lose his dearest, it remains only to cherish, ere yet the blow falls, the lofty thoughts that enoble his little day; disdaining the coward terrors of the slave of Fate, to worship at the shrine that his own hands have built; undismayed by the empire of chance, to preserve a mind free from the wanton tyranny that rules his outward life; proudly defiant of the irresistible forces that tolerate, for a moment, his knowledge and his condemnation, to sustain alone, a weary but unyielding Atlas, the world that his own ideals have fashioned despite the trampling march of unconscious power.[16]

The symbols and concepts are largely antithetical to those

[16] Bertrand Russell, *Mysticism and Logic*, New York, Doubleday, Anchor Books, 1957, p. 54.

we are most accustomed to calling *religious*; but all the elements of religion are there. Yet basically Russell's commitments are essentially scientific and nonreligious. In his most candid moments and in spite of his antimaterialism in morals he has always claimed that only conceptual accuracy and the control of quantitative processes and relations through the knowledge gained only by scientific methods of inquiry can be effective and reliable in the effort to understand and change men's lives. All problems must be approached, he has insisted, in the mood and method of science or scientific philosophy; for only scientific inquiry and knowledge may discover and in some small measure direct the causal relations in nature. His view of the universe is evidently intended, not to inspire worship, but to emphasize the necessity of logic; and where logic is ineffective, the chief alternatives, he insists, are courage, defiance, and resignation. But even much of this may be regarded as a significant form of religious language based on a clear, if not clearly acknowledged, perception that the pursuit of knowledge is itself always carried on in a context of care and concerns which can hardly be satisfactorily articulated in the logical and quantitative languages of the sciences.

At least in its incipent forms religious language is apparently no less natural and is perhaps as widespread as language itself. But obviously not every person trusts or develops the incipient religious language which he can hardly avoid using. As John Herman Randall has noted, recent analytical philosophy, particularly as represented by G. E. Moore, Ludwig Wittgenstein, and A. J. Ayer is almost completely devoid of the religious overtones which have pervaded the language of most serious philosophy. The claim that every person is religious or makes religious judgments is no less a *petitio principii* than the claim that religion is always a form of superstition or judicially irrelevant and is every bit as dubious as the claim that everyone is in some special and significant sense poet and scientist. It may very well be, as Socrates and Plato taught, that every person *ought* to seek a vision of the ideal in order to fashion his own soul in its image and that the wrong use of words creates evil in the soul. And this claim is surely closely related to, if not inseparable from, the view that all men are, or ought to be, religious. Yet it seems almost beyond question that many men, including distinguished philosophers, artists, and scientists, have spoken significantly about many aspects of existence without sharing or taking seriously the Socratic-Platonic view of the function of ideals and the intimate relation of language to the character of the world and man. Many, like Thomas Hobbes, have clearly regarded all significant linguistic usage as simply a secondary appendage to the sensory processes in the pursuit of knowledge; and other metaphysical systems imply at least that language is completely epiphenomenal or as irrelevant finally to the course of human affairs as the rainbow is to the subsequent behavior of light waves. And it is a defensible view (regardless of how inadequate it may seem to some) that all power is in matter or that concepts and symbols merely reflect but do not guide or influence the tortuous path of human decision and action. It may be that all judgment, whether conceptual or symbolic, is merely a by-product of the intricate relations and convolutions within a totally different and indifferent substratum of being.

But even if symbols and concepts are more effective and more indicative of the total ontological fact than they seem, it is surely nonetheless probable that even as each form of judgment is selective, it also in some manner and degree excludes the others; at least very few persons, if any, judge equally well in all matters and modes. Indeed, it is notoriously the case, for example, that a person's abilities as a chemist are not in the least opened to doubt by the fact that he is insensitive to, or highly critical of, the poetic or religious forms of judgment. Knowledge of sound scientific principles or of the structure and behavior of inanimate matter apparently requires sensitivity to neither the religious dimension of experience nor to the history and values of poetry and painting. But neither (and apparently this is harder for many to accept) does reliability as a scientist confirm a person's competence as a critic of religion. Surely, then, humility may be required of all men, though sensitivity to the principles of a particular mode of judgment, whether religious or scientific, can be demanded of none; and no one deserves censure for doing devotedly the particular tasks he is able to do well.

To all appearances there are, especially when we regard the

substance and demands of gross experience rather than formal matters alone, a number of reliable but distinct modes of judgment. And each evidently contains and reveals vistas and splendors peculiar to itself. Religious languages are apparently no exception. Yet the characteristic qualities of each language or activity may presumably influence or appear in each of the others. Consequently it is no anomaly when a genuine religious quality is found in any effective effort to deal seriously with the complex problems and themes relevant to man's desire to live wisely and well. A person may, as Martin Buber has said, eat and work in holiness as well as pray in holiness. The artist, scientist, and statesman, even as their devotion and achievements may become symbols of the way to excellence for all men, may also reflect profoundly religious qualities in their approach to almost any subject or problem. Yet there are also specifically religious modes of seeking and judging which an individual may or may not employ or understand. But even as no one is castigated for his inability to use or understand the languages of the arts and sciences, neither should one be blamed if he cannot use or understand the languages of the religions.

It is therefore seriously misleading to claim, as Paul Tillich has, that religion *is* ultimate concern or commitment, although the claim is unusually suggestive and important as a recognition of the fact that the divine may appear in art and science or in the burdensome round of daily duties. Tillich further states:

'God' is the answer to the question implied in man's finitude; he is the name for that which concerns man ultimately. This does not mean that first there is a being called God and then the demand that man should be ultimately concerned about him. It means that whatever concerns a man ultimately becomes a god for him, and, conversely, it means that a man can be concerned ultimately only about that which is God for him.[17]

Now apart from the fact that this is an unconventional, though perhaps etymologically sound, mode of making religion equivalent to having or believing in a god or God, this definition stands in a long tradition which has, altogether too sweepingly,

[17] Paul Tillich, *Systematic Theology*, Chicago, The University of Chicago Press, 1951, Vol. I, p. 211.

equated religion with supreme loyalty or devotion to any object or goal and sometimes with fanaticism. This approach is also based on the common but nonetheless serious mistake of identifying religion primarily with a mood or attitude, or posture, rather than with a judicial method employing characteristic symbols and concepts. No such approach can ever be unambiguously just to the character and diversity of religious claims and values.

For concern and commitment—even *ultimate concern* and *commitment*, the terms Tillich most often identifies with *religious* faith—may accompany or become evident in any species of judgment. But strictly, even though perhaps tautologically, speaking, religious concern or commitment occurs and is articulated only religiously or in the context and symbols of a particular religious form or tradition. More generally and less tautologically, religious judgment and the experience and convictions which provoke it and those that are in turn provoked by it are inseparable from the presence or the supposed presence of the divine or inviolable and the faith that persons or events are influenced by or responsive to particular and irreducible symbols and symbolic activities. To identify religion with simply *any* ultimate concern is not altogether different in method from equating moral judgment with pragmatic decisions, the perception of beauty with incipient sexual interests, or all truth with scientific truth. All such claims are at best equivocal; they identify things which are sometimes clearly distinct on the basis that the one perhaps always influences the other.

Religious concern and commitment may of course be ultimate for many persons, and all ultimate concerns are probably always subject to influence by religious concepts, symbols, and activities. But clearly not every ultimate concern is religious in any specific or concrete sense, and religion may sometimes be less than an ultimate, though still a genuine, concern. Apparently for some men all of the time and perhaps sometimes for all men there is no sense or conviction of the sacredness or the intrinsic and ultimate worth of anything at all. Furthermore, when the problems of science, art, and politics are unique, profound, and urgent and all visions of consequences limited and uncertain, the ultimate concern and commitment of the individual may often and justifiably take no form other than sincere, if humble, dedication to the development of the forms of judgment in which he is most competent. The artist, whose ultimate concern may be to develop revolutionary and revealing techniques and themes in a particular medium, need not abandon all religious tradition, though it is equally true that he may. So even as we should heed Whitehead's warning and not uncritically associate religion with goodness, so we should also not yield when tempted to claim that every ultimate commitment is a religious commitment. Even if it is true that all ultimate concerns share something of the quality of religious experience and judgment and that religion may often share in some respects the logical rigor of science and the aesthetic excellence of the arts, it is still a travesty on ordinary language and experience to label the ultimate concern of the scientist or artist, although he is inspired and the source of extraordinary value, as inevitably religious.

Indeed, in spite of the fact that Tillich, in defining religion as ultimate concern, points to a quality perhaps common to all instances of highly serious endeavor, this definition also plainly shares all the faults of any extremely generalized and reductive approach to any problem or feature of existence. Art and science, for example, no less than religion, are pervasive forms of culture or dimensions of the spiritual life of man and presumably both might be so defined that all men would turn out to be scientific and artistic, in spite of the fact that ordinary conceptual practice dictates otherwise. But the distinctive aspects of scientific and artistic activities, their respective character, powers, and limits, would of course not be affected in the least. A life dedicated distinctively to science, to art, or to both would still be among the different options open or closed to particular individuals. Each might still be appropriately or inappropriately valued and promoted. Likewise, the definition of religion as ultimate concern cannot change the fact that many persons are convinced, both theoretically and practically, that religion in all its traditional and specific forms—including the form which, significantly, Tillich himself practices—is completely dispensable in an intelligently ordered life.

The definition of religion as *ultimate concern,* if this is supposed to clarify or describe any concrete aspects of religious experience and behavior, is therefore reductive and meaningless in much the same manner as the *dialectics of history* when the latter is offered as clarification or description of the common basis of various and incommensurable practices in politics, science, the arts, philosophy, and religion. For when religion is identified with every ultimate concern, and presumably every person is ultimately concerned about this or that, and thus either consciously or unconsciously identifies a god or God, then both *religion* and *god*, like the *dialectics of history*, become so omnipresent that they cannot possibly play any distinctive role in the vocabulary of deliberate judgment. It is not wholly unfair to suggest, then, that this is essentially only another method, though perhaps an unusually persuasive one, of begging critical questions about the precise function and worth of the specifically religious modes of judgment. In making religion an aspect of every notable achievement and feature of man's life, the characteristic values and faults of the traditional religious forms and commitments are effectively, if not deliberately, ignored. In spite of such question-begging procedures, however, each mode of judgment remains nonetheless distinctive, subject of course to profound influence by and conflict with each of the others. And each mode may on occasion be marked by an urgency, ideal or practical, which demands no less than the ultimate concern and commitment of those who are capable of significant judgment in its terms.

SOME SUMMARY REMARKS

Religion . . . should not be a substitute for dreams and wish-fulfillment; it should resemble neither the holding of a ticket in a lottery, nor the holding of a policy in an insurance company.
                                                    KARL POPPER

Man discovers himself on the solid earth, suspended in the midst of planets and stars which exceed, in both immensity of

number and intricate detail, the greatest stretch of his own
amazing imagination. Intensely aware of good and evil and the
splendor and the misery which surround and pervade his own
being, he knows also that he is now the heir to prodigious and
in some respects prodigiously successful efforts to sound the complex mysteries of existence. Yet he is nonetheless largely ignorant
and deeply concerned about his own nature and possibilities. Man
may be, modern science and philosophy to the contrary not withstanding, the special creation of an eternal and omnipotent God.
Or he may be, traditional religious thought to the contrary not
withstanding, an accidental combination of atoms—the fortuitous
product of an unimaginable cosmic accident. His career may be
almost finished, ravaged beyond recovery by the incredible and
violent powers which his own genius has wrung from nature; or
he may be only beginning the explorations that will lead to an
ever greater understanding of himself and the universe he inhabits.
Some of these are perhaps much more reasonable conclusions than
the others. But neither science nor religion can give assurance in
such matters.

Yet the fact that man questions nature is itself impressive
evidence of the great scope of his own judicial capacities and the
most prophetic witness to the awesome resources of the infinite
and complex order, whether basically material or spiritual, which
produces and sustains the living intellect. That man inquires, that
he is in desperate need of some vision of his own origin and end
and preoccupied with the antecedents and consequences of his
own judgments are apocalyptic facts which, without presuming
any satisfactory answers to the questions they arouse, reveal the
perplexing ambiguity of man's place in the world. The achievement of precise and effective knowledge, which is still surrounded
by mystery, often only intensifies the demand for qualitative satisfactions or emphasizes both the necessity of specific commitments
and the precarious but amazing tenure of man in nature. Questions and commitments are clearly unavoidable but their modes
are many and their consequences various and often unpredictable.

Religion is required, if required it is, by the dual fact (1) that
life is at every moment a qualitative experience, including the
sense of the sacred or holy, as well as a quantitative duration;

and (2) that the judgments an individual *must* make are also commitments with complex implications for the future quality of experience. That the quality of life is man's most certain reward and that the symbolic recognition of the sacred is necessary to secure the most desirable qualities are assumptions implicit in every religion.

Within most religious traditions, however, there are two different groups and attitudes which should be carefully distinguished: (1) those who regard symbols and creeds as a kind of magic which enables them to ignore the prudential labors required to solve critical problems; and (2) those who recognize that the domain and power of religious judgment, though truly significant and precious, are nonetheless limited. Those who accuse the religions of encouraging superstition and false hopes are surely not wholly mistaken. But superstition is essentially only the uncompromising conviction that problems can be solved by methods which are totally irrelevant to the actual relations and influences involved. Even science and philosophy are often as susceptible to such convictions as religion and common sense. And not all superstition, in either science or religion, is without reason or altogether vain. If ignorance is sometimes bliss, it is also sometimes terrifying and compulsive. And the only escape from such ignorance may sometimes be by way of completely unjustified confidence in nonexistent causes and unrealistic goals. Consider the origin of chemistry in alchemy and astronomy in astrology or the influence on inquiry into the physics and chemistry of life of Descartes' atrocious theory that animals are nothing but machines which neither think nor suffer.

The values of superstitious or unrealistic religious ideas may not be so obvious. Certainly religious war dances have never won a battle; springtime festivals and rituals of planting have often preceded bad seasons and poor harvests; the most earnest prayers have failed to alter misfortune; and confident conformity to the supposed will of God has no doubt abetted personal and social ruin. Judged only by the clear and observable results, the religions are often the most dubious benefactors of man. Yet even George Santayana, though completely unsympathetic to the view that

existence is basically or ultimately such that it must be described
in religious terms, has suggested that even the most superstitious
religions may mitigate the spiritual evils of the moment or enhance and intensify certain positive values, even when they damage the prospects of life in other respects.

The following chapters will attempt to show, at least by
indirection, that although it need not be said that religious symbols and concepts reflect or reproduce the structure and content
of some "supernatural realm," they are nonetheless certainly, not
only clues *to*, but both judicial forms *within* and constitutive parts
of the world which includes man. Presumably then religion need
not be ever simply or wholly illusory or a fancied escape from the
dangers and terrors of ill health, economic insecurity, or death.
The religions themselves claim, and apparently not altogether
without reason, to be modes of apprehending, creating, and sharing visions of *what* and *how* man is in the world, visions of the
divine, or of man's existence in a setting which arouses and in
some measure satisfies the passion for worship. Consequently religion is reasonably and sharply distinguished from other aspects
of life and often most intense when life is least secure—when
economic existence is precarious and burdensome or when the
good things normally taken for granted are threatened by sudden
disaster or death. When all things are full of worth and the
performance of daily duties is also devotion to what seems most
worth being, doing, and having, there is apparently less need for
the special activities called *religion*, and the religious spirit may
pervade all that one says and does. In the ideal culture there would
perhaps be no special activity called religion, but every act would
be an act of care and worship. In the world as it is, however, the
most secure and dedicated life may have need on occasion for the
singular accents of a particular religious tradition in order to
renew a vision that identifies the world as both an object of
demanding, if tender, care and a temple of worship.

Above all, then, religion evidently does not begin in fear—
for there is nothing to fear where there is nothing to lose—but
in a sensitivity to the world or to some dimension of it as a
mysterium tremendum which must be identified and cherished as

the source or symbol of all that is finally worth being, doing, and having. Of course the fearful, the precarious, and the tragic may greatly affect religions. In tragic and fearful circumstances all commitments and values may surely seem more urgent and momentous, even as memories and friends may become more precious. But if a person becomes more religious in times of crisis, in old age, or in the face of his own or another's death, it is not necessarily or only because he fears death or loss or recognizes more vividly his own impotence. It may also be because he has never before seen so clearly the splendor of the *mysterium tremendum* in which his life is set. Religion is no less indigenous to good times than to bad.

So Francis Bacon was fundamentally right when he suggested that "depth in philosophy bringeth men's minds to religion." For depth in a philosophy is judged not only by its logical coherence and conformity to the objective character of existence, but also by what it reveals and requires of persons. Philosophy calls man to a rigorous critique of all his claims and plagues him into an awareness of the values and standards by which he lives and judges. Therefore the philosopher inevitably faces questions and problems which are intricately related to the qualitative aspects of life and cannot easily avoid the conclusion, as Socrates claimed, that life is justified, not by its length or other quantitative features, but by its qualities. Depth in philosophy brings men's minds to religion because the need and obligation to encourage and share a vision of what and how man is in the world, including a vision of the qualitative possibilities open to choice and commitment, are apparently as great as the need and obligation to produce and share economic goods or to discover and disseminate scientific methods and results. A person may of course live without taking any of these needs and obligations very seriously; but it is at least possible, and quite probable, that he cannot live well without careful attention to them all.

And if religion is, finally, one of several modes in which the meanings of man's life are apprehended, articulated, and modified, it is or may be intimately related to all the intricate facets of his social and moral life, to the creation of art and beauty, or to all the forms of the pursuit of truth. And presumably religion, like the arts and sciences, may speak appropriately, if it speaks carefully, about all the sundry affairs of the heart and intellect. But religion need not seek and should not be allowed the final word on any matter. For in all matters final words are forbidden, and the dialogue between the many forms of experience and judgment is terminated prematurely if terminated at all.

3

On Religion and Morality

We have, because human, an inalienable prerogative of responsibility, which we cannot devolve, no, not as once was thought, even upon the stars. We can share it only with each other.

SIR CHARLES SHERRINGTON

ON MORAL JUDGMENT AND INQUIRY

A being without the consciousness of a moral demand is not human.

PAUL TILLICH

A community of persons, regardless of its origin or aim, is constantly confronted with moral questions and decisions. For in the words of Edmund Husserl, the world is there for man, not "as a mere *world of facts and affairs*, but, with the same immediacy, as a *world of values*, a *world of goods*, a *practical world*."[1] Thus one of the most obvious and pervasive traits of man is that he judges both himself and others. By both word and act he approves and disapproves, praises and blames, even when he declares that his judgments are not moral judgments or dismisses current morality as absurd and irrelevant. Apparently as a matter of necessity as well as choice, each community establishes certain standards and rules, which are clearly neither altogether utili-

[1] Edmund Husserl, *Idea: General Introduction to Pure Phenomenology*, New York, Macmillan, 1931, p. 103.

tarian nor simply aesthetic, to which the character and deeds of its members are expected to conform.

Now the anthropologist and the sociologist can surely discover by observation what the moral rules and standards are in any given community or situation, as well as the circumstances that make many of the rules and standards both desirable and in some sense necessary. Yet man's interest in his own conduct is by no means limited to what he or others actually do or to the circumstantial justification of particular acts. His most radical and significant interest concerns what he *ought* to do, regardless of what he does, and what is required of him as an intelligent creature, regardless of what other men or local and temporal circumstances may define as the expedient or the desired.

Problems of conduct are indeed complex and difficult enough when clearly limited to meeting only the requirements for survival in a specific environment and culture. What one must do in order to provide for the future, if one looks solely to the satisfaction of biological, personal, and social needs, is surely a terribly difficult and precarious project. But the addition of the conviction that conduct must also conform to a universal standard which must not be violated in spite of undesired or even tragic effects on personal interests and ambitions, multiplies and intensifies the problems of conduct almost infinitely. Yet this is undeniably man's view of his own predicament. At least through the ages many of the most perceptive and extraordinary men have declared that there is an order of existence, or universal requirements, to which man's free acts *ought* to conform regardless of the consequences to his personal life and fortunes. Many have insisted that this order, whether called Nature or God, the rational or the divine and whether known by insight, reason, or revelation, imposes discernable duties and specific requirements in every conceivable circumstance. What man thinks he ought to do, in remarkable contrast to what he in fact does, is often the very heaviest burden which his distressed and aspiring spirit must bear.

But when man seeks the *ought* or the grounds of the ought rather than a mere record of habitual acts and their circumstantial justification, anthropology and sociology, as sciences based on observation, can make only the most limited contributions unless the

ought can in fact be reduced to something other than the ought—
to the practical, the expedient, the widely approved, a disguised
struggle for power, or an illusion of one sort or another. For no
acquaintance with the objective and measurable facts of behavior
through sensory observation provides either unambiguous or sufficient premises on which to base the insistent moral claims of experience. If there is to be serious ethical inquiry at all, there must
be at least a tentative premise to the effect that the moral experience—a sense of worth which includes or entails an obligation to
act in one way rather than another—is in some measure veridical or
trustworthy. Furthermore, like sight or hearing or mind itself,
the sense of moral worth—of good and bad, of right and wrong—is
to all appearances not a derivative of something more primitive or
fundamental but an irreducible and inevitable property of the
mind which knows itself and in knowing itself must judge itself.

But whether inexplicable and irreducible or not, moral experience is as much a matter of fact as theoretical and appetitive
powers or even existence itself. And accordingly, ethics has traditionally been, not primarily an attempt to show that man is or must
be moral, but a quest for universal and nonarbitrary standards or
rules for the guidance of choice and voluntary behavior in the
pursuit and preservation of things of worth. Ethics or moral inquiry
is the critical analysis of the facts and implications of moral experience and the effort to elucidate and evaluate in the light of this
analysis the particular moral rules and practices that characterize
the different communities of men. Now such ethical analysis evidently cannot be completed apart from a reliable generalized conception of nature and man. And surely the possibility of this, in the
light of nature's infinite complexity and man's own radical freedom
is seriously in question. But we can nonetheless relate, tentatively
and with whatever wisdom we possess, the various dimensions and
requirements of life to one another, including the sense of worth
which entails moral duties and the sense of the holy which arouses
and sustains the passion for worship.

To be sure, as practically everyone who has seriously considered the matter agrees, ethical inquiry has had very little success
in the search for moral rules and practices that are reliable in all
times and places. Moral confusion and perplexity are not less but

more evident as knowledge and power increase. Increased knowledge and changed modes of living may clearly render long-accepted principles subject to revision or complete rejection; and practices that are highly desirable in one situation may prove to be the bane of another. If ethical inquiry can claim to have made anything at all reasonably certain, it is that both moral principles and specific practices are always subject to critical analysis in the light of new knowledge and altered conditions. It seems in fact increasingly obvious that neither moral questions nor even the answers to questions that do remain largely unchanged are necessarily the same year in and year out. Furthermore, apparently no aspect of life is ever wholly immune to serious and critical analysis by the moralist; and no moralist can expect to separate his problems from the complex of man's current and specific interests and activities. New powers and practices in living raise new moral problems and demand new answers to the old problems. The moral issues relative to the arts and sciences are continually reformulated, and every age must raise imaginative and probing questions concerning the moral implications of its various political and economic enterprises and commitments.

Of course problems in industry, art, science, politics, and religion are not in every respect or even in the most important respects moral problems. Yet there seems nonetheless no escape from the fact that any enterprise or action and its results, in any area of experience and endeavor, may affect other crucial features of the material and spiritual economy, and thereby incur the moral wrath or win the moral approval of those whose sense of worth has been affected. None therefore can claim immunity to moral concern and judgment. No matter how preoccupied a person may become with the purely quantitative, relational, or logical aspects of existence he cannot wholly escape moral problems and decisions. For although a man clearly cannot always choose whether or not to live, he must, if he lives at all, choose to live in one way rather than another. As long as the life of man qua man endures, there is no freedom from choice. And the sense of worth—that some things must or ought to be pursued and others shunned—is directly or indirectly involved in each decision.

Certainly no student of either religion or morality can afford to ignore the intricate and sometimes paradoxical relations between religious and moral judgments, or, for that matter, between moral judgments and all the other forms of action and value.

ON FOUR VIEWS OF MORALITY AND RELIGION

The doctrine of the autonomy of ethics is independent of the problem of religion, but compatible with, or perhaps even necessary for, any religion which respects individual conscience.

KARL POPPER

Without notable exception the major religions have declared themselves the moral mentors of mankind and have claimed that the highest good is unattainable apart from specific religious insights and practices or apart from participation in certain religious disciplines and rituals. The moral claims or commandments of the religions have of course often conflicted both internally and with each other. Yet moral as well as religious philosophers, seeking both consistency and an unchanging or unquestionable basis for moral experience and judgment, have nonetheless sometimes constructed their theories in essentially religious frameworks or agreed with the prophets and priests who have insisted that religious insight and commandments are above both the laws of the state and the claims of reason.

So perhaps the oldest and certainly one of the most persistent claims concerning the specific relation of religion and morality is that religion, conceived often, if inadequately, as obedience to the will of God or gods, is essentially amoral or both the necessary and the sufficient condition of any genuine morality. One clear and instructive, though admittedly extreme, example of thus elevating the *religious* completely above the *moral* is Søren Kierkegaard's claim that religion, or the relation of the individual to God, may in certain situations demand a complete "suspension of the ethical." Identifying the ethical with universal rules such as, "Thou shalt not kill," Kierkegaard insisted that the individual person, because he is "higher" than the universal, may be required by his particular relationship to God to do precisely what the universal ethical rule forbids. Appealing to the biblical story of Abraham's willingness to sacrifice Isaac, his only son, in spite of the fact that the universalized moral principle would condemn him as a murderer, Kierkegaard claimed that the extraordinary and inevitable paradox of genuine religious faith and commitment is that the individual's recognition of the absolute supremacy of God is consummated only when he is willing to violate, if God requires it, all moral requirements based on universal principles or reason. The demands of faith (religion) are the demands of God and therefore not subject to moral judgment conventionally or rationally conceived. In Kierkegaard's own words:

> Either there is an absolute duty toward God, and if so it is the paradox here described, that the individual as the individual is higher than the universal and as the individual stands in an absolute relation to the absolute or else faith never existed . . . or, to put it differently, Abraham is lost. . . .[2]

In other words, the relationship of the individual to God may contradict all requirements of the universal ethical rule, or Abraham, in that moment when he was willing to sacrifice Isaac as a burnt-offering to God, became a murderer.

Generalized, this view claims that the demands of religion—of the holy or God—may supersede or abrogate all the requirements and implications of rational and conventional morality. Or one might say, in this view all strictly moral questions are rendered secondary or irrelevant by the necessity of regarding the injunctions of the divine, no matter what they require, as the only moral demands. This claim is no doubt most compelling in the framework of the Judeo-Christian tradition where there is nothing anomalous in supposing that God somehow speaks directly and unequivocally to individual persons. But in practice if not in theory this claim has informed phases of every religious tradition; and many would perhaps still insist that unless a religion does provoke and sustain such ultimate and unalterable commitments, it is

[2] Søren Kierkegaard, *Fear and Trembling* and *The Sickness Unto Death*, trans. by L. Lowrie, New York, Doubleday, Anchor Books, 1954, p. 91.

superficial or pseudo religion. Unless the requirements of the holy are absolute, it may be argued, then the holy is not truly holy.

But Martin Buber, although more profoundly convinced than most modern men of the possibility that God is personal and may "speak" to an individual, has clearly described the fallacy and the terrible danger of this view, particularly in the extreme form represented by Kierkegaard. Buber observes:

> Kierkegaard here takes for granted something that cannot be taken for granted even in the world of Abraham, much less in ours. He does not take into consideration the fact that the problematics of the decision of faith is preceded by the problematics of the hearing itself. Who is it whose voice one hears? . . . Moloch imitates the voice of God.[3]

In other words, the problematics of hearing, even if there is a God who speaks to man, casts into serious doubt any denial of universal moral rules or principles. As both Jew and philosopher Buber is perhaps doubly aware that our age is one "in which the suspension of the ethical fills the world in a caricaturized form. . . . In the realm of Moloch honest men lie and compassionate men torture. And they really and truly believe that brother-murder will prepare the way for brotherhood! There appears to be no escape from the most evil of all idolatry."[4] And surely none can deny that under the rubric of various synonyms the supposedly holy becomes the excuse for extraordinary duplicity and violence.

Buber's own view of the relation of religion and morality is that of the prophet Micah, who, in Buber's terms, insisted that God requires of "every man (not of Abraham, his chosen one, but of you and me) nothing more than justice and love, and that he 'walk humbly' with Him, with God—in other words, *not much more* than the fundamental ethical."[5] But even if Buber is basically right and the moral content of religion is of utmost significance, it is still profoundly important, if it is possible, to determine the nature and significance of the *"not much more"*

[3] Martin Buber, *The Eclipse of God*, New York, Harper & Row, 1952, pp. 152-153.
[4] *Ibid.*, pp. 154-155.
[5] *Ibid.*, p. 153. Italics added.

in the fundamental and total character and function of religion.

This ancient and recurring view, that religious commandments are the unique and unquestionable demands of the holy
or God and therefore take absolute precedence over moral conventions and reason, has (as Buber suggests) apparently contributed greatly to the havoc which religious fanaticism has so
often worked in human affairs and has consequently stimulated
diametrically opposed views of the relation of religion and
morality. The apparent and catastrophic results of the view that
religion is amoral—the witchhunts, the inquisitions, the many
forms of fanaticism and intolerance—have led some few famous
or infamous moralists to declare unequivocally that religion is in
fact essentially immoral in effect if not by intention or that any
good which might conceivably be credited to religion is utterly
and unmistakably canceled out by the incredible bigotry, intolerance, hatred, and bloodshed which the religions have provoked or aided. Of course, not many moralists have cared or
dared to be as bold as Friedrich Nietzsche who declared that
religion, or more specifically Christianity, by preserving the weak
and rejecting the strong, encourages both meekness and insensi-
tivity in its followers and is thus responsible for a threatened "sublime abortion of mankind."[6]

But it is not an uncommon claim, particularly among those
devoted to science, that the religions characteristically generate
impulses, attitudes, and beliefs which are utterly incompatible
with a tolerant, reasonable, and fruitful approach to the ever
urgent problems which men must solve and the values they ought
to pursue. Every student of contemporary philosophy, psychology,
and sociology has surely encountered, in one of its various forms,
the accusation which charges religion with precipitating personal
and social catastrophes by encouraging attitudes and beliefs which
are presumably antithetical to rational inquiry and intelligent
compromise.

The idea that the religions encourage immoral forms of behavior has rarely been expressed more clearly and devastatingly

6 Friedrich Nietzsche, *Beyond Good and Evil*, Sec. 62. There are several
editions of this work which was first published in 1885.

or with more insight into the fact that this is surely not the whole picture than in David Hume's *Dialogues Concerning Natural Religion*. There Philo, the philosohical sceptic, and often the supposed spokesman of Hume himself, observed:

> If the religious spirit be ever mentioned in any historical narration, we are sure to meet afterwards with a detail of the miseries which attend it. And no period of time can be happier or more prosperous than those in which it is never recognized or heard of.[7]

Moral conduct, he claims, clearly owes much more to "natural honesty and benevolence" than to the "pompous views suggested by theological theories and systems."[8] Indeed, he continues, a great profession of religious devotion, far from indicating the moral integrity of an individual, is only a sign to the prudent to be on their guard, "lest they be cheated and deceived by him." For religion, the argument claims, not only condones but actually inspires deceitful and immoral behavior by insisting on "frivolous observances or rapturous ectasies or a bigoted credulity" which will surely "weaken extremely man's attachment to the natural motives of justice and humanity." The very notion that there is merit or power in such religious practices, Philo suggests, combined with the "preposterous" ideas of praise, blame, rewards, and punishments, and the consequent social necessity of seeming to accept such religious doctrines lead to the "habit of dissimulation," so that in the long run "fraud and falsehood become the predominant principle" supported by religion.[9] Instead of being either amoral or the indispensable basis of morality or even a significant moral force, religion, Hume suggests through the words of Philo, makes immoral hypocrites and liars of many and perhaps deceives the rest.[10]

[7] David Hume, *Dialogues Concerning Natural Religion*, New York, Hafner, 1948, p. 87.

[8] *Ibid.*, p. 88.

[9] *Ibid.*, pp. 89-90.

[10] A more direct expression of Hume's own opinion on this point is found in *The Natural History of Religion*, Sec. X, where he observes that "The greatest crimes have been found, in many instances, compatible with superstitious piety and devotion. Hence, it is justly regarded as unsafe to draw any certain inference in favor of a man's morals, from the fervour or strictness of his religious exercises, even though he himself believes them sincere."

Now no candid and impartial judgment can completely deny the truth of Hume's observations or the fact that religious commitments have sometimes encouraged dissimulation and hindered social as well as scientific reform and progress. Deeply rooted in the sense of the ultimate and inviolable, religion is no doubt peculiarly susceptible to the fallacy that its own claims are the chief, if not the only, legitimate claims and is consequently easily exploited to promote selfish and irrational aims. Excesses of various sorts repeatedly appear in religious persons and movements, particularly in times of religious revival and in the face of economic and social crises. To identify one's own will with the will of God or to admit nothing problematic in the voice one seems to hear or in what one takes to be the requirements of the holy will no doubt often arouse and support the most arrogant enthusiasm, even as the doctrine of complete dependence on God or a thoroughgoing physical determinism may encourage lassitude and indifference in the face of remediable evils.

Yet those who regard religious activities and beliefs as essentially immoral or a stumbling block to morality should not make the mistake of thinking that David Hume was an unambiguous advocate of their cause. Besides observing, as noted earlier, that men without any religion are little better than brutes, Hume also had Philo, the philosophical sceptic it should be remembered, confess that "no one has a deeper sense of religion impressed on his mind, or pays more profound adoration to the Divine Being, as he discovers himself to reason in the inexplicable contrivance and artifice of nature."[11] Philo also quotes, apparently with approval, the saying of Seneca, that "To know God is to worship him," and suggests that the sceptic in philosophy is perhaps worthy above all of the compassion and indulgence of the divine because only he attempts "to suspend all judgment with regard to such sublime and such extraordinary subjects."[12] "To be a philosophical sceptic is," Philo concludes, "in a man of letters, the first and most essential step towards being a sound believing Christian. . . ."[13] Hume made it reasonably clear, not least of all by the care with

[11] David Hume, op. cit., p. 82.
[12] Ibid., pp. 93-94.
[13] Ibid., p. 94.

which he developed, in the dialogues, the positions of both the deist and the orthodox believer, as well as the sceptic, that as he saw it there is no clear case either for or against religion. He seemed to admit finally that the discovery that the religions tend to be far from morally innocent or perfect need not prove their worthlessness, provided religious symbols, actions, and beliefs express or illuminate the condition of man in the world or add to the total value that is possible in human experience. He was no doubt convinced that the objects of religion, like beauty and morals, "are not so properly objects of the understanding as of taste and sentiment";[14] but he also apparently knew, much better than the contemporary positivist, the inestimable harm, both intellectual and moral, of unnecessary and stringent denial in such matters.

And surely, regardless of the outcome of Hume's inquiry, if religion may share at all in the pursuit of truth or contribute to the increase of beauty and joy, it may not be summarily dismissed because of even the most serious moral defects. It is of course quite possible that religious functions and values, though genuine and important considered in themselves, are more dispensable than the enterprises and values which they may conceivably frustrate or destroy. But it is at least equally arguable that although religion has no doubt been deeply and even inevitably involved in the most hateful and immoral practices of man, this fact does not of itself totally condemn its characteristic powers and values. For the powers and values of the religions, in this respect like the powers and values of science and art, are, if potentially beneficent, rightly understood only when they are rightly employed.

Therefore the third and obviously in many respects the most defensible view is that religion and morality are quite independent of one another or have at least no universal or inevitable relation, even though either one may often have the most profound influence on the other. A. E. Taylor has aptly put the matter this way:

[14] David Hume, *An Enquiry Concerning Human Understanding*, Sec. XII, Pt. III. First published in 1748, this work is available in several different editions.

There are persons, not otherwise mentally defective, who seem to be almost devoid of [religious temperament], just as there are others who have little or no sense of humor or feeling for beauty. As many of these persons are ethically excellent, some of them exceptionally so, and as again the religious temperament is often found strongly developed in persons of quite inferior ethical development, there seems to be no direct connection between religious sensibility and moral excellence, though, of course religious feeling is the most powerful of moral influences when it is conjoined in the same person with ethical fervour.[15]

In a very similar vein John Stuart Mill observed that, "Such moral teaching as existed in Greece had very little to do with religion. . . . For the enforcement of human moralities secular inducements were almost exclusively relied on." And he concluded, rightly or wrongly, that the example of Greece provides "a strong presumption that in other cases early religious teaching has owed its power over mankind rather to its being early than to its being religious."[16]

There is in fact widespread agreement among contemporary philosophers, though not always for the same reasons, that morality is autonomous or logically independent of the religious insights, beliefs, and activities which may characterize a person or a culture. This view owes its modern influence largely to David Hume and Immanuel Kant, although the idea is at least as old as Plato's *Euthyphro* and Aristotle's *Nicomachean Ethics*. Kant was himself very much the heir of the long theological tradition which had identified the moral law with the commandments of God. But clearheaded as he was, he could not fail to see that the claim, "Murder is wrong," for example, is utterly different, as Socrates had pointed out in *The Euthyphro*, from the claim that "God disapproves of murder," unless one can go on to show, which seems clearly impossible, that *being wrong* and *being disapproved by God* are indeed logically equivalent or that the former is derivable from the latter. And confronted with Hume's and his own devastat-

---

[15] A. E. Taylor, *Elements of Metaphysics*, London, Methuen, 1903, p. 390.
[16] J. S. Mill, *Nature and Utility of Religion*, New York, Liberal Arts, 1958, pp. 54-55.

ing analysis of the arguments from both reason and experience which purport to prove the existence of God, Kant saw that morality is in any case utterly indefensible in rational terms insofar as it is supposed to depend upon the will of God. Thus Kant was led to the conclusion that, far from being derived from religious or theological principles, the fundamental elements of morality must be derived from reason and that the rational moral principles in turn, combined with moral experience, constitute the most cogent evidence available for postulating the existence of God.

The logic of morals, then, far from depending on religion or on the assumption that God exists, is the very heart of the practical logic by which the existence of God and immortality (fundamental religious beliefs, according to Kant) are made the necessary postulates concerning matters about which no man can discover the whole or ultimate truth. Of course, it cannot be said that Kant himself totally separated morality and religion. He was convinced, however, that the moral law can be discovered through reason alone or without any reference at all to religious experience, insight, belief, or activity as such. Yet he was also convinced that "belief in a God and in another world is so interwoven with my moral sentiment, that as there is little danger of my losing the latter, there is quite as little fear lest I should ever be deprived of the former."[17] But the existence of God is implied, through practical reason, by moral experience and principles, and not vice versa. In fact Kant may be said to have identified religion with morality by insisting that the necessary and sufficient expression of religious faith is obedience to the moral law. A moral life in accordance with reason, he thought, is all that even God can reasonably demand, and "The illusion of being able to accomplish anything . . . through religious acts of worship is religious superstition. . . ."[18] The essence of religion, he in fact said, is to regard moral laws as divine commands—even though the moral law can be derived from reason alone. In Kant, religion as conventionally

[17] Immanuel Kant, *Critique of Pure Reason*, trans. by F. Max Muller, New York, Doubleday, Dolphin Books, 1961, p. 162.

[18] Immanuel Kant, *Religion Within the Limits of Reason Alone*, trans. by T. Greene and H. Hudson, New York, Harper & Row, Harper Torchbooks, 1960, p. 162.

conceived became practically superfluous, though God and immortality remained as postulates required to complete the supposed rational and moral order of the cosmos as a whole.

Kant has influenced both many who are still very close to
his own position and many who differ radically from it but who still
defend the complete autonomy of moral judgment in respect to
religious or theological principles. Among the latter are such
men as Sidney Hook, who, in his most polemical and thoroughgoing treatises against the sects and traditions of the religions,
echoes the sentiments of Nietzsche and Hume's Philo. Defining
religion as "belief in theological dogmas as revealed to an authoritative church," Hook has claimed that "all this theological baggage
is completely superfluous" insofar as one is interested in such
ethical concepts as "the brotherhood of man, democracy, peace,
cooperation, economic security."[19] In an explicit denial of Kierkegaard's interpretation of the biblical account of Abraham and Isaac,
he claims:

> A new moral insight was born when Abraham identified the
> voice which bade him stay his hand as the voice of God. Thus
> the parable illustrates the Feuerbachian contention that men cre-
> ate and worship Gods in their own moral image and confirms
> the Kantian principle of the autonomy of moral reason with respect
> to traditional conceptions of religion and God.[20]

Parenthetically it may be relevant to note however that, contrary
to Feuerbach's thesis, God is not often conceived in exclusively
moral terms; and George Santayana has said, not without insight,
that "No religion has ever given a picture of deity which men could
have imitated without the grossest immorality."[21]

In any case, although Hook is presumably mistaken in regarding belief in the existence of God as central for all religion, this
does not necessarily invalidate his basic position; for his fundamental and recurring thesis, apparently meant to be an empirical

[19] Sidney Hook, "Mr. Toynbee's City of God," 'artisan Review, June,
1948, pp. 694-695.
[20] Sidney Hook, The Quest for Being, New   ork, St. Martin's, 1961,
p. 133.
[21] George Santayana, Reason in Art, Vol .V, in The Life of Reason,
New York, Scribner, 1905, p. 175.

claim, is that the revival of religion is "really part of the more inclusive movement of irrationalism in modern thought."[22] Accordingly, he insists that although philosophical naturalism "is sufficient to gratify all the legitimate needs of the understanding" through scientific inquiry, the fact that naturalism "cannot provide the consolation which the tenderminded must have, if they are to find their existence meaningful and tolerable" is "the perennial and most powerful source of religious belief."[23] The implication is of course clear: religions are really illegitimate modes of satisfying the needs of the understanding or constellations of beliefs and practices which, far from being either sufficient or necessary for judicial processes or moral excellence, are instead only means of frustrating critical intelligence and confidence in scientific inquiry. The only sense in which Hook admits the relevance of *religion* is when the term is used, as in the philosophy of John Dewey, as a very general synonym for *moral* or "a form of natural piety not merely towards existence but to the ideal possibilities of a better existence."[24]

On the other hand are men such as John E. Smith, who, though he begins by insisting on the autonomy of morals in the sense that "The good is to be chosen for its own sake, just as the good life is to be lived for its own sake,"[25] comes nevertheless in the end to the somewhat paradoxical conclusion that religion provides "the meaning and purpose of moral striving"[26] or puts the heart into moral matters. Smith distinguishes clearly between *morality* as the concern with "principles ordering the lives of men in society and the consistent means for remaking society in accordance with . . . ideals"[27] and *religion* as the concern for "the meaning and importance" of "initial certainties arising from the experience of its founders and heroes" in regard to "the ground" and "the final destiny of man."[28] But although he observes that morality as such "neither knows of nor cares for the *ultimate* destinies of the people

[22] Sidney Hook, *op. cit.*, pp. 96-97.
[23] *Ibid.*, p. 98.
[24] Sidney Hook, *Education for Modern Man*, New York, Dial Press, 1946, p. 111.
[25] John E. Smith, *Reason and God*, New Haven, Yale, 1961, p. 197.
[26] *Ibid.*, p. 201.
[27] *Ibid.*, p. 192.
[28] *Ibid.*, p. xiii.

and societies that recognize its commands,"[29] he later insists also that "Just as surely as moral criticism implies moral standards, so moral standards themselves imply some view concerning the final destiny of man."[30]

Unsatisfactory as it is simply to identify religion with any supposed "certainties" in regard to "the ground" and "the final destiny of man," there is no doubt Smith is speaking primarily about the symbolic and conceptual traditions which everyone recognizes as religious. So paradoxical as it seems, it must be said that the autonomy of morality as he conceives it does not imply that morality is ever quite possible apart from religion. "Ultimately, no view of the good life," he in fact says, "no serious doctrine of what man ought to do, is ever possible apart from some view of his final destiny; and such a view introduces the religious element."[31] In spite of the so-called autonomy of morality, then, "morality is necessarily related to religion,"[32] and "in addition to determining the content of morality, religion is the final judge of morality."[33] And although religion must not be an authoritarian force "compelling the good life through fear," the moral life is nonetheless "both unsure and incomplete without a living connection with religious faith."[34] In effect, Smith claims, religion is required to *complete* and *insure* the value of the moral life.

Now surely anyone wishing to maintain a genuine distinction between morality and religion, and at the same time defend the importance of both, will hesitate to choose between the Charybdis of Hook's polemic to the effect that religion is altogether superfluous and the Scylla of Smith's claim that the moral life is *really* impossible without religion. For somewhere between the whirlpool which engulfs religion in accusations of unmitigated "irrelevance, torture, exploitation, terror, and wars of extermination"[35] and the rock of religion standing as a necessary and "ever present guardian, warning morality of its possible pretensions and en-

[29] *Ibid.*, p. 192.
[30] *Ibid.*, p. 200.
[31] *Ibid.*
[32] *Ibid.*, p. 201.
[33] *Ibid.*
[34] *Ibid.*, p. 202.
[35] Sidney Hook, "Mr. Toynbee's City of God," *op. cit.*, p. 694.

abling it to be free from transformation into ideology,"[36] there is
evidently a path where religion is sometimes highly relevant and
sometimes irrelevant, or at least dispensable, a severe and helpful
critic of moral presuppositions and practices but nonetheless subject itself to the most incisive moral analysis and also ever in dire
need of justification.

Hook, in spite of the exaggerations in his polemics against
religion, is plainly right in suggesting that moral insight and
integrity are often totally independent of the specific doctrines
and practices of conventional religions, and would be no less right
if he went on to suggest also, as he consistently might, that the
most sincere and profound morality is altogether possible without
any unwavering views concerning "the ground" and "the final
destiny" of mankind. And Smith obviously claims too much when
he makes religion responsible for both informing and judging the
moral life and certainly fails to indicate how religion, apart from
refusals to face the terrible uncertainties of existence, can—though
he clearly implies that it does—render the moral life sure and
complete. Yet the very fact that he protests too much perhaps bears
witness to a very important matter: there is apparently a dimension of existence, whether eternal or a relatively ephemeral phase
in man's restless and wondrous career, within which religious symbols and concepts are both ontologically real and judicially
relevant.

Consequently, the question whether or not it is possible without religious symbols, concepts, and activities to articulate satisfactorily *what* and *how* man is in the world and reliably promote or
direct all choice and action is much more fundamental and
decisive than the question whether or not it is possible to be moral
without being religious. For surely it is conceivable that a person
might radically and tragically shortchange himself by rejecting
religion simply because he had discovered that moral excellence is
apparently possible without it; for it might indeed be the case
that although moral excellence is altogether possible independent
of religion (as it often is in complete ignorance of scientific
methodology and discovery), it is nonetheless impossible to appre-

[36] John E. Smith, *op. cit.*, p. 201.

hend and articulate certain critical aspects of existence without the religious forms of judgment. And in regard to this more fundamental question of the relevance of religious symbols, concepts, and activities in discovering and articulating radically important dimensions of existence, even John Stuart Mill's appeal to the Greeks as an example of morality without religion does not touch the critical issue. For if the morality of the Greeks was not closely related to their formal religion or ritual, both the religious quality of their experience and their moral ideals were lucidly expressed by their literature and philosophy, especially in the works of Homer and Hesiod, the dramatic tragedies of Euripides and Sophocles, and the dialogues of Plato. In fact no clearer vision of the divine, no more comprehensive concept of man, and no firmer conviction of the essential truth and efficacy of symbolic judgment in the pursuit of qualitative excellence is to be found anywhere. If nothing is more intrinsically religious than faith in symbolic expression of the divine as a mode of articulating and understanding the existential problems of man and thus guiding his conduct towards the highest excellence that is considered possible, then no people has been more religious in their approach to morality than the Greeks unless the surviving examples of literature and philosophy are in fact unbelievably atypical.

It seems indeed almost inescapable that, although religion and morality are always logically and often actually independent of each other, the person who is completely insensitive or indifferent to religious concepts and symbols is also unaware of specific and important dimensions—heights of aspiration and joy, depths of despair and agony, states and objects of consciousness, judicial possibilities and consequences—in the multivalence of being within which man exists and which sound moral judgment cannot always ignore. The phenomenologists and existentialists, no matter what one may think of their most characteristic teachings and postures, have at least made emphatically clear the fact that the actual structure of man's existence, his forms of being and his powers of judging, may transcend infinitely the form and weight of his body and the categories of sense and science. The nonreligious person, or the person devoid of religious concepts and symbols—and the

sensitivities and powers implied therein—may then be as incapable
of certain highly relevant and revealing judgments as the person
ignorant of mathematics is of others.

But if religion and morality are, as they seem, both forms of
existing and judging, their relations may of course be as various
and complex as the relations between any two aspects or areas of
experience. Surely it is recognized, for example, that the person
whose thought and vision are free of narrow and conventional
moral impediments may see and think more clearly in certain
scientific and social matters than those whose thought and conduct
are deeply influenced by uncritical moral assumptions and
prejudices. Similarly, though it is by no means self-evidently or
necessarily so, it may sometimes be true that the religious judgment rendered by the immoral person is more cogent, revealing,
and reliable than the religious claims of the morally scrupulous.
And also in certain instances religious judgments, like some scientific discoveries, may be morally significant or have important
moral implications, even though in other cases a reliable moral
judgment may be possible only by eliminating religious concerns
and qualities. For example, insofar as freedom of religion is a
genuine and justified moral principle, equally as important as any
religious principle or doctrine and not just a matter of political
expedience, our decisions concerning such matters as official
prayers and the reading of sacred books in the public schools can
presumably be consistently moral only as we succeed in disallow-
ing our religious commitments to dictate our position. In other
words, some moral decisions are apparently necessarily independent
of religious perspectives, even though religious perspectives may
sometimes inform or radically transform the moral point of view.

So although many moral decisions are clearly independent
of religious commitment and much religious activity is patently
autonomous in relation to morals as either science or art, the
distinctions between morality and religion need not and must not
deny the frequent and profound influence of each on the other.
Extremely unlike things may, both directly and indirectly, exercise
the greatest influence on each other. As different as painting and
mathematics are, for example, the achievement of the appearance
of normal perspectives and spatial relations on a flat surface was

dependent on mathematical knowledge and gave rise in turn to purely mathematical problems. Also, the logic of physics is clearly one thing and the logic of politics a very different one; yet few inhabitants of the earth today are able to live without being affected by the mutual, and perhaps mutually destructive, influence of physics and politics. The fact that moral and religious judgments are logically or functionally different does not in the least preclude their mutual and profound effects on each other.

Yet the fact that exceptionally moral men have sometimes been indifferent or even hostile to all specifically religious teachings and practices, combined with the obvious fact that practices which are plainly immoral have flourished in the name and with the support of religion, have led to a fourth, and perhaps currently the most prevalent, approach to the relation of morality and religion. This approach insists that, illusion and superstition aside, religion has never been essentially anything other than a form of moral principles and sanctions. Morality is then religion. Or in more traditional terms, religion is nothing other than doing justice and loving mercy. The position of Sidney Hook, described earlier, might in fact be very well interpreted in these terms, except that he obviously, and perhaps correctly, prefers not to characterize himself or his moral philosophy as religious at all.

The widespread contemporary claim that the moral person is *ipso facto* also a religious person stems no doubt in part from the moral elements of ancient Judaism but owes its dominance more directly to the moral emphasis of the Protestant Revolution and, as already suggested, the extraordinary philosophical influence of Immanuel Kant. Whatever else the Protestant movement may have attempted, it was surely an effective moral protest against certain practices of the Church and the clergy. And the spirit of this moral protest, for better or worse, still persists in much of Protestantism and influences many to identify completely the *religious* man with the *good* man. And Kant, we may say, justified the moral emphasis of Protestantism philosophically by suggesting, as indicated earlier, that it is moral experience above all else that makes the existence of God a plausible postulate of human reason. In this world morality and justice, merit and reward, righteousness and happiness, Kant observed, are indeed flagrantly disproportionate, since the righteous so often suffer while the wicked prosper. Unless the world is finally and radically irrational, he concluded, God must be assumed to exist as the judge who is able, in spite of all phenomenal events that suggest the contrary, to reward the righteous or moral man with perfect happiness in an immortal life beyond this one. The ontology of religion becomes simply the ontology suggested to the practical reason by a high sense of moral duty.

Several other factors have of course conspired to force the identity of morality and religion on the uncritical modern mind. The sciences have claimed to have a complete monopoly on "the facts" and have admitted their inability to deal with "values." And religious leaders have often pounced on this idea and asserted their own claim to nothing but "values," as if they had thought of it themselves as a way of maintaining responsible respectability in the terrific competition with science. In addition, religious diversity, combined with technical and social developments which have brought all peoples closer together, apparently makes respect for different creeds and rituals not only an ideal, but a practical necessity. And it is only a short step, though surely not a necessary one, from the respect for different practices and convictions to the conclusion that personal integrity and social responsibility are all that count or that so long as moral and social duties are performed all specifically religious activities and products are essentially superfluous. This view is also reflected in and supported by the current philosophical persuasion that knowledge is wholly the province of morally neutral science or that all substantive claims which cannot be verified by sensory experience are noncognitive or emotive and express essentially only arbitrary needs and distinctions. According to this view, religious as well as artistic, aesthetic, and moral values are judicially irrelevant or intellectually empty.

Insofar as the view that morality is religion represents a tolerant approach to different religious languages and perspectives and so emphasizes the importance of certain rights and prerogatives regardless of personal religious beliefs and activities, it is unquestionably a moral advance over the views which tend to identify religion with revealed and eternal truths or justify extraordinary punishment for those who are unable to believe certain metaphysical and religious claims. But to judge a religion wholly on moral grounds or to identify the moral and the religious seems no less wrongheaded in important respects than the notion that all judgments are in all significant respects moral judgments. Indeed it seems reasonably clear that whatever authority religion may have in the moral life is derived ultimately from its ontological truth. The ontological or metaphysical quest is therefore fundamental in any religious view, and to forsake the rigorous demands of actual discovery in favor of emphasis solely on right conduct is to admit that religion has no firm grip on the truly real. In other words, if religion cannot speak to the contemporary mind as an indispensable mode of articulating the structure and content of existence, of man, and the world, then surely religion cannot speak as a moral teacher at all. For although the moral judgment is never simply a recognition of "facts" as such, sanity in morals no less than in science demands that our judgments take proper account of the complex conditions in which they occur.

Indeed since both the uniqueness and the autonomy of religious judgments are put into question by the tendency to equate the religious with the moral, an extended examination of the issues involved is clearly demanded. For if religion is equivalent to the moral or superfluous except for its moral content, then surely a philosophy of religion that goes beyond the discovery of that fact or fails to discover it is perchance wasted breath and idle labor.

ON JOHN DEWEY'S VIEW OF MORALITY AND RELIGION

And if there is nothing that can so hide the face of our fellow-man as morality can, religion can hide from us as nothing else can the face of God.
                                        MARTIN BUBER

John Dewey's defense of the idea that the religions must be judged primarily on moral grounds or that the moral life and the religious life are largely identical continues and attempts to justify a claim that is as old as the Hebrew prophets and a dominant strain in the entire history of Protestantism. And there is hardly a better way of seeing clearly the issues and their implications than by looking critically at Dewey's moral interpretations and criticism of religious symbols, concepts, and activities. For Dewey, unlike many professional ecclesiastics, was deeply concerned about the logic of inquiry as well as the logic of morals and did not shrink at all from drawing the inferences implied by his premises.

Dewey himself preferred to call his general philosophy *instrumentalism* in order to emphasize that all ideas or claims to knowledge are significant only to the extent that they serve as effective instruments or means for solving problems. And the problems with which philosophy can characteristically deal, he thought, are social and political rather than metaphysical or religious in the traditional sense. Convinced that man is a highly complicated but thoroughly natural creature, and in no sense a transcendent spirit struggling with an alien world, he believed that knowledge is basically the result of the interaction between a living organism and its environment, rather than the achievement of an independent mind or a detached spectator who turns away from the world to receive from some extraordinary dimension of existence a revelation of eternal truth. Man learns by doing, by living, by experimenting. Ideas are not idly entertained but used. The aim of inquiry is the solution of concrete and specific problems, not a comprehensive vision of things *sub specie aeternitas*. Ideas and beliefs are justified primarily as guides of action, and not by either a quality intrinsic to themselves or as replicas of objective structures and qualities. Even art, traditionally the epitome of achievement for its own sake, may be said to be justified instrumentally, according to Dewey, as a mode of producing and sustaining certain qualities of experience.

There can also be little doubt that the basis of Dewey's philosophy of instrumentalism was his profound moral sensitivity and conviction. He was, no matter what theme or problem he pursued, as the late Irwin Edman once said, an "incorrigible moralist," always devoted to clarifying issues related either directly or indirectly to the right and the good. But moral problems, Dewey insisted, are not unique in either their origin or their demands on intellectual or other special powers. Rather, moral problems arise in precisely the same manner and contexts and are solved in essentially the same way as practical and scientific problems. Whether an act is right or wrong is never due simply to its conformity to a priori rules or arbitrary standards but to its effect on character and events in a particular situation. Moral problems are generated by specific circumstances and must be solved in the terms or acts demanded by the circumstances.

But this does not mean, Dewey claimed, that moral problems are nebulous or less important and objective than other types of problems. The very existence of man requires certain supporting conditions, including economic and cultural institutions. And the economic and cultural environment, with its specific requirements and corresponding benefits, he insisted, is no less a matter of fact than the planets in their orbits. So the principles which define and presumably signify the conditions that sustain social processes and structures are no more mysterious or nondiscoverable—though they may be more complex—than the laws which describe the physical world. But even the physical world, Dewey recognized, is a "mixture of the regular and dependable and the unsettled and uncertain,"[37] or a "union of the hazardous and the stable, of the incomplete and the recurrent. . . ."[38] The principles that are applicable in one community, then, need not and will not be altogether or precisely relevant in another where knowledge, interests, and material conditions are different. As in all inquiry, the fundamental problem in moral judgment is not to discover or establish unchanging laws and standards but to develop methods which will be effective in dealing with a multitude of situations and problems. And the scientific method, with its rejection of arbitrary authority, its emphasis on freedom and change, and on systematic inquiry and experimental testing, Dewey thought, is the most reliable guide in morals as well as in other matters.

And because the religions have traditionally been both authoritarian and the advocates of eternal and inalienable laws of conduct,

[37] John Dewey, *Experience and Nature*, London, Allen & Unwin, 1929, p. 56.
[38] *Ibid.*, p. 62.

Dewey was for the most part of his long career unconcerned
with the religions or the religious dimensions of experience. He said
late in life that he had "not been able to attach much importance
to religion as a philosophic problem"[39] and had suggested earlier
that the strange paradoxes of religious morality render the subject
unworthy of the serious moral philosopher. But when he finally
gave the Terry Lectures at Yale University, he turned a mature
mind to some of the important contemporary problems in religion
and the philosophy of religion. The result, published under the
title of A Common Faith, was a short and penetrating, though certainly limited, analysis of the "institutions of religion" as distinguished from and in many respects opposed to "the religious
aspects of experience." Both in what he said and in what he omitted
this brief book pointed up then current, and still influential, approaches to the relation of the moral and the religious.

The most fundamental distinction in A Common Faith was
between "religion" and "the religious aspect of experience."[40] Religion, Dewey said, is essentially an institution with "a special
body of beliefs and practices."[41] And the beliefs and practices of
the religions, he observed, have been so various and "so shocking"
that the noun "religion" cannot possibly imply anything very
specific or morally desirable. Emphasizing the mottled moral
history of the religions, he suggested that the supernatural, for
example, "has been conceived in a multitude of incompatible
ways,"[42] that "there is no conceivable purpose for which rites have
not been employed,"[43] and that "there is no discernable unity in
the moral motivations appealed to and utilized."[44] Disregarding
the very significant possibility that such disparate facts, instead
of being imaginary trivia, may bear witness to the overwhelming
importance of the symbols and practices of religion, he dismissed
religion primarily because the term "applies equally to the most

[39] John Dewey, "From Absolutism to Experimentalism," in On Experience, Nature, and Freedom, R. Bernstein, ed., New York, Bobbs-Merrill, 1960,
p. 11.
[40] John Dewey, A Common Faith, New Haven, Yale, 1934, Chap. I.
[41] Ibid., p. 9.
[42] Ibid., p. 4.
[43] Ibid., p. 5.
[44] Ibid., p. 7.

savage and degraded beliefs and practices that have related to unseen powers and to noble ideals of a religion having the greatest
share of moral content."[45] And to distinguish unmistakably between his own subject of inquiry and the "savage and degraded
beliefs and practices," Dewey limited his discussion primarily to
"the religious quality of experience." This distinction, inspired
in part surely by the Protestant tradition which has emphasized
the inseparability of *the religious* from *the good,* was no doubt
meant to suggest that religion (institutionalized rituals and beliefs in unseen powers) is always superfluous if not actually immoral and that one important step towards realizing the genuine
"religious quality of experience" is to get rid of the religions.

The "religious quality of experience" was accordingly defined
almost wholly in moral terms: "Any activity pursued in behalf
of an ideal end against obstacles and in spite of threats of personal
loss because of conviction of its general and enduring value is
religious in quality."[46] The "ideal end" is no doubt a moral notion,
although perhaps not altogether ontologically insignificant, for
Dewey. But unless the *ideal* is defined differently from the way
in which he ordinarily defined it (as an imaginative possibility
suggested by the actual), many aims and movements (such as
Fascism, Communism, and white supremacy), which Dewey clearly
would have found no less "savage and degraded" than the practices
of primitive and fanatic religions, might surely be described by
their proponents in precisely the terms he used to define "the
religious." Yet the intent of his definition is clear: The immoral
practices of the religions must not be allowed to taint the concept
of "the religious," and no worthy and difficult enterprise or achievement may be altogether excluded.

That Dewey's primary concern and categories are fundamentally moral is further evident in his treatment of certain traditional religious beliefs, especially in his view of the motives and
consequences of believing in the existence of God as a supernatural power on which human destiny depends. He clearly did not
wish to identify himself with the militant atheists, who, as he
described them, assume an attitude of defiance towards a sup-

[45] *Ibid.,* p. 27.
[46] *Ibid.,* p. 53.

posedly "indifferent and hostile world"[47] and thus ignore the fact that the life and efforts of the individual are supported by both nature and other men. Dewey himself apparently felt a profound piety towards the sustaining conditions, natural and social, of human existence. But he did not wish to give the slightest aid and comfort to traditional Christian notions of sin and salvation or to acquiesce to the claim that the "isolated and lonely soul" of the individual will be ultimately rescued by a supernatural God. He insisted that nothing in experience justifies the belief that God is an actual being and suggested that such belief is only the result of hypostatizing what is really only an imaginative construct. He pointed out also that neither mysticism nor any religious experience can be said to prove the existence of a supernatural God unless "the conditions, of whatever sort, that produce the effects are called "God.' "[48]

Yet for Dewey the strongest argument against belief in the supernatural (and the religions that depend upon and nurture this belief) was neither the fact that the empirical evidence is inconclusive nor that the logical and mystical proofs assume all they prove. Belief in the existence of the supernatural is unacceptable above all because of its effects on the practical and moral affairs of men. "Men have never fully used the powers they possess to advance the good life," he declared, "because they have waited upon some power external to themselves and to nature to do the work they are responsible for doing. Dependence upon an external power is the counterpart of surrender of human endeavor."[49] The most urgent problems of man, he claimed, depend for their solution on the development of intelligent and humane methods of understanding and controlling his own behavior and social relationships. For without such understanding and control, he thought, the catastrophes of war, economic depression, and tyranny are bound to continue. He was also convinced that:

> Such understanding will not develop unless we strive for it. The assumption that only supernatural agencies can give control is a

[47] *Ibid.*, p. 12.
[48] *Ibid.*, p. 46.
[49] *Ibid.*, p. 76.

sure method of retarding this effort. It is as sure to be a hindering force now with respect to social intelligence, as the similar appeal was earlier an obstruction in the development of physical knowledge.[50]

Belief in the supernatural is then not only the result of irrational fear and a rationalization of normal indolence, but also a specific cause of fear and of acquiescence in the face of problems that might be solved by a more realistic sense of power and responsibility directed by intelligence. Belief in the existence of the supernatural and the institutions of religion which support it are then *morally condemned* by the fact that they stand "in the way of an effective realization of the sweep and depth of the implications of natural human relations" and "in the way of using the means that are in our power to make radical changes in these relations."[51] Thus where Kant had suggested that only moral experience renders belief in the existence of God at all plausible, Dewey insisted that genuine moral experience and achievement demand the recognition that God is essentially, if not only, a moral ideal, suggested by the actual, which may guide intelligent decision and action.

Consequently Dewey recommended that "God" should be frankly and explicitly defined primarily in moral terms. ". . . 'God' means the ideal ends that at a given time and place one acknowledges as having authority over his volition and emotion, the values to which one is supremely devoted, as far as these ends, through imagination, take on unity."[52] Again, " 'God' represents a unification of ideal values that is essentially imaginative in origin when the imagination supervenes in conduct."[53] And emphasizing that ideals are not simply or wholly subjective and that "God" is more than a rootless fantasy of the individual mind, he wrote, "There are forces in nature and society that generate and support the ideals. They are further unified by the action that gives them coherence and solidity. It is this active relation between ideal and actual to which I would give the name 'God.' "[54] In answer to those who might conceivably suppose that any use of the word

[50] *Ibid.*, p. 80.
[51] *Ibid.*, p. 42.
[52] *Ibid.*, p. 43.
[53] *Ibid.*, p. 51.
[54] *Ibid.*, p. 53.

"God" would lead to the misconception that he was making concessions to the theistic traditions of the religions, he also offered a thoroughly moral defense of his terminology: "Use of the words 'God' or 'divine' to convey the union of actual with ideal may protect man from a sense of isolation and from consequent despair and defiance."[55]

Dewey's critique of religion was then plainly and thoroughly moral, though presumably supported also by certain epistemological and metaphysical claims. The concepts and practices of the traditional religions, he thought, have not aided but have instead seriously hindered the achievement of the moral ideals which have been generated in the minds of men. It is this, and not their metaphysical falsity, that ultimately condemns them. Because of reliance on creeds and rituals, men have neglected the only effective methods of solving problems and rendering their ideals actual. Thus in place of faith in the supernatural or in dogmas and rituals, Dewey proposed faith "in the continual disclosing of truth through directed cooperative human endeavor, which is more religious in quality than is any faith in a completed revelation."[56] For it is chiefly in seeking through the methods of scientific inquiry to improve the lot of mankind, according to Dewey, that the individual may experience a sense of high purpose, difficulty, and fulfillment that is genuinely religious and not illusory in its quality and outcome. And the basis of the religious experience is neither the confrontation of the holy, nor the intrinsic quality of the imagined ideals, nor the elevated conviction that the ideals are already actual in some bright empyrean beyond the reach of ordinary experience. The religious quality of experience, as Dewey conceived it, is not a part of the primitive data of human existence but a *product* of struggles against obstacles and the sense of achievement that attends the genuine improvement of human affairs. A rhetorical question emphasized the secondary, pervasive, noninstitutional, and moral character of the religious as Dewey conceived it: "What would be the consequences upon the values of human association," he asked, "if intrinsic and immanent satisfactions and opportunities were clearly held to and cultivated

---

[55] *Ibid.*, p. 26.
[56] *Ibid.*, p. 71.

with the ardor and the devotion that have at times marked historic religions?"[57] But morally relevant as this question was, and still is, the implications are not as unambiguous as Dewey apparently thought. The implications he saw are inseparable from the conviction that the religious experience requires no special nurture, methods, or attitudes and reveals no unique or actual dimensions of existence. On this assumption the moral rejection of religion is of course justified.

In view of the fact that Dewey defined the religious as a quality of experience, however, and elsewhere emphasized that qualities in fact have very basic and dominant logical functions as well as "existential reality," it may seem less than just to claim that he actually regarded religion as both thoroughly moral in function and a secondary product of experience. Certainly one cannot consistently claim, as Dewey did, that qualities "demand certain distinctions,"[58] produce "functional connection,"[59] "run through" and "give meaning to"[60] the objects of experience without also recognizing that qualities are judicially and ontologically significant in the most fundamental sense. And Dewey's recognition of this was indeed most explicit and straightforward, *except in relation to religion*. He wrote, for example, "The immediate existence of quality, and of dominant and pervasive quality, is the background, the point of departure, and the regulative principle of all thinking. Thought which denies the existential reality of qualitative things is therefore bound to end in self-contradiction and in denying itself." It would consequently seem incumbent on him to develop the judicial and ontological implications of "the religious quality of experience" which, he said, "introduces genuine perspective"[61] and produces attitudes which harmonize the self and "lend deep and enduring support to the processes of living."[62] Presumably such qualities, perspectives, and attitudes should be treated not only as the products of certain activities

[57] John Dewey, "Qualitative Thought," in *On Experience, Nature, and Freedom*, R. Bernstein, ed., New York, Bobbs-Merrill, 1960, p. 186.
[58] *Ibid.*, p. 193.
[59] *Ibid.*, p. 179.
[60] *Ibid.*, p. 198.
[61] John Dewey, A *Common Faith*, *op. cit.*, p. 24.
[62] *Ibid.*, p. 15.

but also as the source of "religions" and "religious judgments," even as "aesthetic" and "artistic" qualities and needs may be said to be not only the products but the *sine qua non* of museums and schools of art, or even as the qualities and demands of the social life may be said to be not only the results but also causes of certain processes and institutions of government. But in spite of his recognition that qualities are generally determinants of thought and action, Dewey treated the religious experience as an exception, as an instance in which the quality is almost wholly derivative, an effect rather than "the point of departure" and "the regulative principle of thought." Far from regarding "the religious quality of experience" as a determinant of thought and judgment, he claimed instead that "The actual religious quality . . . is the effect produced, the better adjustment in life and its conditions, not the manner and cause of its production."[63]

In summary, Dewey insisted that *religion* is inseparable from institutions with questionable interests, practices, and aims, but that the genuinely *religious* is a quality of experience which may be realized in any persistent effort, in the face of difficulties, to improve the condition of man. And at least by omission he implied that neither the pursuit of truth nor the increase of beauty is a direct or essential element in the religious enterprise—though both scientific inquiry and artistic creation, along with social and economic activities, may be consummated by experiences that are religious in quality. But apparently the possibility never occurred to him that such symbolic activities as religious music, poetry, ritual, and prayer, the behavior and products inspired by "the religious quality of experience," or the traditional attempts to articulate the sense and the demands of the holy are other than misguided and futile attempts to escape both real and supposed dangers or to secure both actual and imagined benefits. He was therefore only following the logic of his basic thesis when he distinguished sharply between the ecclesiastical organizations whose moral history is at best dubious and the religious as a quality of experience. And if the religious is only a quality of experience which results from the appropriate employment of other methods of inquiry and activity, and is not itself a

[63] *Ibid.*, p. 14.

unique and effective mode of judging or informing and directing judgment there can surely be no defense of institutions or persons that aim primarily to promote or nurture the religious experience. For if this is the case, institutionalized religion can only attempt, with no basis at all for success, to reproduce or recall a quality that is actually inseparable from the fulfillment of life through the very methods and activities that are neglected in the act of worship or symbolic expression. And if this is so, then religion is of course not only superfluous but may also prevent the achievement of basic goods, including the religious quality of experience.

ON THE NONMORAL DIMENSIONS OF RELIGION

Conduct is a by-product of religion—an inevitable
by-product, but not the main point.
                                        A. N. Whitehead

It seems an inescapable conclusion that John Dewey was so convinced a priori of the essentially superfluous and immoral character of the religions that he wanted no part of specifically religious institutions, functions, meanings, and powers. Or as J. H. Randall has said, Dewey simply failed to understand "the host of institutionalized techniques the religious arts of the past have normally employed."[64] Yet Dewey, it may be said, surely presented unequivocally, though not altogether consistently, the logical consequences of identifying the religious with the moral. If his critique of institutionalized religion, its rituals and creeds, is at all mistaken, it is precisely because his concept of religion is woefully inadequate. One who begins with the thesis that doing justice and loving mercy is altogether equivalent to being religious and that creeds and rituals have neither a cognitive nor a religious function can never hope to avoid conclusions similar to those Dewey defended. The reasonable inference from such

[64] John H. Randall, Jr., "The Religion of Shared Experience," in *The Philosopher of the Common Man: Essays in Honor of John Dewey to Celebrate His Eightieth Birthday*, New York, Putnam, 1940, p. 114.

premises is, as he saw, that religious institutions, if they should continue to exist at all, must be transformed into organizations concerned exclusively with charity, social reform, and scientific or philosophical projects. There would be no place in Dewey's intelligent, well-ordered, and thoroughly democratic society for the nurture of specifically religious activities.

Now important as charity, social reform, scientific, and philosophical projects no doubt are, Dewey's claims fall considerably short of complete cogency if one admits that religious judgments, including institutions, creeds, rituals, myths, and symbolic activity, are ever based on anything other than pure imagination or sheer illusion. And even Dewey himself said in one place, "The most fantastic views ever entertained by superstitious people had some basis in experienced fact."[65] Yet in claiming that science, as a method of deliberate inquiry, is always the most significant, reliable, and appropriate basis and form of judgment, he had no clear logical alternative except to conceive the religious experience and judgment as essentially secondary, or derivative and illusory, and therefore to reject its own estimate of itself as a source of unique, necessary, and dependable insights and judgments. In this he was of course only combining the clear implications of the Protestant tendency to identify morality and religion with the growing conviction that science exemplifies the only warranted method of discovering and describing the actual character of any aspect of existence. In other words, he was simply carrying to its logical conclusion the claim, already subscribed to by a significant number of both religious and nonreligious individuals, that all judgments except value judgments, with which the sciences acknowledge they cannot deal, are under the jurisdiction of the various forms of scientific inquiry and verification. And religion itself, as noted earlier, confronted with the conspicuous success and challenge of the sciences, was already attempting to preserve its own self-respect and the confidence of others by limiting its claims to what the sciences candidly admit is beyond their reach.

Such limitation is of course *in a measure* both necessary and honorable. For religious judgments are neither disguised nor

[65] John Dewey, *Experience and Nature, op. cit.,* p. 32.

pseudoscientific claims, and it is radically ill-conceived for the religions to pretend to compete with the sciences. But it is nonetheless premature, altogether unjustified, and in all probability a profound mistake to suppose that every aspect of existence except value is in every respect subject to scientific analysis and judgment or to imagine that value judgments have no ontological or irreducible basis in existence and are strictly secondary and irrelevant to the executive—but nonetheless permissive—order of nature. For facts and values, as Dewey himself was very much aware, can by no means be distinguished as sharply as this claim presupposes. A strict and consistent separation of facts and values is indeed bound to claim ultimately that facts are worthless and to commit values to a nebulous realm that is neither actual nor ideal.

Yet the defenders of both religion and science are often addicted to the view that the former is concerned only with values, or the moral life, and that the latter has a monopoly on the facts, although neither has any conception of what either a fact or a value is independent of the other. And significantly Dewey himself, at least in this particular context, avoided both the problem of the factual basis of religious judgment and the difficulty of conceiving of neutral or value-free facts not by denying the existential sources of the religious experience, but by rejecting a priori the possibility that the "religious quality of experience" is itself a source of legitimate and illuminating forms of judgment. However, it may be said that, indirectly and inadvertently, he demonstrated to those who are sensitive to its traditional forms and values that religion cannot abandon the pursuit of truth and beauty or find genuine and sufficient justification for its claims on man's limited time and energy in a concern simply for moral character and judgment. For it has long been evident to many that moral excellence is altogether possible without any explicit religious symbols and commitments.

And surely if religion is important at all in the sense in which it has been taken to be important through the ages, it is even desperately concerned, not simply with some nebulous realm of values, but with the facts—luminous and awesome—which are the basis, the content, and the aim of the judicial processes by which matters of intrinsic and inviolable worth are discriminated, protected, and nurtured. And if such judicial processes are not recognitions of "fact" there is plainly something profoundly misleading about the general use of this word. For if religion is successfully concerned with anything at all, it may surely claim to be concerned with *facts*, even though it may take only minor notice of the analyzable and measurable matters which the sciences investigate. Religion can indeed be judicial—or a mode of guiding and influencing the moral and spiritual economy of life —only by somehow reflecting a radical dimension of the actual, or facts. If the religions are *in any measure* effective modes of judgment, the nature of existence, including both facts and values, must make this so.

Indeed the religions have always claimed, implicitly or explicitly, that there are dimensions of existence which can be apprehended only through religious acts and symbols or through the consciousness which creates and recognizes the meanings of such acts and symbols. And if these meanings could be fully articulated philosophically or scientifically, that would of course mean that religion is not fundamentally important because what it says can be said in other terms. But presumably the religious symbol is always employed on the assumption that the otherwise inexpressible is expressed or the otherwise inapprehensible is apprehended— not simply the symbol itself but rather the invisible world, the divine, God, the order of splendor which both includes and sustains the manifold reality revealed by a complex of judicial instruments and processes. Indeed to assume that men acquire from religious experiences and activities any ideas, ideals, or attitudes—or powers, methods, and directions—by which their vital and judicial careers may be maintained or guided is to assume that religion bears witness to and participates in the factual complex of being.

But what are the facts and complexes apprehended and revealed through religious judgments? There is clearly no satisfactory answer to this question apart from the religious symbols and activities themselves. The religious facts and complexes are fully available, if at all, only in or through the perspectives, symbols, and actions which are themselves religious. It should perhaps be pointed out, however, that there is nothing at all unique or unusual in the claim that it is impossible to say more directly or in other terms what the subject matter of religious judgment is. In the last analysis one must see in order that anything be revealed through sight, and nothing that is available through the ears is in the same respects an object of sight; likewise one must understand the language of science before the scientist can speak to him about the content of science, except in a roundabout and highly unsatisfactory way. Similarly, there is nothing paradoxical or absurd in the claim that it is necessary to understand the language of religion in order to know the reality which sustains, demands, and justifies the use of religious symbols, though this reality may be referred to philosophically in a summary but never wholly satisfactory manner as the holy, the sacred, the divine, God, or the order of splendor.

But that religion is not simply a variation on moral sensitivity and judgment is more particularly evident from even a cursory examination of religious literature, activity, and conviction. From the strictly moral point of view, nothing is more obviously superfluous than many religious practices and teachings. Also nothing is more obvious than the fact that every major religious movement in history has been based upon explicit cosmological and metaphysical claims and has included, in addition to moral commands and directives, judgments about the nature and limits of knowledge and eloquent testimonies to the beauty, tragedy, glory, vanity, and briefness of life. The holy must be known if it is to be worshipped, even if worship is the most effective way of knowing it. Consequently description of the world and of *how* man is in the world and *what* he is and can hope for are no less fundamental and functional elements in the religious perspective than are prescriptions concerning what ought and ought not to be done or the formulae of salvation. It may of course be the case, as many claim, that the sciences and philosophy can deal with every aspect of such problems better than the religions. But to claim this without a great deal more evidence than is now available, no less than to claim the contrary, is an inexcusable begging of the question.

In any case the religions have always insisted that not only

can man not know what he ought to do, but also that he cannot
know himself or the world apart from religious symbols and concepts. And if the moral element has often been dominant in such
symbols and concepts, it is only because moral qualities and
categories have proved so inescapable in man's confrontation and
judgment of himself and the world. And surely, regardless of
whether they are permanently relevant, such conceptual-symbols
as, for example, *sin* and *salvation* (to say nothing of *God*, the
cross, etc.), far from being clearly and simply either superstitious
nonsense or completely moral categories, reflect and express, at
least in the one case, man's unconditioned responsibility for the
character of certain of his deeds and propensities, and, in the
other, both his capacity for hope and his sense for ideal possibilities within himself and others. Also, it is not rhetorically or
in any weak sense symbolically that *Genesis* proclaims that "In
the beginning God created the heavens and the earth," or that
the Psalmist says, "As for man, his days are as grass: as a flower
of the field, so he flourisheth. For the wind passeth over it, and
it is gone; and the place thereof shall know it no more." These
are presumably descriptions which, in *Genesis*, call our attention
to "the heavens and the earth" as bearing within themselves
evidence of divinity and, in the Psalmist, remind us of the
poignancy of man's life, so bright and important in itself, an
intimate part of the place in which it grows and yet so brief and
so quickly and totally eclipsed. There are no obviously moral
overtones in the petition, "Give us this day our daily bread" or
in the assertion, "The heavens declare the glory of God; and the
firmament showeth his handiwork." Nor is it strictly a moral
judgment for a man to say of himself, "I am fearfully and wonder-
fully made." Although by no means all religious judgments may
be construed as assertions or claims, neither petition, praise, nor
prescription occurs in religious contexts without the presumption
of supporting facts.

Thus very few, if any, religious symbols, acts, or claims can
be treated simply as moral judgments but must be regarded in
the most basic respects as recognitions and articulations, in various
forms, of the existential-qualitative complex which man is and
in which he must live and judge. And if a religion could somehow

abdicate all its claims, implicit and explicit, concerning the existential-qualitative complex, whatever relevance and authority it might have in the moral life would surely be lost. For on the one hand, the passion for worship—like the quest for improved theoretical schemes and practical tools—can be maintained only when evidently supported and justified by objective and enduring conditions; and on the other, reliable moral judgments are plainly no less dependent on discriminating the actual conditions of existence—in terms of common sense, science, and art no less than in terms of religion—than on the power to choose one course of action rather than another. Without an ontology, or an objective basis, religion will surely falter and fail, though not due anymore to casting a distorting light on moral problems and choices than to making the world, man, and judicial powers appear other than they in fact are. The ontological character and relevance of religious symbols and acts are then clearly more basic matters and in some respects more certain ones than the power of religions to support or sanction moral standards and judgments. For if religious judgments are altogether illusory, then no one can safely submit his moral decisions to their influence, while it is quite possible that although the moral relevance of religion may be altogether indirect and enormously exaggerated, the power of religious symbols and activities to articulate and enlighten and thus inform are unparalleled and indispensable.

ON NONRELIGIOUS MORALITY

The actual existence of secular morals and of purely secular systems of ethical doctrine ... make it a futile academic gesture to insist, as some moralists still do, that religion is a necessary foundation of morals.

H. W. Schneider

Moral judgments are comprised of the behavioral, conceptual, and symbolic acts which presumably express both a sense of worth and a consequent obligation to perform certain acts or to refrain from others. Now those who maintain that morality is impossible apart from religion or that moral and religious judgments are equivalent are bound to insist either that moral judgments are derivatives from religious categories (the holy, the divine, the sacred), that moral and religious judgments are finally different only in degree, or that the religious judgment is derived from, or is only a special case of, the moral judgment.

But obviously, though the moral and the religious are sometimes clearly related, all of these possibilities fail to provide a way of satisfactorily characterizing some moral and religious judgments. For the moral experience or the conviction that some things are good or desirable and ought to be sought or protected appears to be quite different not only in degree but also in kind from the conviction of being in the presence or under the jurisdiction of the divine or holy. On the one hand this seems quite evident in the fact that the most important categories and principles of moral judgment may be largely defended, though perhaps not derived, in conceptual terms from the combined rational and social character and experience of man. At least the recognition by the individual that he is a rational member of mankind, dependent upon others, and responsible—at least in the sense that he inevitably *responds* in some way—to others and they to him, is surely a sufficient basis for the defense of rigorous and demanding moral rules or principles. The very minimum conditions of man's existence—of his rationality, freedom, and many of his most basic powers and satisfactions—quite clearly demand a moral code or a largely settled and satisfactory manner of deliberately pursuing and sharing possible goods and evading the evils which are ever near. Thus anyone who reflects, after reasonable experience, on the requirements of man's life would surely discover the inevitability, if not also the generalized form and content, of the fundamental moral principles. For moral requirements are apparently necessitated by the structure and problematics and guided by the successes and failures of man's life and experience as a rational and social creature and may therefore be formulated almost wholly in conceptual terms.

From the other side, the disparity of the two forms of judgment is evident in the fact that religion, like so many of the very greatest things in life—such as music, poetry, pure science, philosophy, and architecture—is added to man's existence largely, not as a basic necessity, but as a crowning glory. The individual, and perhaps even some communities, may never develop their potentialities in any of these forms of possible greatness. Religion, though perhaps less so in certain respects than music, philosophy, and pure science, transcends in important respects the limits and necessities of empirical existence. And so as Rudolf Otto has written, "The object of *religious* awe or reverence—the *tremendum* and *augustum*, cannot be fully determined conceptually: it is nonrational, as is the beauty of a musical composition, which no less eludes complete conceptual analysis."[66]

The fact and character of nonreligious moral sensitivity and judgment are perhaps nowhere better or more directly evident than in the United Nations Educational, Scientific, and Cultural Organization, which, representing many religious and nonreligious aspects of various cultures and traditions, has declared that there are certain rights and responsibilities which accrue to every individual person simply by virtue of his humanity. The facts of human rationality and interdependence, this declaration reasonably implies, without any appeal to the divine or sacred, seem a sufficient basis for the claim that each person, who has unavoidably received much from others, is responsible for helping to provide the minimum requirements for a decent and happy life for all, insofar as these can be provided by human ingenuity and effort. Thus secular morality is based simply but firmly on the claim that the facts of human rationality and interdependence, in a world of precarious and limited goods, make every person responsible, if he values his own life at all, for being in some measure and manner a good Samaritan.

Yet interdependence, contrary to the claims of many contemporary moralists, by no means implies that morality is wholly social in origin, that outside society all moral distinctions vanish, or that moral action is justified chiefly by the fact, as Kurt Baier phrases it, that sometimes "it is in the interest of everyone alike

---

[66] Rudolf Otto, *The Idea of the Holy*, trans. by J. Harvey, New York, Oxford, 1958, p. 59.

that everyone should set aside his interest."[67] From one point of view all moral judgments are of course social in origin, though some are evidently not social in function. Man's life and especially his power of language and reason on which moral discrimination and judgment depend are presumably possible only in society. But in this sense society is a no less necessary condition of scientific inquiry, though surely no one seriously believes that society rather than the structures and relations of the objective world constitute the validating matrix of scientific claims.

Admittedly, many moral judgments are social in a sense in which few, if any, scientific claims are. But at least theoretically a person permanently separated from society may also be immoral, even as he may be illogical, color-blind, or mistaken about causes and consequences. For evidently man is in important respects no less responsible to and for himself than he is to and for others; or at least if one cannot find within himself an intrinsic reason for moral conduct, he will never find an extrinsic justification in his relation to others. And if we heed the formidable wisdom of Aristotle, we may say that a man becomes immoral, not only by violating rules formulated for the benefit of everyone, but also by the failure to live in the way in which a man—a creature with characteristic needs and powers—must live in order to be himself. "For virtue preserves, while vice destroys, that intuitive perception of the true end of life which is the starting point in conduct."[68] The immoral act is condemned, according to Aristotle, precisely by the fact that it is a step on the way towards that *beastly* condition in which an individual will no longer be able to make moral distinctions. Or following Kant in the same matter, it may be said that morality is justified by the fact that each person confronts in himself and others a rational will or a will to rationality which cannot be conceived except as an end (or good) in itself. And from this is derived the practical moral maxim to treat mankind, whether in *oneself* or another, always as an end and never as a means only. Either one recognizes the inviolability of human life

[67] Kurt Baier,*The Moral Point of View*, Ithaca, Cornell, 1958, p. 314.
[68] Aristotle, *The Nicomachean Ethics*, trans. by J. A. K. Thomson, London, Allen & Unwin, Bk. VII, Chap. viii. There are of course many other translations of this classic work on morals.

and happiness, including one's own, because of intrinsic qualities or else abstains from selfishness and murder only because of the fear of the power of others.

Thus following either Aristotle or Kant, it must be said that the moral character of man produces certain social demands no less surely than his social nature imposes certain moral requirements or that certain moral decisions and actions were, for example, no less possible to Robinson Crusoe when he was alone on his island than when he was aboard ship or after the arrival of Friday. And if this is not the case we must face the peculiar consequence of defending the claim that although in the presence of each other both Crusoe and Friday were subject to various and serious moral transgressions, either could defend himself from the threat of moral culpability by the very simple expedience of murdering the other. There is then no possible basis for genuine morality except man—the individual—himself; but a man is a social creature set down in the midst of and sustained by cosmic events and processes. Morality is of course *conditioned* by such facts. Morality can be *required*, however, only by the fact that the individual person has imposing and specifiable powers and potentialities which, though they may be happily actualized in many ways, may also warp, torment, or destroy either oneself or others when wrongly employed. And morality is possible without religious symbols, concepts, and activities simply because religion is only one of the forms through which a man may fully actualize his potentiality for integrity and discovery through judicial excellence.

So the moral philosophers who have insisted on the independence of morality and religion are essentially right, although unfortunately this view is often defended in a spirit of antireligious feeling or complete indifference to religious values, which seriously misrepresents the fruitful interaction that is possible, and has often occurred between the moral and the religious forms of judgment. Certainly a moral theory need not be antireligious any more than it need be antimusical or pro-middle class. Both the meaning and the demands of religious symbols and concepts, as well as certain religious practices, may indeed conflict with the canons of apparently reasonable moral theory or judgment. Also the specific character of either morality or religion is best seen and understood without reference to the other. Yet religion and morality may be nonetheless equally important elements of the wholly judicious life. It is then evidently a serious mistake in philosophical analysis to make either religion or morality the logical or ontological basis or equivalent of the other—although the average person may have no need or may even find it a serious hindrance to make sharp distinctions between them. For there can be little doubt that they are in some important respects mutually influential and sometimes existentially interdependent. But precisely the same relations may obtain of course between morality and the arts or sciences.

ON THE INTERACTION OF MORALITY AND RELIGION

In every highly developed religion the appreciation of moral obligation and duty . . . has been developed side by side with the religious feeling itself. Nonetheless a . . . recognition of 'the holy' may occur . . . without being always or definitely charged or infused with the sense of moral demands.

RUDOLF OTTO

Religious judgment, rooted in the recognition of the holy or sacred, attempts to inform and modify human character and destiny through discoveries which are presumably inseparable from the qualitative character and effects of certain symbols and acts. And anyone who imagines that the idea of the holy or the modes of recognizing it originated as simply the demand of the moral order or primarily as a means of enforcing moral injunctions has surely missed altogether the mystery, majesty, and loveliness at the heart of existence. For morality is essentially only conduct in accordance with principles that are regarded as binding for the sake of any object of worth to either the individual or the community.

Indeed religion and morality must not be regarded as either completely interdependent, identical, or mutually exclusive. On the one hand, moral judgment, though no doubt possible apart from religious concepts and symbols, can hardly be in all respects independent of the recognition of the sacred, if the sacred is recognized at all, and may often be based on it. But insofar as the discovery, the presence, and the articulation of the holy constitute only a part of life and only one, even if the highest, form of value, not all moral judgments will be directly related to religious judgments. On the other hand, religion as a dominant form of human activity and association which demands significant expenditures of energy and other resources and has more or less distinct consequences is surely in some respects subject to moral approval and disapproval. If religion, as some cogently claim, must often serve as the guilty conscience of secular morality, it is nonetheless true that, at its best, secular morality is an equally effective guilty conscience of the religious demands and practices. No less important than the fact that religion may provide sanctions for moral principles and decisions is the fact that religion itself must sometimes be judged morally.

But it is of course only indirectly and peripherally that moral judgment is applicable to religion, even as it is only indirectly and peripherally that the arts and sciences may be judged morally or that religion and art are subject to scientific description and analysis. Yet surely a religion, like the arts and sciences, may sometimes have undesirable effects, or a person devoted to religion or to art or science, for that matter, may, in the pursuit of some particular value or end, obviously neglect some more fundamental requirement of life or excellence. Such consequences and conduct are plainly not less subject to moral disapproval than the actions of the father who unnecessarily and tragically neglects his children or the conduct of the person who fulfills his own laudable ambitions at the expense of others. But although religion, like art and science, is from one perspective subject to moral judgment, to make this aspect of religion fundamental is to lose sight of its own judicial functions or of the fact that its primary aim is to reveal and celebrate—to intensify awareness of the fact and implications of—the existence of the divine. The religious judgment is not, anymore than the artistic creation or the scientific claim, a moral judgment, even though every judgment may rest ultimately on discriminations of value. And to judge a religion solely by its conformity to accepted moral principles or by the moral character and consequences of the actions it inspires is not more appropriate or less appropriate than applying exclusively moral criteria to the creations and discoveries —and their subsequent uses—of the arts and sciences.

There is in fact almost overwhelming evidence that the religions, far from being the voice or condition of all moral authority, may be, even as art or science or domestic arrangements, either the supreme fulfillment of the moral life or the cruelest enemy of the good. Only the blind or dogmatic can deny that religion has often stood on the side of tyranny, privilege, and even brutality. The sense of the sacred, especially when it is most intense as, for example, in the Christian hermits or St. Francis of Assisi, may distract men from any effective concern for even the fundamentals of the moral life. The religious life, like the artistic or scientific life, may be intensified at the expense of bodily health, social duties, and philosophic understanding. As Brand Blanshard has observed, Saint Francis achieved "remarkable things. . . . What he did not succeed in showing is that the spiritual life, if lived intensely enough, can afford to ignore the conditions under which nature has appointed that it must be lived."[69]

But it is equally important to point out that such equivocal results of profound religious sensitivity and commitment do not necessarily invalidate the religious judgment, since it may nonetheless recognize, articulate, or reveal existential dimensions and extraordinary judicial possibilities, even as artistic and scientific products and judgments are not invalidated by their sometimes unfortunate concomitants. In the broadest sense, the moralist and the moral decisions of the prudent individual aim

[69] Brand Blanshard, *Reason and Goodness*, London, Allen & Unwin, 1961, p. 65.

at the compatibility or harmony of all activities and values. But the practitioner of a particular mode of judgment (whether art, science, or religion) may employ its powers most effectively when he employs them most ruthlessly. Thus again it may be relevant to note that great things may often enter into life accompanied by a curse.

But although religion is often nonmoral, or even sometimes immoral, there may be a religion of morality: an effort to encourage or create through appropriate symbolic expression the conviction that the moral law alone is sacred and to bring into being the kind of world that is demanded by moral insight and principles. But such a religion, though perhaps a great deal more than merely a moral theory, will not (because of the stringent preconceptions imposed on itself) adequately perform the functions the religions have traditionally claimed for themselves— those of revealing not only moral requirements but, more importantly, the extraordinary elements and dimensions of existence which account for the richly qualitative and spiritual phenomena of life. If there is any justification at all for claiming such revelatory functions, a religion preoccupied with moral necessities is presumably shortsighted in regard to its own powers and potentialities. And if religions do reveal some otherwise unrecognized dimension of man's existential structure and need or provide the instruments and conditions for reliable and otherwise unattainable instances and forms of judgment, the most serious and profound concern for necessary moral principles and sanctions should not be allowed to obscure or minimize such facts. But equally important, to make a religion of morality is generally unjustified precisely by the fact that morality does not for the most part require the support of the religious forms of judgment; and the unnecessary introduction of religious symbols and concepts into the defense of moral principles and ideals will very often prove not only vain, but also confusing and obstructive.

Yet the fact that religion is concerned primarily with qualitative and spiritual elements and perspectives makes it peculiarly able to influence and in some respects promote the moral life. But it is utterly insufficient and misleading to say, as Stephen Toulmin said in his recent *Reason in Ethics*, that "religion helps us to put our hearts into" the moral choice.[70] The basis of this claim is the assumption that religion is primarily a form of psychological reassurance rather than a form of judgment with ontological foundations. But although it is no doubt true that religion provides some psychological reassurance, this does not in itself indicate anything either specific or unique about the relation of religion and morality; for it may also be said that the arts and the sciences sometimes enable "us to put our hearts into" the moral decision. At least the arts may encourage and sustain a particular moral choice by presenting a similar one in a context of great beauty or heroism; and scientific inquiry may surely persuade a person to favor a specific moral course or choice by offering evidence that certain factual assumptions and presumed consequences are highly justified.

But any fundamental contribution of religion or of art and science to moral decision can never be, as Toulmin's remark suggests, simply to increase and sustain enthusiasm or psychological assurance. Any genuine relevance of nonmoral judgments to the moral decision (unless the moral decision can be derived from nonmoral premises) must depend upon their contribution to the envisagement of the total quantitative-qualitative, or fact-value, complex in which such decisions must occur. For sound moral judgment is notoriously a product of a very careful balancing of the various claims of experience against each other in the light of the *goods* that are possible or the *demands* which are unavoidable. There is then significantly more than a merely preferential or pragmatic basis for the claim that the prophet is best justified in discovering and articulating the character of the holy, the artist in producing works of art, and the scientist in demonstrating causal relations or verifying theories, rather than in seeking primarily to render their respective judgments harmonious with prevailing or conventional moral standards. For moral judgments can hardly be more relevant or more reliable than the total view of existence of which they are part; and so the claims of a religion concerning moral obligation and choice can be no better justified or sounder than the religious claims about *what is*. Thus

[70] Stephen Toulmin, *Reason in Ethics*, Cambridge, Cambridge University Press, 1961, p. 219.

unless a religion does in fact contribute to the envisagement of the existential complex, it can hardly be expected to make positive or enduring contributions to moral sensitivity and judgment. And only insofar as religion contributes *more* than the arts and sciences to the total and defensible view of *what* and *how* man is in the world, or of qualitative possibility and necessity, can it be reasonably supposed that it is *more relevant* to moral decision and action. But it is at least highly debatable that any form of judgment is *in every respect* more effective or more necessary than another in discovering and properly manipulating the things in man's power or the areas in which moral judgment is possible and necessary.

The moral relevance of a religion is then inseparable from the judicial reliability of the materials (meanings, methods, qualities, etc.) apprehended or assimilated in religious activities—in communal worship, prayer, contemplation, or reading sacred writings. Yet it is surely a mistake to suppose that the apprehended and assimilated are limited simply to the words, music, icons, images, and ideas—which are after all incidental in the sense that other words, music, and ideas, or other forms and objects of worship might function equally well if cultural traditions and personal needs were different. Even as persons are known not altogether or simply by the particular words they use, but by the general manner and cogency of their speech and action, so the existential discovery that occurs in religion, and also in the arts and even to a great extent in the sciences, does not depend wholly on the particular symbols, concepts, and practices. In some measure it may be said of all religious and artistic objects, as Shakespeare said of sadness, that:

> . . . how I caught it, found it, or came by it,
> What stuff 'tis made of, whereof it is born,
> I am to learn;
> And such a want-wit sadness makes of me
> That I have much ado to know myself.

Yet love and joy, the sad and the tragic, the presence of the holy and the awe-full may be communicated and may surely influence and even guide judgment in many ways. So although *what* a religious symbol is and says cannot be said without the symbol itself, it seems clear that from communal worship, for example, no matter what the particular form, one may apprehend, as in no other experience or association, the quality—the joy, the anguish, and the urgency—of certain shared concerns, fears, convictions, and hopes. And man's very existence as well as his judging, it seems plain, is by no means separable from such qualitative complexes. At the very least, then, the religious judgment or act may be said to recognize and communicate certain attributes of the ultimate and total qualitative-existential complex which man is.

The moral importance of religion is then surely not simply that it helps the individual to put his heart into the moral decision; for it may also help him, particularly when he fails to see clearly, to put his heart into the immoral decision. Religion is morally important primarily because it may reveal as well as help to create the subject-object of decision: man in community intensely aware of divine splendor and enormous tragedy, of sheer anguish and immense possibility. The judgment pronounced and the truth shared in the religious perception or act reveals, but does not explain, celebrates, but does not conclude, the drama of man in nature. From this perspective, religious truths may be as various and as unharmonious as the truths of the sciences; also it may well be that in both realms the greatest discoveries are yet to come. And the religious judgment or discovery, even as beauty and truth in other forms, may indeed be justified chiefly by its own existence and should be morally censored only when it prevents or frustrates what is clearly a greater and possible value.

But to claim that religion may help to reveal the total context of moral decision is not to describe all the possible functions of religion in relation to morality. A religion which articulates matters of ultimate worth may also contribute significantly to the development of genuine moral sensitivity and thus to the persistence of moral resolve and decision. Apparently only a sense of intrinsic but ever precarious worth can transform the basically rational moral principle or deduction from a prosaic imperative or utilitarian requirement into an urgent but beneficent encouragement to excellence. Now certainly the religions have no

monopoly on the sense or presence of intrinsic worth and purpose and no doubt a positive and reliable morality is altogether
possible independent of any religious perspective or sense of the
holy. But the tendency of purely rational and empirical morality,
especially if antireligious and even if simply indifferent to religious
symbols and concepts, is nonetheless to rely almost wholly on
either purely practical principles or on highly abstract logic and
the quantitative and relational concepts of the natural and social
sciences as the basis and criteria of ethical rules. Morality so based,
ripe in wisdom as it may sometimes be, is always threatened by
grossly utilitarian motives or by the dangers implicit in the claim
that the good is the desired and the uncritical supposition that
the satisfaction of the desires of the greatest number is always the
ultimate appeal in moral issues. The danger is that utilitarian
logic, followed to its inevitable conclusion, suggests that the good
can be infallibly discovered by consulting the members of the
community concerning their desires and achieved by following
the wishes of the majority. Even John Stuart Mill, though
surely aware that the most important "goods" cannot be measured
in quantitative terms, claimed, "Of two pleasures, if there be one
to which all or almost all who have experience of both give a
decided preference, irrespective of any feeling of moral obligation
to prefer it, that is the more desirable pleasure."[71] Thus *numbers*
become both the unilluminating means and the dubious end of
moral judgment. The logic of utilitarian morality is made possible precisely by making morality only a matter of measurable
quantities.

But ever since Socrates, who saw that the good is logically
independent of the gods who may approve it, and Aristotle, who
insisted that only a good man can be expected to recognize the
good consistently, ethical analysis has been unable to escape the
conclusion that moral judgments cannot be logically the result of
any inquiry that begins with nonmoral premises. Even John
Dewey, though he emphasized primarily the organic and social
context of morals, insisted that it is futile to expect our goals or
ends to realize qualities which we ignore in our means or in-

[71] J. S. Mill, *Utilitarianism, Liberty and Representative Government*, New
York, Dutton, 1910, p. 8.

struments. Moral judgment must apparently be rooted in an ir-reducible sense of worth. For without a sense of worth, which is essentially qualitative and is qualitatively communicated if communicated at all, the knowledge of facts and relation is only dead ashes in the mouth. And evidently the sense of worth can be increased in depth and scope, if at all, only through the nurture of qualitative modes of judgment. So although formal and utilitarian morality may require essentially only a character formed and sustained by good habits and rational decision, the arts and religions may be the most effective, if not the only, means of supporting, broadening, and deepening the sense of worth when habits and logic are frustrated, as they so often are, by either unprecedented tragedy or good fortune. For obviously existence is not simply a logical and practical matter, and evidently a moral theory which appeals only to logical powers and practical necessities is altogether too meagre for all but the most unimaginative of men. And effective moral inquiries, like illuminating scientific theories and artistic products, must continually reject conventional assumptions and practices in order to identify and cultivate the specific insights, needs, and feelings of a particular age and thus locate their requirements in the unique discriminations of worth and possibility which are evidently at the heart of both personal individuality and the distinctive qualities of a civilization. And religion, precisely because it is a mode in which judicial powers are imaginatively employed in behalf of individual persons and the qualities that are possible as well as actual in a culture, is often an effective framework for moral judgment.

Consequently it is no anomaly that the sense of the sacred—of the awesome majesty and power of the divine—and the most profound and precise sense of the moral law and justice were first developed by the same people, the ancient Hebrews who, incidentally, used the same word for loving and knowing and so suggested, as much subsequent thought has also assumed, that all illuminating and veridical judgment is based ultimately on love. And it is a plausible view, though of course not a necessary one, that nothing essential—or more than gilding and superfluous myth—has been added since except as ways and means of articulating and sharing the force and significance of their basic and extraordinary ideas with persons whose own sense of the sacred and the good is less direct and intense.

Apparently, then, although morality is altogether possible apart from religion and religion is itself sometimes immoral, it may be concluded that it is not simply coincidental, John Stuart Mill to the contrary notwithstanding, that religion and morality are so often conjoined. On the one hand, moral conduct is a necessary condition for the existence of any community in which cooperative activities, including religious activities, can be carried on. In this sense and measure, moral principles and practices are plainly more fundamental than and logically independent of religion. But on the other hand, the religious (or any symbolic, conceptual, or judicial) enterprise may stimulate, develop, inform, and guide the sense of the good and the just by identifying, creating, intensifying, and protecting that which otherwise would be missed or neglected. If religion reveals or teaches anything at all it may surely illuminate, although clearly it cannot by itself define or complete, the context and the character of every aspect of moral right and responsibility.

And if *moral value* is considered in still broader terms, as is often the case, as the very general quality and condition which may be said to distinguish vital and humane life from the stagnant and brutish, additional and important influences of religion become possible and defensible. A. N. Whitehead argues persuasively, for example, that neither tradition nor complete novelty but a constant and precarious tension or balance between the two is one of the most fundamental requirements of civilization. In his words, man apparently requires "both the advantage of social preservation, and the contrary stimulus of the heterogeneity derived from freedom."[72] And the very first step towards the required social wisdom, he continued, is "to recognize that the major advances in civilization all but wreck the societies in which they occur: like unto an arrow in the hands of a child. The art of free society consists first in the maintainence of the symbolic code; and secondly in fearlessness of revision, to secure that the code serves those purposes which satisfy an enlightened reason." Thus the alternatives to a

[72] A. N. Whitehead, *Symbolism*, New York, Putnam, Capricorn Books, 1959, p. 65.

combination of *reverence for symbols* and the *freedom of symbolic revision*, he claimed, is either decay "from anarchy, or from the slow atrophy of a life stifled by useless shadows."[73]

Now although religion has no doubt sometimes abetted both the anarchy which arises from the failure to revere the symbols which identify or support the truly holy, and the atrophy of life caused by mistaking shadows for substance, it is also difficult to deny completely the value of either the emphasis in so many religions on the enduring worth of particular "truths" and "certainties" or the importance of the novel meanings and experiences introduced into life by the religions. Simply by emphasizing the supposedly permanent value of specific doctrines, rituals, and attitudes, as well as by the sometimes conspicuous opposition to less than radical changes in conduct and belief, religion may often increase the stability (and not only or simply the slow atrophy) of even the nonreligious institutions and social practices. Precisely this aspect of religion led Henri Bergson, in *The Two Sources of Morality and Religion*, to claim that religion is, on one side, "a defensive reaction of nature against the dissolvent powers of intelligence."[74] Bergson was convinced, and not without impressive evidence, that if all the novel and progress-producing insights which come to men were adopted immediately and without serious reservation, even though they might be immeasurably superior to prevailing manners and beliefs, the social and intellectual life of man would be in many respects seriously disrupted and perhaps destroyed.

On the basis of such stabilizing influence, some of even the most notorious instances of the inflexibility of religious belief and practice may be afforded some defense. Such examples as the attitude and behavior of Christians in the face of the Copernican hypothesis and Darwin's theory of evolution (the most famous, though perhaps not the most important, chapters in the history of the relation of religion and science) may be seen as neither simply perverse nor altogether unintelligent and inexcusable. For apart from the fact that the evidence for these theories long

[73] *Ibid.*, p. 88.
[74] Henri Bergson, *The Two Sources of Morality and Religion*, New York, Doubleday, Anchor Books, 1954, p. 122.

seemed insufficient, not only to educated clergymen but also to many knowledgeable and honest representatives of the scientific community, there were obvious and genuine dangers (as Bergson might have pointed out) to intellectual values as well as to moral and social assumptions and practices (which were at least pragmatically necessary) in any wholesale and immediate approval of theories so inconsistent with long-established perspectives and habits of thought. Although profound changes in customs and thought may be clearly desirable and even necessary for progress, they are ambivalent goods when they threaten or destroy already established and largely satisfactory modes of thought and action. Or from a slightly different point of view, the primary mistake of the Christians was not, under the circumstances, in opposing the Copernican and Darwinian theories but in presuming that the truth and relevance of the religious life and judgment are completely dependent on a specific view of the universe and man's place in it.

But that religion is in fact distinguished by the novel meanings and values which it introduces into experience or contributes to civilization may seem much less obvious than that religion stabilizes (and sometimes atrophies) both ideas and conduct, especially to the observer of modern life and in the light of recent developments in science and philosophy. Yet in spite of the record of the last few centuries, the most superficial understanding of Western history must recognize that the religions, although often the most conservative forces, have also in fact introduced and supported the most radical and effective changes in belief and custom. The theological and ethical teachings of the Jews, the metaphysical doctrines and moral ideals of Jesus and his earliest disciples, the concepts of man, *agape*, and complete dependence on God as proposed by Saint Paul and developed by Saint Augustine, the medieval synthesis in a religious framework of Greek rationality and Hebrew inspiration and insight, and the Protestant Revolution, no matter how commonplace they now may seem, are undeniably among the most crucial and revolutionary turning points of thought and experience which, for better or worse, have made the modern world what it is.

Fortunately, the religiously orthodox and the ever-present reformers, whether liberal or reactionary, within the framework of the religions themselves, serve in some measure respectively the need for stability and the equal need for constant criticism and the vitality produced by the frequent necessity of adjusting to changing circumstances and increasing knowledge.

Finally, religion and morality, though always logically and often existentially separable, may nonetheless interact in many ways. But if it is remembered that needs are not always necessities, we may say in conclusion, with Bronislaw Malinowski, that "Religion needs the community as a whole [including of course moral concepts and rules] so that its members may worship in common its sacred things and its divinities, and society needs religion for the maintainence of moral law and order."[75] But even as in the case of science and music, this conclusion does not at all preclude the possibility that religion will sometimes be used to pursue ends and promote practices that are immoral or inimical to the best interests of the individuals in a given community; or that some individuals and communities can best maintain their own moral integrity and discharge their responsibilities by remaining free of the distracting demands and influence of religious vision and commitment. Human life as a whole may surely be tempered by the presence of the divine even though not every individual is responsible for recognizing and articulating this presence.

SOME SUMMARY REMARKS

I have merged, like the bird, with the bright air,
And my thought flies to the place by the bo-tree;
Being, not doing, is my first joy.
                              THEODORE ROETHKE

One noteworthy consequence which both witnesses to and flows from the basic difference between religious and moral judg-

[75] Bronislaw Malinowski, *Magic, Science, and Religion*, New York, Doubleday, Anchor Books, 1954, p. 54.

ments is that religion *as such* affects the life of the individual only to the extent that he opens himself to it or participates voluntarily in religious forms of thought and activity. On the other hand, moral judgments are most appropriate when the effects of conduct are essentially suffered rather than chosen. To a significant degree man is *compelled* by circumstances, including the requirements of his own character, to be moral; and moral values are in important respects negative. To a similar degree he is *persuaded* to be religious; and religious values are almost wholly positive. Of course there is a sense—indeed a very fundamental sense—in which one chooses to be moral or immoral. The glutton surely chooses the pleasures of eating and drinking, and the liar chooses to lie. But neither the glutton nor the liar chooses the conditions or the consequences which render gluttony and lying incompatible with the good or undesirable both in themselves and because of their personal and social results. Thus Immanuel Kant was profoundly right in insisting that the moral act, when it is executed morally, is performed essentially out of a sense of duty or obligation rather than from a sense of pleasure or pure choice. Morality prescribes or may prescribe both arduous means and undesired consequences.

But in religion, it may be said, both the means and the end, if not altogether the product of pure choice, are at least non-obligatory. Religious vision and commitment are effected only by persuasion and relatively complete freedom. And it is never basically or simply a duty but rather an extraordinary privilege to share in religious vision and judgment; seen in this light the Christian doctrine of salvation by grace, far from being capricious, is simply a consequence of the fundamentally gratuitous character of the religious experience. And accordingly, the demand for religious freedom has increased historically as sensitivity to and concern for the rights and privileges of the individual have increased. In contrast, however, and primarily because moral action is often secured only by stringent sanctions, deepened concern for inalienable moral rights and personal responsibility has widely resulted in the gradual regulation by legal penalties of ever more of the aspects of conduct that may be regarded as moral or that inevitably affect the character and welfare of both the performer and others. Conduct in its strictly moral dimension is subject to control by legislation simply because the community, in its solidarity, suffers from the wrongdoing of the individual. Of course, to compel a person to act morally does not make him altogether moral; but it is at least more effective and more justifiable than the effort to impose a religion. For as Aristotle emphasized, moral action is required partly in order to give the "good-in-itself" a chance. But religion, if it is one form of the "good-in-itself," ceases to be religion as soon as it ceases to be essentially voluntary. To compel a person to be religious is indeed as impossible as to compel him to be happy or a mathematical genius, though apparently religious sensitivity even as happiness and mathematical intuition may be nurtured by appropriate habits and exercises.

But although moral conduct is in many respects subject to control by law, it is nonetheless radically mistaken for a community or a government to undertake to extend legal jurisdiction to the whole of the moral life. For over and beyond the fact that the highest morality is self-imposed, certain features of the moral life can never be successfully controlled by legal penalties. As Aristotle saw, it is therefore unwise in some instances and impossible in others to provide effective legal sanctions for actions which may be morally required or condemned. And no doubt a large part of the confusion about the relation of morality and religion is due directly to the fact that religions have so very often provided sanctions for the regulation of conduct that is beyond the reach of the law. But such sanctions are the fortunate and sometimes unfortunate by-products of the religions and by no means the chief or the whole of their functions.

Yet it bears repeating that in spite of important—perhaps sometimes even indispensable—contributions to knowledge of the complex of being, to moral sensitivity, to social stability, and even to the revolutionary thought which may radically transform the community, religion is neither the necessary basis nor even the most authentic voice of moral authority. There are always moral issues to which self-knowledge, friendly interest, scientific information, and insights derived from social and political experience may be both more necessary and more revealing than religious vision, belief, and judgment. The parent, usually better than the religious advisor, can direct his child in personal relations and responsibilities; the informed and intelligent sociologist or psychologist, better than the prophet, may foresee the genuine dangers of certain sexual customs or of widespread dishonesty among public officials; and the biologist, better than the minister, may identify and warn against the disastrous results of intemperance.

In fact religious vision and commitment alone can hardly render any action or project morally acceptable. A religious ethic may be positively dangerous, unless based on wide knowledge of man and his environment and buttressed by sound social and political structures. A religion that attempts to stand alone, regards itself as wholly sufficient in either moral or intellectual matters, or claims to be the special or only channel for the revelation of ultimate and unquestionable truth may do irreparable damage to other basic interests, capacities, and ideals of man. Religion may pervade but must not monopolize the lives of men who are also capable of other forms of profound experience and judgment. The life completely dominated by religion so that other dimensions of life are tragically neglected or frustrated is hardly better and may be much worse than the life dominated by other single passions or pursuits. This of course does not mean that greatness is not possible in the religious life but only that the religious life is not the only or necessarily the highest form of greatness.

In many respects religion belongs most clearly and significantly to the holiday life of man, to the hours, both joyful and tragic, not filled by necessary labors and to the mind that is free to examine the awesome conditions and values of its own existence and to contemplate the marvels which surround it, including man's own excellent works. Thus Aristotle observed, "It appears that the ancient sacrifices and ceremonies have come to take place after the harvest as a festival for the dedicating of first-fruits, because it used to be at these seasons that people had most leisure."[76] And F. J. E. Woodbridge has written, "Conventionally, from the savage to the civilized, religious exercises come as inter-

[76] Aristotle. *op. cit.*, Bk. VIII, Chap. ix.

ruptions in the daily round, like grace before meat, going to church on Sunday, or opening a wholly secular meeting with prayer."[77] But great tragedy and sorrow, even more profoundly than leisure and the celebration of good fortune, interrupt normal routine and demand examination of the conditions and values of existence. And to regard religious exercises as *simply* interruptions or as superfluous amenities which may add a little to the limited joys of life is of course radically mistaken. For the religious exercises may inform and influence every dimension of existence or every mode and instance of judgment, by revealing or intensifying the splendor which tragedy need not wholly conceal or weariness altogether miss.

The most urgent moral task of religion concerns less what we do than what we are and see and is surely not to determine or legislate rules in regard to right and wrong, good and bad. Such rules, insofar as they are appropriate at all, must be summary products of all that men know through every mode of experience and judgment, including above all the intuition that some things are and others are not worth being, doing, and having for their own sake—an intuition which may of course be modified or rejected in the light of further experience or critical analysis. Even so moral rules will probably always be precariously established and uncertain in their consequences. In any case, moral inquiry and decision almost always involve aspects of life with which religion is not equipped to deal directly or thoroughly. The features of life, splendid and awe-full, which provoke and justify the passion for worship do not provide either the details or the depth and breadth of knowledge or even the first principles which reliable moral decision almost always demands. A religion itself must surely be justified, if it is justified at all, not only by the perspectives that sustain worship, but also by the fruits which it bears in the world. Yet it is only by distortion that the religious symbol or vision becomes a moral imperative or the moral decision a religious judgment.

Religion, art, science, and common sense, as well as social and economic experience and need, interact in many and complex

---

[77] F. J. E. Woodbridge, *An Essay on Nature*, New York, Columbia, 1940, p. 312.

ways; and each may make appropriate demands and suggestions when the moral dilemma or decision is faced. But the genuine moral relevance of each in any particular instance can be determined only in terms of its disclosures concerning what is, what is worth being, doing, and having, and what is at the same time possible. The fact that makes religion truly important is not that its symbols, concepts, and methods are more relevant to moral decision than are the arts and sciences, but that they are equally justified as judicial instruments and ontological discoveries. Thus it is neither more nor less a duty to be religious than to be scientific or poetic, and the judicial integrity of religion itself is bound to remain in serious jeopardy as long as it claims that the moral life is peculiarly dependent on the religious life or that there is a necessary lapse of moral integrity in the person who is not religious. For the evidence that morality is independent of religious symbols and concepts is really so overwhelming that special pleading or a serious confusion of categories is bound to be suspected wherever the two are made either inseparable or identical. If this means that the moral authority of religion is severely limited, it also suggests that religion, even the most primitive rites and rituals and the religious concepts most alien to science, may not be cavalierly dismissed in the name of reason as so much superstition or even in the interest of some special set of moral principles or standards unless it is quite clear that the quality and direction of life are hindered by judgments which are obviously mistaken about the way the world is.

4

On Religion and Art

Since brass, nor stone, nor earth, nor bound-
less sea,
But sad mortality o'ersways their power,
How with this rage shall beauty hold a plea,
Whose action is no stronger than a flower?
WILLIAM SHAKESPEARE

AN HISTORICAL SKETCH

The exploration of the artist is no less truthful
and strenuous than that of the scientist.
J. BRONOWSKI

Through imaginative constructs, unusual insight, and skillful manipulation, the artistic judgment, it was suggested earlier, makes more readily available to oneself or others an unprecedented complex of qualities and symbols which both reveal and increase aesthetic and judicial possibilities. The arts are modes of discovering, articulating, and thus also modifying the powers of nature and mind. No less than the farmer who tills the soil carefully and breeds animals selectively or the physicist who discovers new forms and powers in the atomic structure of matter, the original poet and painter may also discover, reveal, and exploit creatively the amazing powers in existence or the extraordinary aesthetic and symbolic powers of certain forms and qualities.

Both the arts and the religions are then fundamentally symbolic, perhaps equally so. And this similarity alone sometimes makes terribly difficult the task of identifying and relating their separate judicial powers and functions. Apparently both are profoundly dependent, in their origin, on unusual combinations of perception, imagination, insight, and feeling. Furthermore, every great and extended religious judgment is evidently in some sense and measure a work of art, though it seems equally evident that not every great or important work of art may be called religious. Consequently extremes of theory concerning their relations, including both the claim that religion is identical with poetry and that all great art is religious, has complicated the efforts to distinguish the characteristic features of religious experience and judgment from the generic qualities of aesthetic experience and artistic creativity.

Although it is frequently acknowledged that the arts and religions are closely related, the specific similarities and differences are not often seriously worked out by either the orthodox or the liberal religious thinkers or by the so-called aestheticians who are concerned with the theory of art. The aestheticians want their art pure and generally disclaim any important relations between the two. And the strictest representatives of orthodoxy, committed to a matter-of-fact approach to many of the most poetic and iconic elements of their heritage, and recognizing that much secular art is concerned with the admittedly imaginative and fictional, find it virtually impossible to discover any other than superficial similarities between the arts and religions. Some traditions, notably the Catholic, have of course used the arts deliberately and effectively. But such traditions have usually insisted on a more or less arbitrary, sharp, and ineradicable distinction between the religious and the artistic elements, exemplified best perhaps in the Thomistic doctrine that art is concerned primarily with making, a notion derived of course from Aristotle, while religion is inseparable from certain revealed and eternal truths. But it is also true that such traditions have sometimes claimed that all great art is *ipso facto* religious art or has at least a religious quality.

Religious liberals, however, are by and large less perceptive than the orthodox where the arts are concerned. The orthodox in practically every religious tradition has made abundant if not deliberate use of the arts. But liberals, in an effort to render religion reasonable, cautious, and "scientifically" respectable, have frequently ignored and even rebuked the rich artistic heritage embodied in, and perhaps inseparable from, the religious traditions. Religious liberals have attempted, particularly in recent decades, to speak largely in logical prose—the prose of the social sciences and psychology or of philosophy when it is least poetic. The liberals' neglect of the arts has of course often been supposedly justified by pointing to the dangers presumably inherent in the passionate and imaginative predilections of the arts. And the orthodoxies, the liberals suppose, are grossly at fault in failing to distinguish carefully between the "literal truth" (scientifically discovered and expressed) and the "emotionally charged products of the religious imagination." The notion of "literal truth" is at best difficult to define and defend. But even if there should be some truth in this supposition, it is still a crucial question whether such extreme caution and stringent "literalism" are not worse than the threat. If religion is inseparable from the attempt to apprehend (or receive) and articulate (or make available) certain dimensions of existence or truth through symbolic judgments which may inform and alter the quality of life, there is obvious reason to suspect that poverty of expression, almost inevitable in the absence of the arts, is both the evidence and the cause of barrenness in religion.

Actually the claim that the arts and religions are closely or even inextricably related is very old and persistent. A critical tradition all the way from Plato to the present claims that the aesthetic experience and the religious experience are highly similar or that what the artistic symbols and the religious symbols express or reveal is ultimately the same reality. If this tradition began formally with Plato's claim that the poets suffer a "divine madness" in order to speak better the wisdom of the gods, it may be said to have culminated in various contemporary views to the effect that there is little or no fundamental difference between artistic and religious temperament and sensibility or between the nature and function of artistic and religious symbols and activities. Thus Sigmund Freud has characterized both religion and art as forms of illusion, the escapes of the neurotic, and different chiefly in the fact that while religion claims to be true, art, except in a few people "obsessed by Art," "does not seek to be anything but an illusion."[1] John Dewey has emphasized the similarity, if not the identity, of the two by claiming that both are significant primarily only as ways of idealizing the actual or as the quality or consummation of experience which results when any task that is worth doing is done well. Paul Tillich has claimed that the arts reveal indirectly the "ultimate reality" which is, according to him, directly revealed in religion. And even the positivists or logical empiricists, it may be said, have suggested a basic likeness between the two by denying that, cognitively speaking, either religion or art is more than gibberish or an emotive (intellectually and judicially meaningless) response to certain circumstances. But the poet or artist, according to the positivists, does possess the intellectual virtue of knowing that his symbols or products are irrelevant to the actual character of existence while the religionist blindly claims that his nonsense is the highest truth.

Other writers have described similar but perhaps more plausible views. The religious character of the tragic drama, especially, has suggested itself to many. Among the more noteworthy, Friedrich Nietzsche, in *The Birth of Tragedy*, claimed that the Greek form of this art was derived from the fusion of the contemplative spirit or the worship of Apollo (most directly expressed in sculpture) with the mystical and orgiastic cults of Dionysus. Apollo, the god of light and reason, was the symbol of perfect individuality as revealed by rational insight; and Dionysus, the god of the vine and fertility, represented the unified vitality of all nature. The classic art of tragedy, said Nietzsche, combined the religious vision of the ideal person in his essential individuality (Apollonian worship) with the passion and excitement of the religious festivals which sought an ecstatic, mystical, and self-annihilating union of the self with nature (the Dionysian mysteries). Jane Harrison, after long and intense study of Greek culture, also reached a similar conclusion and declared that, at least in the beginning, it

---

[1] Sigmund Freud, *New Introductory Lectures on Psycho-analysis*, New York, Norton, 1933, p. 219.

is "one and the same impulse that sends a man to church and to the theatre."[2] Likewise, Edith Hamilton has pointed to the intrinsically religious quality of the Greek tragedy by observing that in the theatre of the fifth century "the great mystery, human life, was presented through the power of great art. Poets and actors and audience were conscious of a higher presence. They were gathered there in an act of worship, all sharing in the same experience."[3] And even Jean-Paul Sartre, writing from a perspective which is radically critical of practically all conventional religious concepts and symbols, has admitted that drama and the theatre are nonetheless "religious" in quality.[4]

In his published speeches on religion Friedrich Schleiermacher suggested a more general relation between the arts and religion by claiming that "In all the arts, all great works are religious representations, and that . . . in all religions, Christianity not excepted, hostility to art involves barrenness and coldness."[5] A decline in the seriousness of either religion or art, he concluded, will be followed by a similar decline in the other. But Walt Whitman, from the perspective of the poet rather than that of the religious philosopher, reversed Schleiermacher's claim and wrote in "Democratic Vistas" that "The altitude of literature and poetry has always been religion—and always will be."[6] And Matthew Arnold, on the basis of a very similar (and more critical but nonetheless superficial) analysis, defined religion as "ethics heightened, enkindled, lit up by feeling," or as "morality touched by emotion."[7] Disillusioned with traditional religious beliefs because of their apparent conflict with the discoveries of science, Arnold

[2] Jane Harrison, *Ancient Art and Ritual*, New York, Holt, Rinehart and Winston, 1913, pp. 9-10.

[3] Edith Hamilton, *The Greek Way To Western Civilization*, New York, Mentor Books, 1948, p. 166.

[4] Jean-Paul Sartre, "Forgers of Myths," *Theatre Arts*, June, 1946, p. 332. Sartre's exact words are, "To us a play should not seem too *familiar*. Its greatness derives from its social and, in a certain sense, religious functions: it must remain a rite." Italics in the original.

[5] Friedrich Schleiermacher, *On Religion: Speeches to Its Cultured Despisers*, New York, Harper & Row, Harper Torchbooks, 1958, p. 146.

[6] Walt Whitman, "Collect," in *Complete Prose Works*, New York, Appleton-Century-Crofts, 1908, p. 242.

[7] Matthew Arnold, *Literature and Dogma*, New York, Macmillan, 1898, p. 18.

claimed that it is precisely and characteristically literary language that has the power of enkindling, heightening, and communicating emotion. So biblical or typically religious language, he added, "is literary, not scientific language; language *thrown out* at an object of consciousness not fully grasped, which inspired emotion."[8] And eventually religion, as conventionally conceived, Arnold was convinced, will be replaced by poetry which claims to be nothing but literature and will yet fulfill the essential functions of religion without presuming to compete with science in its characteristic power of describing the way thě world is.

More recently Martin Heidegger has said, "It is poetry which first makes language possible," that. "The essence of language must be understood through the essence of poetry,"[9] that "Writing of poetry is the fundamental naming of the gods,"[10] or that "The poet names what is holy."[11] And it is through language, according to Heidegger, that "man's departure into being" takes place, and "The great poetry by which a people enters into history initiates the molding of its language."[12] If Heidegger's case for poetry, which names the holy as the fundamental or primitive source of language, and for language as the very basis of man's existence, is at all sound, then not only religion but the whole of the life of man is radically dependent on poetic or artistic creativity. And Martin Buber also has said that the arts are fundamental forms of man's existence. But partly in reaction to Heidegger's emphasis on the isolation and loneliness of the individual, he insists that all art is dialogue, and that "Poetry is the soul's announcement that even when it is alone on the narrowest ridge it is thinking not of itself but of the Being which is not itself, and that this Being which is not itself is visiting it there, perplexing and blessing it."[13]

Finally, though perhaps with more flourish than insight,

[8] *Ibid.*, p. 36.
[9] Martin Heidegger, *Existence and Being*, Chicago, Henry Regnery Company, 1949, pp. 283-284.
[10] *Ibid.*, p. 287.
[11] *Ibid.*
[12] Martin Heidegger, *An Introduction to Metaphysics*, trans. by R. Manheim, New York, Doubleday, Anchor Books, 1961, p. 144.
[13] Martin Buber, *Between Man and Man*, trans. by R. G. Smith, Boston, Beacon Press, 1955, p. 180.

Walter Kaufmann has very recently suggested that "Shakespeare and Beethoven pose at least as profound a problem for the future of religion as Copernicus and Darwin."[14] This claim may be superficially true of course simply for the reason that neither art nor science is a very clear or serious threat to religion. But Kaufmann considers the claim important because he regards poetry as "vision without rational scrutiny" and religion as, among other things, "poetry turned authoritarian."[15] So the great tragedies and symphonies, he clearly implies, put the future of religion in question because they are sources of exactly the same values as religious symbols, systems, and activities but are free of the romantic superstition and deadly authoritarianism which he believes are inseparable from the religions.

This sketch of notable claims and possible relations is by no means exhaustive, though it is presumably typical of the profoundly different views and possibilities in regard to the relations of the arts and religions. Apparently, then, these relations are complex and surely various. For otherwise there would hardly be so many different and in some respects plausible accounts of the characteristic functions and the relative importance of each. Yet it seems hardly possible, complex as the arts and religions so obviously are, that each of these views is simply and only a partial account of the total fact, no more and no less accurate than the others. And so it is necessary to try to see more clearly the distinctive elements and functions of both art and religion by examining some of the more complete and influential views.

[14] Walter Kaufmann, *Critique of Religion and Philosophy*, New York, Doubleday, Anchor Books, 1961, p. 361.
[15] *Ibid.*, p. 362.

ON SANTAYANA'S VIEWS OF THE ARTS AND RELIGION

Now the history of mankind will show us that whenever spirits at once lofty and intense have seemed to attain the highest joys, they have envisaged and attained them in religion.

GEORGE SANTAYANA

Among contemporary philosophers George Santayana made a very exceptional effort, no matter how well or badly it succeeds, to define and articulate the subtle relations of the arts, especially poetry, and religion. His central thesis was that "Poetry is called religion when it intervenes in life, and religion, when it merely supervenes upon life, is seen to be nothing but poetry."[16] Now no doubt his treatment of both art and religion is in some respects uncritical, ambiguous, and quite misleading. Yet there are good and compelling reasons for considering his views carefully. First of all, his is one of very few recent nonreligious philosophies in which the values of both the arts and the religions are nonetheless the most serious and central themes. Second, he was unusually sensitive to many of the profound and distinctive values of each. Third, he faced more candidly, sympathetically, and imaginatively than most contemporary philosophers the results of the widely shared conclusion that religious perspectives or claims are fundamentally illusory or false. And finally, he provides at the very least an illuminating background against which it is possible to construct and defend judgments that are essentially opposed to his own claims while retaining the insights and values which his sensitivity and eloquent mastery of language so clearly revealed.

Santayana was a self-confessed materialist. He insisted that all existence is inextricably rooted in what is commonly called matter, though he candidly admitted that matter may itself be variously

[16] George Santayana, *Interpretations of Poetry and Religion*, New York, Scribner, 1900, p. v.

defined or identified with energy, a tension in the ether, or simply dark fertility. In calling himself a materialist he wished mainly to emphasize that *mind* or *spirit*, as he conceived it, is never an immaterial entity or power, independent of the body, which may influence the course of nature or even a part thereof. Out of the dark movements and arrangements of matter, he thought, come life and ideas no less than the hills, the rivers, and the stars. But ideas are only the passing effects—the epiphenomenal and ephemeral glow—of complex order and motion in matter and never themselves factors in effecting changes in nature, society, or the individual. He compared mind and ideas to incense which "rises from burning coals, but . . . is itself no conflagration, and will produce none."[17] And less figuratively, the "mind is not the cause of our actions but an effect, collateral with our actions, of bodily growth and organization."[18]

Yet the mind or spirit, as Santayana saw it, is not simply a passive recording of the shapes, patterns, and movements of external objects. "Perception points to what it does not, save by pointing, know to exist."[19] But besides the power of perception, man has also the gift of imagination. The movements and arrangements of the material elements within him give rise to images and ideas which have no conceivable counterparts in the external world. Thus man is truly endowed with *spirit*, or mind, viewing itself and its imaginative products as functionally independent of its material embodiment. And although such independence is not actually a fact, the illusion of it, according to Santayana, is intimately related to the intrinsic qualities and the worth of life. For it is only in the life of the spirit—in the visions, joys, feelings, and interests which are irrelevant to actual and external events—that man becomes acquainted with his own and the world's implicit but unattainable perfections. It is the spirit that delights in the discovery of the truths of logic and mathematics which bring no practical benefits or in observing the intricate patterns and processes of the physical world. But the chief delights of the

[17] George Santayana, *Reason in Science*, Vol. V in *The Life of Reason*, New York, Scribner, 1905, p. 215.

[18] George Santayana, *Winds of Doctrine*, New York, Scribner, 1913, p. 7.

[19] George Santayana, *Scepticism and Animal Faith*, New York, Scribner, 1923, p. 283.

spirit are the sensuous forms and qualities of the arts and especially the highly imaginative and idealistic vistas of poetry and religion.

Properly protected and nourished, man's psyche becomes the habitat of the spirit or the recipient of the gift of detached observation and develops the capacity of envisaging and living in the presence of the ideal. But the ideals which occur to the spirit have no reality or function except as imaginary or fictional entities. The primacy of matter and the imaginative character of the arts and religions mean precisely that nothing real—nothing with executive power or influence—can be discovered in or through the religious and artistic enterprises. They do not represent realities and they do not constitute or affect judicial processes. The values of the arts and religions, however, are, Santayana claims, quite compatible with the fact that they reveal or express no reality or truth. For such fictions are "the best of things and signs, when clear and beautiful, of a life being led in harmony with nature."[20] The arts and religions are not powers or methods which transform either man's life or his ways of seeing and judging the world, but are rather the nonetheless valuable results of an already established or automatic harmony within the individual and between him and the world.

Thus there is, Santayana insisted, no actual or fundamental difference between the arts and religions. Each is constituted primarily of imaginative vistas and ideals, both formal and qualitative, made possible and actualized by the harmonious functioning of the various and intricate material complexes on which life so obviously depends. The apparent and superficial difference is that the arts are generally recognized as congenial fictions while religious symbols and ideals are accepted as literal presentations of cosmic truth or as reliable moral perspectives and guides. But religion no less than the arts is in fact only an *imaginative* envisagement—even though it speaks of the debt a person owes to the powers and conditions that create and sustain him (piety), of the ideals towards which he aspires (spirituality), and of the rights and privileges that belong to others (charity).[21] But para-

[20] *The Letters of George Santayana*, Daniel Cory, ed., New York, Scribner, 1955, p. 413.
[21] George Santayana, *Reason in Religion*, Vol. III in *The Life of Reason*, New York, Scribner, 1905, Chaps. X, XI, and XII.

doxical as it may seem, the genuine values of a religion are by no means dependent on an accurate conception of the origin and character of such debts, ideals, and the rights of others. For the truth in such matters, according to Santayana, can indeed be no more than an established and congenial convention. And so religion as an imaginative interpretation of experience demands no more in the way of proof or justification than the specious facts of a novel or a poem. Religious values are different from purely artistic values only in the attitudes taken towards them, and the visions and ideals that represent the religious commitments of one age may be only objects of art to another. The philosopher, freed of illusion by the recognition that all is ultimately illusion, may look on the different religious perspectives, whether ancient "myths" or contemporary "beliefs," with profound sympathy and appreciation. But he will also recognize that religion cannot be distinguished from poetry—or any religious art from the nonreligious—except by the fact that the religions are *regarded* as true and morally significant while the arts are recognized for the imaginative illusions which they are.

But in spite of his conviction that religions are primarily products of imagination, Santayana defended the idea that a religion must claim a matter-of-fact validity in order to be morally and spiritually significant for most persons. Consequently he agreed with the fundamentalist Christians that to assert that the virgin birth, the resurrection, and the miracles of Jesus are only symbols is a denial of the very heart of Christianity.[22] For the imaginative, or artistic and poetic, symbols and concepts actually become or can function as religious symbols, he claimed, only when they are believed to be representations of actual fact. The denial of the *literal* truth of a religious claim is an admission that it is poetry, and the acceptance of it as poetry is a rejection of its imputed metaphysical and moral truth. He recognized of course that the intrinsic value of poetic sounds and symbols is not necessarily increased when they are regarded as signs of independent and existential facts. But most men, he said, are simply not capable of understanding that the highest values are moral and spiritual

[22] See especially, "Modernism and Christianity," in *Winds of Doctrine*, New York, Scribner, 1913, pp. 54 ff.

or that moral and spiritual values need not be based on any specific claims concerning the ultimate character of existence. Truth itself is not required for happiness, even though most men are unable to live except on the uncritical assumption that their claims and actions are justified by the actual character of the objective world. And only a belief in another world, independent and substantial, he thought, enables the unimaginative person or the person who does not know that he has imagination to transcend spiritually the actual but unattractive world in which he must labor and suffer. Religion is neither true nor instrumental, Santayana thought, but most men can discover the extraordinary and genuine value of it only when they regard it as both.

"Another world to live in," which, Santayana said, is the essence of religion,[23] has in fact, he claimed, no effect on the destiny of man in either this world or a world beyond. Yet this other and imaginative world may reflect, and in reflecting satisfy, the hopes and expectations of the believer or be the paradigm of excellence and splendor for both the believer and the unbeliever. So although the religious vision is only an inevitable product of the gratuitous harmonies in complex material processes, it may nonetheless be also the most redeeming feature of an intractable world which suggests perfections that are never realized and makes promises that are rarely kept. Even though neither religion nor art can affect the actual character and fortunes of man, each may in its own way redeem the moment from the blind tyranny of matter in motion by providing ideal objects for contemplation. But only matter possesses the power to effect genuine changes in the world or the individual; and material processes run their relentless course regardless of human hopes and plans and pleas. If man affects the course of nature at all, then, it is *not* through his ideas and ideals; for these are themselves completely dependent finally on the arrangements and motions of matter for their existence. So ultimately any changes which man may work in the world are all due to the universal material forces which work through him.

Thus a religion is never a power or instrument to build or

[23] George Santayana, *Reason in Religion*, Vol. III in *The Life of Reason*, New York, Scribner, 1905, p. 6.

rebuild the world in which man must live or even an approximate or symbolic account of actual and independent dimensions of existence, but an ideal superstructure raised above the world—an imaginary and congenial refuge that makes the ways of the world bearable. The importance of religion is therefore due wholly to the fact that only the spiritual (the imaginative and aesthetic) values can rescue the life of man from utter vanity. Concern with material facts and instruments for reforming and controlling the world can at best discover or secure the conditions of life. And although bodily health and favorable circumstances are necessary for the organism and the flamelike appearance of the spirit, there is nothing intrinsically valuable in the materials and conditions that make life and the spirit possible. The enjoyment of formal and sensuous beauties and especially the contemplation of ideals, are, according to Santayana, the intrinsic and highest values of life.

Religions and the arts are, then, the most free and perfect expressions of the spiritual life. They must not attempt to be more. A purely spiritual religion—even if its symbols are taken literally—must not seek to reform the world but only to wean the spirit away from the aspects of the world that are alien to its own vision of perfection. So the spirituality of Christianity, Santayana claimed, is best evident not in its zealous but futile attempts to reform the world, but rather in the doctrine that the Christian is "chosen out of the world." The spirit can only watch and pray; it cannot and need not remake a world that is already sufficient for those who live spiritually. Religion is a splendid spectrum, "the sunny pleasure-dome" of the spirit, the refracted light of the material patterns and processes that sustain the spirit in its inevitable and impatient bondage to the world and the flesh. The immediate and intrinsic value of religion is immeasurable but it offers no evidence of actualities either present or to come, though its visions are often mistaken for the ultimately real. So far as judgment, truth, existence, and the destiny of man are concerned, Santayana concludes, religion is as irrelevant as the fairy tales that delight imaginative children.

ON THE INADEQUACIES OF SANTAYANA'S VIEWS

*... although beliefs are not directly responsible
for more than a small part of our actions, the actions for which they are responsible are among the
most important, and largely determine the general structure of our lives.*

BERTRAND RUSSELL

Few men have appreciated more than Santayana the aesthetic
and imaginative vistas possible to the spirit in its religious and
artistic expressions. And his sympathies in such matters were both
discriminating and, contrary to some interpretations, generous.
Yet almost no one has attached less existential or ontological significance to the spirit and the objects which are most clearly
spiritual. Spirit redeems life from vanity but only momentarily
before it is swallowed again into the dark fertility of the matter
whence it came. The "phases of human progress" or the development of reason and spirit are episodic and apparently doomed to
eventual and final extinction. But even more important, nothing
within the spiritual or (as it is called here) the judicial power of
man can either hasten or delay the hour of doom. Paradoxical as
it may seem, the highest values are finally the least significant.
For they are epiphenomenal and the most ephemeral of things.

It is clear that Santayana saw best and appreciated most the
aesthetic surface of both art and religion, even though he also
emphasized that both may reflect and celebrate the good or the
moral burden of experience. He was never profoundly influenced
by the critical concern of his contemporaries with myth and
symbol and their growing significance in the analysis of judgment and knowledge. He of course wrote a great deal about *myth*
and *symbol*. But he used these terms primarily in their conventional and most superficial meanings, in which *myth* refers to
any false but elaborate and poetic story with more than one
level of meaning and a symbol is only a sign or a symptom of the

underlying mechanisms of nature. Consequently he regarded the problems of the relation of religious and artistic symbols to judgment and knowledge as strictly a dilemma: either religious myth and artistic symbols are to be taken as more or less accurate accounts of matters of fact which exist altogether independently (and may be apprehended apart from) the myths and symbols or else they are to be considered important aesthetically and spiritually but altogether irrelevant to the effort to understand, judge, or control either natural or human events and complexes.

But the crucial problems do not seem nearly so simple or clear-cut. The existential import and the judicial relevance of religious and artistic concepts and symbols are not clearly either so easily discovered or dismissed. It is not necessarily or obviously the case that one must accept religious symbols and artistic creations as simply accounts of matters of completely independent fact in order to claim that they are existentially and judicially significant or elements effectively determining the issue of human affairs in highly important respects. Mathematical axioms and methods, as everyone must surely admit, are not matters of fact in the same sense that mountains, oceans, and cities built by men are matters of fact. Yet mathematical axioms and methods are certainly far from mere fictions or irrelevant to effective accounts or judgments of the physical world; they are, rather, apparently inseparable from any extended knowledge of quantitative relations and processes. The symbols and methods of the arts and religions are perhaps similarly and equally indispensable in any objective and enduring judgments or communicable knowledge of man's qualitative experience and dynamic life. For no matter how well and completely physics and chemistry may tell of the shapes and sizes, the intricate motions and relations, and the amazing powers of the various material or quantitative elements of existence, the story is (as Santayana himself bore eloquent witness) radically incomplete without some account of the splendor and anguish which dwell, perhaps inseparably, in the very heart of man's experience. And this is presumably the story told so inimitably by the arts and the religions.

But Santayana, apparently more than most modern men, had a profound sense and conviction of being carried along by (without in any measure affecting) the irresistible march of events. And in the last analysis there is surely no absolutely clear and cogent reason for maintaining the contrary. Yet the sense that man shapes his world in at least limited ways, and is not only shaped by it, is surely the stronger conviction of most men. And surely if man has only a fraction of the freedom he has attributed to himself in the idea that through the sciences and technology he can turn the world closer to the heart's desire, his qualitative concerns and their effects on his decisions are not altogether secondary or wholly irrelevant to the shape of things to come. How incongruous even to attempt to account for the existence of cathedrals, museums, poems, hymns, and paintings without reference to the causal efficacy, partial though it is, of religious and artistic sensibilities and the objects and acts which nurture them! The claim that the arts and religions are ultimately only signs or symptoms of material organization and harmony, and not themselves genuine modes of being and judging, or ways in which the cognitive and judicial capacities and behavior of man are actualized, must be based on the reductive notion that what seems most important in the development of culture is not important at all, and that neither religion nor art belongs in any measure to the causal order of existence.

It is perhaps most surprising, however, that Santayana, with his extraordinary sensitivity and experience, did not distinguish more clearly between art that is concerned primarily with the merely sensuous qualities or aesthetic surface of its own medium and the art, both within and without the religious traditions, which obviously attempts to come to grips with the most urgent and baffling problems of men. The difference is not clearly or simply a matter of attitudes and beliefs or not merely a matter of mistakenly regarding the symbolic as the literal and independent truth. Serious and complex themes, unprecedented methods and insights, and extraordinary sensitivity not only to unusual aesthetic qualities but also to perplexing moral and intellectual problems and moods indicate without much question that such works of art are not intended and do not function, except in quite minor respects, as objects of pure and detached aesthetic enjoyment. They attempt at least to stimulate, to clarify

and intensify, to broaden and deepen man's awareness of himself
and the world he inhabits; and they are to all appearances often
the most radical, effective, and enduring judgments which man
passes on himself and the world. And there is in fact a great
deal in Santayana's own writings, too often ignored by his unfriendly critics, which suggests that he was not unaware of the
depth and effectiveness of such artistic and religious symbols
and systems. Yet he gave no distinctive treatment to such art or
to religion. Ambivalence plagues his reader: art and religion grow
out of the conditions of existence and are in a sense, he admits,
"profoundly just."[24] But in man's effort to apprehend or know
and judicially alter either the order of nature or human events
they are profoundly useless.

Santayana's view of the arts and religions was of course closely
related to, if not demanded by, his metaphysics. A highly mecha-
nistic and thoroughgoing materialism cannot consistently admit
more than an ultimately illusory character to the apparent objects
and judicial processes of the arts and religions or even the sciences.
Yet a person as sensitive as Santayana was in such matters can
hardly miss either their beauty or their apparent judicial relevance.
So as a sensitive but uncompromising materialist Santayana could
neither altogether deny the effects of religious and artistic methods
and values nor frankly admit their relevance in the executive warp
and woof of human decision and activity. For the spirit (or
intelligence), as he conceived it, is only a by-product of material
atoms dancing purposelessly in space; and *religion* and *art* are only
the names of the spirit's inevitable, though ephemeral and non-
objective, perspectives. The religious perspectives, although they
celebrate the good in both its actual and ideal forms, are never
altogether free from illusion, superstition, and unjustified hopes.
For without these religion becomes poetry, a poetry burdened
perhaps with anguish and moral insight, but also joyous and free
from the illusion that artistic achievements or religious symbols
and commitments will ever in fact guide or alter either the quality
or the inevitable outcome of human affairs.

If his materialism is inadequate as a metaphysics (and there
are many reasons to believe it is), Santayana's views are im-

[24] *Ibid.*, p. 4.

portant chiefly as a background for certain important questions concerning the arts and religions and their relations to each other. Does religion contain and nurture no insights and values not also found in the arts? Are the arts and religions ontologically derivative from material facts or functions and relationships? Or if so, does this mean that judicially they are completely ineffective? Are the values of either the arts or religions as illusory and ephemeral as Santayana suggests? And what are the respective functions of the arts and religions which make them perhaps equally but nonetheless distinctively important elements of culture?

It would of course be presumptuous to suggest that definitive answers can actually be given to such questions. It does seem clear, however, that categorically reducing the one to the other only avoids the decisive problems and is not the most illuminating way to envision their entangled relations. Certainly it is more difficult to account for both the *similar* and the *singular* features, concerns, and values of each. But also such an inquiry may surely prove more fruitful than either the attempt to reduce the meaning and value of one to the other or the exposition (which in certain moods is perhaps inevitable) that delights chiefly in noting how precious but brief and illusory the values of both are.

ON MEANING IN ART AND RELIGION

... every gained power is a delightful discovery of one's own power and of the wonders of the world.
                                                            JOHN DEWEY

Poetry fettered, fetters the human race.
                                                            WILLIAM BLAKE

Although a few men, such as Whitman and Schleiermacher, have claimed in altogether too brief remarks on the subject, that all great art is religious, this claim is much too ambiguous to be taken seriously. For the claim as usually made does not indicate

whether the generic elements of art or of religion are to be considered fundamental. Consequently there is only one extreme
view, other than the claim that religion is simply poetry or a form
of art, which must be described and criticized in the present context. This is the view that, when each is considered in terms of
its generic and essential traits, the character and functions of art
and religion are totally different. This view, although implicit
in practically all recent theories of art for art's sake, as well
as in all claims that religious truth is based on special and infallible
revelation, is perhaps best and most explicitly developed with
attention to both religion and art in Ernst Cassirer's theory of
symbolic forms.

Compared with Santayana's identification of religion with
poetry, Cassirer's attempt to describe the different forms and
functions of each is, especially in regard to the problem of meaning, a distinct advance. At least Cassirer's metaphysics is such that
neither religion nor art is merely epiphenomenal, and neither can
be reduced to the other. The fundamental theme of his *Weltanschauung* is that all experienced reality is determined by the nature
of the experiencing organism, and that consequently the real world
for man is a spiritual world—a world composed of linguistic forms
and distinctions, myths, artistic images, religious symbols and
rites, and scientific concepts. These are the spiritual or symbolic
forms which constitute the human self and through which it is
created and expressed. So the world in which man must live, according to Cassirer, is not so much a world of hard and irreducible data in the sense of objective matters of fact but a world of
meaning, a world interpreted, or perhaps more accurately, constructed; it is a world which, strictly speaking, would not exist
at all apart from the symbolic forms which the structure and
experience of the organism generate and which in turn inform
the experience of the world. Language, myth, religion, art, and
science are thus fundamentally autonomous ways of *humanizing*
the universe or ways of constructing the only world which man
can know and in which he must live.

Within this context Cassirer sometimes seems to treat the
arts as forms of genuine knowledge and suggests that compared
with the sciences they provide "a richer, more vivid and colorful

image of reality, and a more profound insight into its formal structure."[25] And indeed there is no theoretical basis in his system for distinguishing at all between the epistemological and metaphysical relevance and validity of the various symbolic forms. Yet his most persistent emphasis contrasts, very sharply and explicitly, the "aesthetic trend" in the arts with the "cognitive" and "existential" claims of both the sciences and the religions.

In a consideration of Schleiermacher's religious philosophy, for example, he observed that the very "highest religious truth remains attached to sensuous existence, to the world of images as well as things," even though religion's "intelligible purpose strives to cast off and reject" this attachment. The distinctive feature of religion, he insists, is not at all the sensuous image but the *meaning* of the image or "the relation to the universe which it obtains in religious feeling and thought."[26] And the religious pursuit of meaning free of sensuous fact or of meaning without a symbolic image or form, he claims, gives rise to an insoluble conflict between *meaning* and *existence*. And this conflict, he continues, is the basis of the profound and distinctive religious concern with the question of *what it means to be or to exist*. Is the image or symbol itself the only reality? religion asks. Or is the fact that meaning seems to struggle (in the consciousness of the religious person) to be free of any particular embodiment indicative of a realm of existence not characterized by the limits that belong to the ordinary forms of human existence and knowledge? In this question, precipitated by the conflict between the image (or symbol) and its meaning, said Cassirer, religion "faces the problem of 'existence' in all its harshness."[27] Religion, in other words, cannot avoid metaphysical questions and commitments.

But in art—or rather in the "aesthetic trend" exemplified and promoted by the arts—, he wrote, "the image is recognized purely as such" and "to fulfill its function it need give up none of itself and its content." The sensuous embodiment is the very essence of artistic creation, and consequently the artistic or aesthetic con-

---

[25] Ernst Cassirer, *An Essay on Man*, New Haven, Yale, 1944, p. 170.
[26] Ernst Cassirer, *The Philosophy of Symbolic Forms*, trans. by R. Manheim, New Haven, Yale, 1955, Vol. Two, p. 260.
[27] *Ibid.*, p. 261.

sciousness knows no conflict at all between image and meaning; for in fact, says Cassirer, it seeks neither meaning nor existence. The images produced by the artistic spirit "confess themselves to be illusion" and thereby "become for the spirit a pure expression of its own creative powers."[28]

The fundamental difference between art and religion is then distinct and explicit.

> The involvement and opposition of meaning and image are the essential condition of religion. If this involvement and opposition were ever replaced by a pure and perfect equilibrium, the inner tension of religion, on which rests its significance as a symbolic form, would be negated.[29]

In other words, the sense of depth, of existence beyond the image itself, created by the tension in the conflict between the sensuous form and the symbolic meaning of the form, is the source, the distinctive quality, and the strength of the religious experience. On the other hand, in art there is absolutely no problem of either meaning or existence. The only aim of the artist qua artist is to produce a congenial illusion or to facilitate and enhance perceptual discrimination and appreciation of the formal and sensuous properties of his medium, without concern for either meaning or existence. Art may intensify the perception of the formal structures and sensuous qualities of actual objects and events or it may create imaginary forms and landscapes which give aesthetic satisfaction. But art neither reveals existential powers and dimensions, nor increases man's capacity for knowing, nor radically affects his character or involvement in the actual structures and processs of nature. The symbol or the image in art signifies or means nothing.

In another context Cassirer observed that "Religion and art are so close to one another in their purely historical development, and so permeate one another, that sometimes the two seem indistinguishable in content and in their inner formative principle."[30] But he also notes again in a later work that ultimately the princi-

---

[28] *Ibid.*
[29] *Ibid.*, p. 260.
[30] Ernst Cassirer, *The Philosophy of Symbolic Forms*, trans. by R. Manheim, New Haven, Yale, 1953, Vol. One, p. 82.

ple which distinguishes religion from art is that the "religious image can never be treated as merely a picture, as an arbitrary play of the powers of imagination."[31] The implication of course is clearly that the arts are essentially sensuous and illusory images produced arbitrarily.

If all this seems to contradict claims in the chapter on art in Cassirer's later work, *An Essay on Man*, it is only because of the ambiguities there in the claim that art has a logic and a truth of its own. *Logic* and *truth* do not there mean what they ordinarily mean, even to Cassirer, and refer not to genuinely existential matters but only to appearances. So although he says art is "a peculiar and specific" kind of knowledge, that "The plastic arts make us see the sensible world in all its richness and multifariousness," and "Poetry is ... the revelation of our personal life," he also sharply contrasts art with science and morality by noting that "Science gives us order in thoughts; morality gives us order in actions; art gives us order in the apprehension of visible, tangible, and audible *appearances*."[32] The emphasis is clearly on appearances, and he never claims for art that it is judicially necessary, ontologically noteworthy, or that it symbolizes some actual aspect of empirical and enduring existence; art presents only secondary or nonefficient forms of appearance and illusion. Cassirer in fact says in *The Philosophy of Symbolic Forms:*

> What distinguishes empirical reality, the constant core of objective being, from the mere world of representation or imagination is that in it the permanent is more and more clearly differentiated from the fluid, the constant from the variable. The particular sense impression is not simply taken for what it is and gives [as is preëminently the case in art]; instead we ask: will it be confirmed by experience as a whole? Only if it stands up under this question and this critical test can we say that it has been received into the realm of reality and determinate objective existence.[33]

In spite of the genuine likelihood that absolutely nothing is in fact ever *confirmed by experience as a whole*, the existential and

---

[31] Ernst Cassirer, *The Problem of Knowledge*, trans. by W. Woglom and C. Hendel, New Haven, Yale, 1950, p. 295.

[32] Ernst Cassirer, *An Essay on Man, op. cit.*, pp. 168-169. Italics added.

[33] Ernst Cassirer, *The Philosophy of Symbolic Forms,* trans. by R. Manheim, New Haven, Yale, 1955, Vol. Two, p. 31.

judicial relevance of the arts is nonetheless supposedly denied by this test. Thus in *The Myth of the State* he observes, "A poet lives in the world of his imagination; and a great religious poet, like Dante or Milton, also lives in a world of prophetic vision. But he does not take these visions for realities; nor does he make of them a philosophy of history."[34] Art deals not with empirical reality or existents, but with appearances.

The logic and truth of the arts are then significant and effective only within the very special world of the artist or in aesthetic perception and imaginative construction. And important as it may be for man to actualize his creative powers through making and appreciating works of art, the arts are nonetheless irrelevant to the truly judicial capacities and processes by which he may identify or apprehend the ontological dimensions of himself and the world or modify his existential character and situation.

This is not of course an unusual view of the differences between religion and art. Another version of it was assumed and developed by Sigmund Freud when he wrote, "Art is almost always harmless and beneficent" because "it does not seek to be anything else but an illusion.... Art ... never dares to make any attacks on the realm of reality." But in regard to religion Freud of course claimed that although "the truth of religion may be altogether disregarded," it "is a really serious enemy" because it seeks "reality" in the "illusion" which "falls in with our instinctual desires."[35] Thus art confesses itself an illusion but religion persists in the most dangerous illusion that illusion is itself the truth. And R. G. Collingwood at one time defended a version that is still closer to that of Cassirer. He claimed that "Art ... is pure imagination"[36] but "Religion, relatively to art, is the discovery of reality"[37] or "art asserting its object. The object of art is the beautiful, and therefore the holy is the beautiful asserted as real."[38]

[34] Ernst Cassirer, *The Myth of the State*, New Haven, Yale, 1946, pp. 289-290.
[35] Sigmund Freud, *op. cit.*, pp. 219 and 239.
[36] R. G. Collingwood, *Speculum Mentis*, Oxford, Oxford University Press, 1936, p. 61.
[37] *Ibid.*, p. 112.
[38] *Ibid.*, p. 120.

Now surely the claim that the religions but not the arts are concerned with problems of meaning and existence has much to recommend it. The arts are often quite frankly "imaginative" and "fanciful"; and their products are frequently described as "fictitious," or as "myths," "cloud-castles," "inventions," "moonshine," or "make-believe." And of course such terms sustain and promote the notion among many that, on account of serious and profound concern for existential problems, religion is immeasurably superior to the arts, both morally and intellectually. Yet conversely, some partisans of the arts are apparently convinced that it is precisely because the arts have no interest at all in existential matters, and so harbor no unrecognized illusions, that they are greatly to be preferred to religion.

But Cassirer's analysis in particular and the others insofar as they are similar seem radically mistaken or inadequate on at least two counts. In the first place, although Cassirer admits the necessity, he seriously underestimates the profound importance of the purely sensuous and formal values in religious symbolism and ritual. Although nothing is further from the religious life than purely aesthetic appreciation and detachment, nothing is closer to the sense of the holy than the sense of beauty. A world without beauty, if at all possible, might provoke serious questions about the grounds of existence but could hardly arouse the passion for worship. Even truth in a world without beauty would apparently have chiefly utilitarian or instrumental value. And a religion without beauty, true only in the most narrow pragmatic sense, would be a religion in name only.

The second difficulty is that the supposed purity of sensuous and formal elements and the corresponding absence of cognitive content implied by Cassirer's analysis characterize at most only very special and limited genre, such as the purely decorative arts and playful or nonsensical poetry. Few if any of the major arts are ever concerned primarily with only formal and sensuous values or mere appearance. Even architecture, the most practical and often the least expressive of the arts, is by no means limited artistically to the enhancement of practical with sensuous and structural values. The buildings of a community—temples, churches, libraries, museums, and even purely utilitarian structures

—may in fact embody and express, not only economic values, technical skills, and an extraordinary sense of beauty, but may also emphasize selected elements of a religious, scientific, or moral tradition and so pass enduring judgment on certain values of the tradition.

Of course, if meaning is limited to a tripartite relation between a sign or symbol, a subject, and an object—if there is *meaning* only when a sign stands for an object in the experience of a knowing subject—then surely many important artistic products and images, as well as many religious activities and symbols, and even scientific concepts, are not meaningful. But the claim that all meanings involve such tripartite relations depends itself on the assumption that all symbolism and language are essentially nounal and is (as Cassirer knew) much too naïve and uncritical. For symbolism and language are then only varieties of independent and diaphanous pointing, and genuine and unambiguous meaning is confined to instances where the sign and the signified are clear and distinct. Now a very modest sensitivity to the complex functions and nuances of language and its relations to other symbols and activities should detect at once that such a theory is inadequate. Meaning pervades man's relations to tools, concepts, and objects. The meaning of a hammer, however, is not a referent but the activities which it enables one to perform. The meaning of a number is not something to which it points but its place in the numerical order and the processes of counting and measuring which it makes possible. And the meaning of a loaf of bread is primarily that it may be assimilated to satisfy taste and hunger. Meaning, as Justus Buchler has persuasively argued, may occur in any process of judging (accepting, rejecting, manipulating, describing, or modifying) actions, beliefs, or objects.

Consequently meaning is by no means confined to language conventionally conceived but may belong to any object, sign, quality, symbol, concept, or complex which either affects or is instrumental within the judicial processes by which the quality and direction of an individual life are maintained. Indeed language, far from being the condition in terms of which meaning is possible, is itself apparently grounded in meanings which are always in some measure *beyond* the power of language to articulate.

For example, if artistic powers and products are not only instances of intrinsic value but may also influence both the modes and substance of subsequent and deliberate thought and action (or judgment) they must surely be regarded as cognitive and meaningful in a manner quite impossible to language. And even the use of *illusion*—which has a reality of its own not altogether independent of the rest of existence—may sometimes be an indispensable mode of deliberately articulating certain meanings and serving the interests of sustained and reliable judgment.

The denial of the judicial power and meaning of the arts can in fact be based finally only on either a thoroughgoing materialistic determinism or on the equally fantastic and arbitrary assumption that experience and existence are sharply divided into efficient and nonefficient categories or into areas where reasonable judgment is, and others where it is not, effective. But to all appearances the artist, no less than the prophet and the scientist, may lead men to modify radically their habitual ways of seeing and conceiving the world. Cold and silent marble may *speak* eloquently about or reveal important aspects of man. And in the case of the artist himself, the medium he chooses, as well as his style, is of course already a judgment which influences his own, and perhaps others', subsequent decisions concerning both certain facts and values. For both what the artist or anyone else, for that matter, sees and what he finds worth sustained care and exploration plainly depends in significant part on prior decisions, whether implicit or explicit, in regard to medium, style, talents, and other similar matters of artistic importance.

So only in an age when science or religion has inspired undue confidence in its own methods and discoveries as the final word on existential and procedural matters can it be widely and seriously denied, by neglect if not by explicit claim, that the arts are among the judicious discriminations by which man *discovers, maintains,* and *modifies* his precarious posture and direction in nature. The aesthetic values of the arts are no doubt often dominant; and these values are in a sense less necessary than the practical and conceptual values on which human existence is radically dependent. But aesthetic values and the arts which nurture them are not always as irrelevant to practical and conceptual judgments as is often thought.

In poetry, for example, the patterns of words, sounds, symbols, and ideas must be acceptable not only to what may narrowly be called "the aesthetic sense" of the poet but also to his logical insight and entire sense of value and reality. And obviously the very habits of thought and expression developed in reading and writing poetry are parts of the complex substance of his being and will be reflected not only in further reading and writing but also in other intellectual and practical matters. The poet—and even the lover of poetry—may be profoundly poetic in almost all that he is, sees, and does. Poetry exemplifies elements of existence and not simply ways of speaking.

Likewise, although in sculpture the marble, wood, or metal may be shaped primarily to accentuate or create significant elements of form and surface, the results may also express, as no other medium can, aspects of character and concern such that the total mood and interests of the spectator's life may be, at least for the moment, radically changed. Colors and shapes in painting are not only colors and shapes but modes of seeing, of emphasis and de-emphasis, of discovery and choice; so both the process and the results of painting are judgments, whether basically discoveries or inventions, which may provoke verbal responses and related thoughts, gestures, attitudes, and actions regardless of whether one finds painting a significant commentary on the nonformal and nonsensuous aspects of life. And music, by the very fact that it may be either appropriate or inappropriate, an invitation to joyful celebration or solemn reflection, the voice of hope or of impending tragedy, is evidently a mode of judging events and total situations—and in some respects modifying them—as well as a delightful or remarkable arrangement of sounds and tones which may qualify subsequent tonal experience and musical creativity.

Any consistent denial that the arts bear or contain meanings which may promote and modify judgment must insist that there is something completely illusory in the choices or decisions which the arts and artistic qualities apparently provoke and sustain. Either the art is not the genuine basis of the choice, the denial implies, or the judgment could have taken a different and more direct form. Now assuming that any attempt to account for artistic judgments in terms of nonartistic causes or factors may also apply *mutatis mutandis* to scientific, religious, and moral judgments, it is clearly impossible to take seriously such a *reductio ad absurdum*. Thus the claim that truth or reality is obtainable only through a particular form of judgment seems to express a preference rather than an obvious truth. For each mode of judgment apparently has its own objects and limits as well as its own methods and powers. Even as physics deals with *measurable objects and processes* but not at all with *concepts of measurement*, the arts and the religions are appropriately concerned only with the qualities, commitments, and results which can be realized or articulated through their media and methods. If it were possible to know physics without mathematical formulae and controlled experiments, the mathematical language and the experiments would be, though surely not in all respects meaningless, clearly superfluous in relation to physics. And if it were possible to render more directly and effectively the judgments or to realize the facts and values disclosed or achieved in painting and poetry without painting and poetry, such products could perhaps be regarded as judicially or cognitively superfluous or meaningless. But the fact that the meaning or significance of a work of art is intrinsic and grasped immediately without any struggle to translate it into nonartistic terms or to discover something to which it refers, far from implying that absolute illusions are either expected or satisfying in the arts, only bears witness that in the supreme work of art the image and meaning are bound into an inseparable union. As surely as the hydrogen and oxygen separated out of water do not possess the qualities or powers of water, so the image and meaning of a work of art do not exist *as such* apart from each other. And the sensitive observer, far from considering the artistic image an illusion in any fundamental sense, may realize or grasp for the first time a meaning that has never been more fully or lucidly presented. The arts are surely not any less concerned with *meanings* and *existence* than is religion, though they may often take seriously different dimensions of existence or objects and meanings which the religions regard as trivial or even profane.

Thus the analysis of religion as primarily existential concern, or as the product of conflict between image and meaning, and of art as congenial illusion, disregards the judicial importance of both the aesthetic dimensions of religious symbols and the profound existential relevance of the arts. The analysis is perhaps just to the discontent of many religious persons with the particularity (and thus the illusion) inherent in all symbols but not to the fact that neither the particularity nor the illusion can be sharply or wholly separated from the total value of a religion. The analysis is perhaps also just to the perceptual and aesthetic values of artistic achievement but not to the artist's own struggle with existential problems, meanings, and values. Dramatists and novelists especially, but also lyric poets, painters, sculptors, musicians, and even architects—judging both by their own testimony and that of their audiences—articulate and provoke, deliberately and effectively, existential concern and decision as well as imaginative and aesthetic vistas and values. To treat art as primarily illusion and religion as nothing but existential concern in effect completely denies the validity of Aristotle's claim that tragedy is a mode of apprehending and expressing universal truths about the quality and consequences of character and action, as well as the relevance of Santayana's claim that one important function of religion is to provide an imaginative refuge from a world whose tragic and ugly events are so often too much with us. Yet experience suggests and reflection confirms, so far as reflection can, that neither Aristotle nor Santayana, incomplete and partially mistaken as their accounts may be, wholly missed or completely misrepresented the facts.

The conflict or tension between the sensuous form of the religious symbol and its meaning, contrary to Cassirer's analysis in particular, is apparently different only in degree from the tension in all judgment between sensory experience and ideas, passion and action, or the given and the created. Disparity or incommensurability and consequent tension are surely present in some degree in all instances of the power or capacity by which sensory, emotional, and introspective experiences are transformed into objective and highly effective forms of communication and action. The tension occurs in both art and science and underlies the controversies between art-for-art's sake and art as a form of existential meaning and truth, as well as the fundamental disagreements between rationalists and empiricists in science and philosophy. The degree of tension is apparently proportionate to the degree of mystery or incommensurability admitted or stimulated.

And ultimately of course religious symbols or judgments are not any more mysterious in either origin or function and so should not produce more tension than the symbols and judgments of ordinary speech, science, philosophy, and art. Yet the reason for the common failure to confront mystery, and therefore to arouse tensions, in art and science is not far to seek. The arts are now so rarely taken seriously as forms of authentic judgment and the concepts and symbols of science are so carefully related, at least in theory, to experimental or observational evidence that special effort is required to discern their mystery or the incommensurability between the source, the concept or symbol, and the meaning. To deny that the arts are meaningful judgments or to imagine that science is completely verified by observational and experimental results, almost invariably obscures, though it does not remove, one of the poles of mystery and wonder and so mitigates or destroys the doubt and tension which should rightly characterize every supposedly fundamental judgment passed by the finite mind. But even as the arts can be regarded as congenial illusions only by one who has already completely dismissed their judicial relevance, the idea of an unusual tension between the religious symbols and their meaning can occur only to one who confronts and yet doubts their judicial power and adequacy. To the person who is tenaciously or unquestioningly confident of the power and relevance of a particular symbol or concept, there is no question about meaning and no tension; for others the tension arises from the fact that they know, even though they may not always admit, that they see only through a glass darkly.

ON ART, RELIGION, AND METAPHYSICS

There are facts of existence which can be expressed only in such terms as the language of poetry, art, morals, and religion employ. It is difficult to see how these languages could be if there were nothing in existence to support them.
                                    FREDERICK J. E. WOODBRIDGE

As should be expected from the facts and theories noted in the previous section, religion is almost universally regarded, whether correctly or incorrectly, as a more serious and metaphysically significant phenomenon than the arts. As indicated by the quotations from Sigmund Freud, for example, even those who dismiss any possibility of religious truth often regard religion as a very serious matter—as an inevitable neurosis to be treated, a demon to be fought, or a social necessity. On the other hand very few have been favorably impressed by Friedrich Nietzsche's protest against "the habit of looking at art merely as a merry diversion, a light carillon sounding on the edge of earnest pursuits, easily dispensed with." Still fewer have agreed with his more positive claim that "Art is the highest human task, the true metaphysical activity."[39] Most philosophers, including religious philosophers and theologians, have been convinced that logic, the categories of the sciences, of morals, and of religion may all have profound ontological significance but that the arts need not be taken seriously in metaphysical inquiries, though they may be highly relevant in the psychology and sociology of perception and taste. So the philosophers have usually added a theory of art or aesthetics to their *Weltanschauung*, if at all, only as an afterthought or in order to round out their systems. Schopenhauer and Nietzsche are perhaps the most notable modern exceptions to this practice.

And much of art so-called is of course largely decorative or

[39] Friedrich Nietzsche, in the "Preface to Richard Wagner" for *The Birth of Tragedy*, trans. by F. Golffing, New York, Doubleday, Anchor Books, 1956, pp. 16-17.

even frivolous or absorbed in the sheer delight of the sensuous and formal qualities of a medium. Artistic perspectives are often admittedly the products of sheer invention and playful fancy. Of course there are indeed persuasive, if inconclusive, reasons supporting the claim that the arts always aspire towards technical but unsubstantial perfection and virtuosity or splendid irrelevance in "mere grace and feeling and music and cloud-castles and frolic." Yet ultimately, in spite of the burden of philosophic practice to the contrary, there seems to be no indubitable facts or assumptions which altogether justify excluding fancy and frolic from the matters which must be *seriously* accounted for or included in any metaphysical scheme which pretends to be adequate. Man is no less the creature that plays and laughs than the creature that labors and weeps. And although the arts have only rarely been regarded as absolute necessities and have generally been tolerated on the periphery of earnest endeavors as pleasant and perhaps harmless diversions, no great civilization has existed without great art. Men are in fact artists long before the necessities of organic life are fulfilled or in circumstances which do not encourage and barely allow any genuine fancy and frolic. Consequently it seems radically mistaken to claim that the arts are fundamentally illusory or have no important effects beyond their power to delight, especially if this implies the conclusion that the delight they bring is due to an appearance which passes without in any way revealing or influencing the basic ontology of the world-which-includes-man.

Indeed, there are perfectly sound reasons for supposing that the arts are irreducible forms of being and judging, even as the sciences, the religions, and moral actions are irreducible forms of being and judging. And if Aristotle was, as he seems, essentially right, and it is the intelligibility of the world that makes the many forms of man's intelligence possible and his own character-in-the-world that demands and defines the moral, it is surely not too much to claim that the artist also only apprehends and actualizes forms and qualities already implicit in nature and himself, and that neither logic nor science nor religion is more indicative than the arts of *what is* in the world or of what the world in fact is. A genuine aspect of existence not otherwise evident at all, it may then be said, is revealed through each of the arts or even in each instance of original poetry, music, painting, drama, etc.—an aspect of man himself and of the world in which he has his extraordinary career. And surely there is little reason to deny that to judge the world artistically is to discover or create qualitative objects which may influence subsequent experiences of seeing, hearing, and thinking or that the arts do in fact reveal genuine possibilities of sight, sound, and meaning within the complex of existence. Thus the creation of a work of art is never merely the expression of personal feeling or the actualization of the capacity of an individual but also, and equally, a revelation or discovery of the potentiality of a universe that produces men who write poems, paint pictures, and compose symphonies. So the universe, it should be said, may be known and judged artistically even as it is known and judged mathematically and chemically. Or the universe may be called a universe of artistic creativity and aesthetic experience with as much right as it is called a universe of physical law and chemical reaction. And that it is more widely called a physical and chemical universe than an artistic or religious one reflects not simply or so much "the facts" as "the value" of the facts in the eyes of the age.

In summary, it is not as illusion that the arts are most significant but as the vivid and eloquent, and even terrifying, availability of forms and qualities for seeing, assimilating, and rejecting —or judging and being. If man heeds the arts as he should in constructing his metaphysics, he will not make the mistake of supposing that nature is simply mechanical and repetitious or less than wonderful or that there is any strict limit on the forms of perfection and perversity which may be actualized by nature or by chance and human choice. And to take the arts seriously as ways of revealing the "infinite variety" of actuality and possibility or as decisive existential forms and judicial modes need not mitigate, as some have seemed to fear, the sense of seriousness and reality which the holy has everywhere inspired in the minds of men. Or in other words, the arts may surely be metaphysically and judicially significant without in any way compromising the genuine importance of religion and the other basic forms of experience and judgment.

ON THE SIMILAR POWERS OF THE ARTS AND RELIGIONS

For beauty being the best of all we know
Sums up the unsearchable and secret aim of
nature.

ROBERT BRIDGES

A part of the momentous value of both the arts and religion is clearly aesthetic. It is also at least highly plausible that beauty in its simplest forms—that which is immediately pleasing to the eyes and ears—is much more influential in practically all modes of judgment and patterns of behavior than is generally recognized or even imagined. Religious activities and ideas, in any case, are often clearly and intimately related to the creation of beauty in music, painting, architecture, sculpture, and poetry. It would in fact be difficult to overemphasize either the extent to which the religions have encouraged, refined, and satisfied the basically aesthetic sensibilities of man or the influence of the sense of beauty on the cultural and judicial functions of the religions. From the psalms of David to the magnificent marble images of the many Greek divinities; from the great epic vision of Dante to the simple miracle plays of the fifteenth and sixteenth centuries; from the powerful choral music of Bach to the haunting hymns and spirituals of the Negro American, religion has often and obviously provided a framework and inspired the creation of the most elevated art and beauty. And apparently the arts, as both objects of great beauty and the expression of insights and judgments which can be articulated in no other way, have in turn moved men to both artistic and nonartistic commitments or to labors dedicated to actualizing in other ways the ideas and ideals which were originally conceived and expressed only artistically. André Malraux has said:

> Almost all the great works of the past have this in common: their submission to the dialogue, impassioned or serene, maintained by

each with that part of his soul which the artist deemed the holiest. . . . In times when man feels stranded and alone [art] assures to its votaries that deep communion which would else have passed away with the passing of the gods.[40]

And even "The arts of the religions in which we do not believe," he has also said, "act more strongly on us than nonreligious arts or those of religions which have lapsed into mere convention."[41] No matter how profoundly religion differs from art, the aesthetic dimensions of religion and the influence of artistic methods and aesthetic values on the whole of man's life must not be minimized.

There is of course a sense in which a work of art is simply a work of art and in which it is no more intelligible to call it religious than to call it scientific. But at least many, if not all, works of art may also appeal to more than technical values and the values of sensuous and formal perception and become significant parts of the moral and intellectual or spiritual life. It was undoubtedly for this reason that Leonardo da Vinci claimed that painting, far from being simply the use of color and form in the demonstration of sensuous and formal values, "is a form of poetry made to be seen," and Malraux has added, "Far from excluding poetry from painting, we should do better to realize that all great works of plastic art are steeped in poetry."[42] Surely neither Leonardo nor Malraux is proposing that poetry as such is the highest of the arts. But if "the poetic" as they conceived it may be defined as the fusing of various elements and values—sensuous, formal, symbolic, and conceptual—into the irreducible and significant meanings which become available in a work of art and which can never be exhausted in any precise correlations between a symbol or concept and its presumed object, then practically all religious judgments may be said to be poetic. Such poetic qualities apparently pervade primitive religious chants and rituals as well as technical theological speculations. A poetic judgment occurs in the dances and incantations of the rainmakers and also in the

[40] André Malraux, The Voices of Silence, New York, Doubleday, 1953, p. 639.
[41] Ibid., p. 527.
[42] Ibid., pp. 54, 58.

elaborate and passionate arguments of a Pascal or Kierkegaard. Even by the most severe secular standards much of the best poetry is found in sacred books. And at least much of this presumably found its way into the sacred canons not because it dealt with elevated themes or the experience of the holy, but because the most common and simplest matters become radiant in the hands of the poet.

The arts, at the very least, transform the most commonplace features of life into singular and unforgettable events. In a landscape by Van Gogh or in lines as unembellished as the following by Tennyson, unremarkable scenes and events become the occasions of the most memorable concepts, concerns, and insights.

> Flower in the crannied wall,
> I pluck you out of the crannies,
> I hold you here, root and all, in my hand,
> Little flower—but *if* I could understand
> What you are, root and all, and all in all,
> I should know what God and man is.

The simple or ordinary landscape transformed by painting is no less astonishing—no less luminous, liberating, and revelatory—than the most elaborate and detailed cosmology; and the lines by Tennyson accentuate the same sense of weight and extraordinary significance—though it is not long sustained—which experience gains in the great tragedies such as Sophocles' *Antigone* and in religious classics such as *The Book of Job*.

The work of art—poem or painting or symphony—if it makes no notable changes in the objective world, may at least modify habits of thought and perception. And in this respect, if in no other, the effect of the artistic judgment may indeed be radical and enduring. Even Santayana ascribed such power to poetry and to religion in his discussion of prayer. Describing prayer as the most distinctive religious activity, he wrote (paradoxical as it may seem for a thoroughgoing materialist to write in such terms) that "Strange as it may sound to the rationalist who thinks prayer ridiculous, the only perfectly rational form of life for a spirit that has attained self-knowledge is the life of prayer."[43] For prayer

[43] George Santayana, *The Realms of Being*, New York, Scribner, 1942, p. 801.

is justified, he thought, by its threefold function: it expresses or defines the ideal towards which the soul aspires; it enables the soul through the act of expression to become more like the envisaged ideal; and finally, it reconciles the soul to the alien and unavoidable circumstances in which it may be caught. The "soul" here means of course only self-consciousness or the fact that an organism reflects on its own nature and conditions; and to say that prayer "functions" in these various ways is not, for Santayana, to attribute genuine efficacy to prayer but only to note that prayer accompanies certain aspirations, processes, and attitudes. Santayana was fully aware that he saw in prayer or in religion only the values and powers that others have associated chiefly with the arts. And like many who admit that the arts have such powers, he never explicitly acknowledged that the changes in the inward man may be reflected in objective relations, judgments, and decisions. He was as reluctant to emphasize the transforming and reconciling powers of religion as many contemporary critics are to deal seriously with the nonaesthetic or nonformal aspects, influences, and implications of the arts. Santayana's reluctance was of course justified by his frank metaphysical materialism which is clearly incompatible with any genuine or enduring consequences from the arts; but this is a defense that few current critics would explicitly claim.

Yet no matter how important the purely formal and sensuous elements may seem, few who take the arts seriously can wholly escape, though they may often try, the idea that at least one highly significant function of the arts is that they provide standards and stimuli for nonartistic judgments and activities. In the *Saturday Review* some years ago, John Ciardi, in an editorial entitled "Literature Undefended," set out to develop the theme that literature needs no nonliterary, or nonaesthetic, defense. But his most impressive claim was that:

> A savage, after all, is simply a human organism that has not received enough news from the human race. Literature is one most fundamental part of that news. One needs to hear Job lift his question into the wind; it is after all, every man's question at some time. One needs to stand by Oedipus and to hold the knife of his own most terrible resolution. One needs to come out of his

own Hell with Dante and hear that voice of joy hailing the sight of his own stars returned-to. One needs to run with Falstaff, roaring with his own appetites and weeping into his own pathos. What one learns from these voices is his own humanity. . . . Until he has heard these voices deeply within himself, what man can have any sizable idea of himself?[44]

One needs to hear such voices, in other words, because they transform the savage organism into a soul that has heard the most significant news of mankind. Literature informs man and the intimate and profound relation between being informed and reformed or transformed hardly needs to be labored, although it is no doubt too often overlooked or taken altogether too lightly. But the informing, and therefore the reforming, power of the arts is not widely or explicitly admitted in an age when educated men generally shun the acknowledgment of any form of mystery or "nonscientific" influences more carefully than they shun death. Yet the idea that art, or more particularly the tragic drama, has the power to inform man and thus to reconcile him to inevitable defeat was of course effectively argued long ago by Aristotle. The art of tragedy, he observed, makes the fate of the tragic hero and all who identify themselves with him intelligible and therefore bearable. The understanding generated by the exhibition of his passions, motives, and inevitable failures or by the symbols and concepts presented provide no control or security. Yet the moral supremacy and the magnificence of man, said Aristotle, is established by his consciousness of the inexorable events that destroy him. Life understood is life reconciled to its limits and made aware of its dignity. And tragedy, Aristotle concluded, is a better mode of understanding man than is history.

Few who grant such powers in the arts would altogether deny them in the religions or deny that the powers of the religions are in some respects highly similar to and even dependent upon the powers of the arts. When the Lord is said to answer Job "out of the whirlwind," to question and to command, "Who is this that darkeneth counsel by words without knowledge? Gird up now thy loins like a man; for I will demand of thee, and answer thou me.

[44] John Ciardi, "Literature Undefended," *Saturday Review*, January 31, 1959, p. 22.

Where wast thou when I laid the foundations of the earth? declare if thou hast understanding," the effect produced is hardly less dependent on the quality of the language than on the sudden and abysmal darkness into which thought is plunged by symbol and concept and the sense of utter mystery and dependence which this may generate.[45]

Both art and religion are apparently modes of apprehending, creating, and communicating, both symbolically and conceptually, aspects of existence that are essentially qualitative rather than quantitative. Both may inspire and inform and thus reform or transform the inward life of man. And if the inward man is reflected in objective decisions and actions, both the arts and the religions may influence profoundly the shape of the world that man builds and in which he must live. But in spite of some highly similar and interdependent powers and functions, religion and art seem to be nonetheless essentially different approaches to the constant demands in man's life for the judicial and judicious use of the diverse and awesome powers of correlative assimilation and manipulation with which he is endowed. It is to the distinct differences between the two that we must now turn.

ON THE DISSIMILARITIES OF THE ARTS AND RELIGIONS

The intellect of man is forced to choose
Perfection of the life, or of the work.
                            WILLIAM BUTLER YEATS

The most obvious thing to be said in distinguishing the arts from the religions is that the arts are clearly possible without any conviction or sense of the presence of the holy or divine. Conse-

[45] Compare the following example from Rudolf Otto: " 'Eye hath not seen, nor ear heard, neither have entered into the heart of man, the things which God hath prepared for them that love him.' Who does not feel the exalted sound of these words and the 'Dionysiac' element of transport and fervour in them." *The Idea of the Holy*, trans. by J. Harvey, New York, Oxford, Galaxy Books, 1958, p. 34. One could of course cite many such examples from both the Old and New Testaments.

quently there is perhaps also sufficient reason for claiming that the only fundamental difference between the work of art and the religious symbol is a functional one, comparable to the difference between an outstretched palm and a closed fist. But even if this is so, it must still be said that two quite different and distinct things are involved. For even as an outstretched palm is not the same thing as a closed fist though there is no difference in substance, the art object neither is nor means the same as the identical object functioning as a religious symbol, though in both instances it is most surely something meaningful.

The fundamental difference between the two is borne out by the fact that the most powerful religious symbols are often artistically very bad while the most impressive work of art may offend the religious conscience. So although it is no doubt impossible to say, apart from their actual functions, that *this* object is a religious symbol and *that* one a work of art, it is nonetheless possible to distinguish between the object functioning religiously (or the religious meaning) and the same or similar object functioning artistically and aesthetically (or the artistic meaning). And although an individual may sometimes regard the religious symbols of cultures and religions other than his own as only works of art, few have any insuperable difficulties in distinguishing between the objects or complexes which function religiously and those that function artistically in their own culture, even when many objects function almost equally as both. And this is apparently not simply a matter of knowing the import of sacred scriptures so-called or the general form and content of a religious tradition or that certain things are considered appropriate and others inappropriate in recognized places and on occasions of worship. Certain symbols, moods, and gestures seem to bear a religious burden or accent which makes them recognizable as such even in nonreligious contexts, even though they may depart radically from the form and content of familiar traditions, and which enables even the outsider to identify the religious symbols of a particular culture. Also there are clearly works of art which, at least in our own civilization, under no circumstances would be regarded as religious, even though they may carry significant nonartistic meanings.

Dante's *Divine Comedy*, for example, is not only a great work of art but a devout allegory which is at least always potentially, though surely not exclusively, religious in power and function while Shakespeare's *Antony and Cleopatra*, though equally impressive simply as a work of art, is as intrinsically secular as it is splendid. The same sort of contrast is implicit in Michelangelo's *Creation* on the one hand and a still life by Cezanne on the other or in the music of Bach in relation to that of Gilbert and Sullivan. And although it is true that the meaning of a work of art is due in part to its contextual uses, its uses are apparently determined at least in part by its intrinsic qualities.

When these facts—that some religious images or symbols are clearly not works of art, that some works of art cannot conceivably function religiously, and that some works of art are, or are potentially, religious—are recognized, it becomes quite plausible, if not altogether certain, that to the religious person the nonartistic and nonaesthetic values of religion are always its chief and often its only values. Yet the religious consciousness apparently sometimes looks *through* the art object into a religious meaning or complex, even as the astronomer looks *through* the telescope into the heavens or as the microbiologist looks *through* the microscope into the normally invisible world. And in each instance *meaning* is intimately related to the instrument of discovery. But even as the basic principles of telescopy and microscopy are altogether different from the basic principles of astronomy and microbiology, so art (in the proper sense of the term) and religion are radically different enterprises. But obviously this analogy, even if pushed much further, does not contradict the claim that the religions and the arts are often closely related in the sense that they may greatly influence each other and are in some cases not only indistinguishable but actually interdependent.

The characteristic power and function of the arts, however, is to reveal, to exhibit or show, particular things and relations, whether actual or ideal, in their manifold and qualitative distinctiveness. Thus the artist may patiently and carefully develop and intensify the sensuous and formal qualities of ordinary language, sounds, lines, masses, forms, and colors, or experiment with metaphor, simile, and perspective. Art may be only exceedingly clever, beautiful, and fascinating, inviting one simply to come, see, and hear. In other words, that art begins and ends in extraordinary perceptual sensitivity and delight combined with exceptional technical skills is a defensible, though presumably an incomplete, view and is justified in part at least by the fact that artistic products rarely lose altogether their purely artistic or aesthetic powers and values when the intellectual and cultural elements which they may have originally carried are lost or abandoned. There is a purely perceptual or aesthetic dimension possible in experience which the arts may and often do legitimately exploit and develop. But that this is not the only or entire function of the arts seems equally evident.

That joy and sadness, shame and anguish, despair and hate, in their specific and multiple forms, are qualitative elements which belong to the most basic ontology of man and can be communicated only in the qualitative languages of the arts has already been argued. It may be added here that the artist may also exhibit in a unique and highly personal language, which many others may nonetheless come to understand and share, his own conceptual framework, including his deepest concerns, commitments, and objects of devotion. The poems of Donne and Blake and Hopkins, Picasso's Guernica, the novels and plays of Camus, and the poetic drama of T. S. Eliot are only among the more notable works which obviously intend to be and are not only artistically and aesthetically excellent, but also judgments that are not only artistically but also philosophically—though not simply logically—defensible. But the primary function of art as such is still to present or exhibit the qualitative actualities and possibilities in the manner that is most effective and impressive. The fact that this can only rarely be done without the introduction or intrusion of elaborate conceptual and symbolic assumptions and meanings, which perhaps inevitably express personal preferences and basic commitments, is both an increased power and an ever-present danger or distraction in artistic judgment.

In relation to art, the quite different and distinctive aim and function of religion is expressed by A. N. Whitehead when he describes religion as "a system of general truths which have the effect of transforming character when they are sincerely held and vividly apprehended."[46] The religious symbol or set of symbols which constitutes a religious view of existence both *invites* and *urges* the individual not only to come, see, and hear but also to change his life. Religion in articulating a vision of the holy also presents specific ontological, procedural, and moral standards by which the individual must judge his own life. Even though one may be intelligent and judicious without religion and the moral needs and character of man are not the basic religious facts, every religion entails specific judicial procedures and moral standards of its own. So instead of the perceptual sensitivity, technical skill, and delight in qualitative perspectives for their own sake which characterize works of art, religion requires ontological and moral commitments or categorical claims concerning what, in the light of the holy, is above all worth being, doing, and having. Therefore religion is never simply clever, charming, and fascinating or never without a nonartistic and nonaesthetic burden and must watch its logic and existential commitments as well as develop its powers of presenting and articulating the actual and the possible in the light of divine requirements. The arts aim at seeing for its own sake, whether with the eye of the mind or the senses; but the aim of a religion is a life formed and guided according to the specific requirements of a particular envisagement of the holy. Religion sustains, sanctifies, and criticizes the personal and the communal life of man.

Yet if the arts—like morality and science—do not demand a sense of the presence of the holy or a nonartistic burden or commitment, every aspect of life, including the arts, may be nonetheless influenced by the presence of the divine. And when freighted with existential and moral issues and traditions or when concerned with cosmic questions as in the Greek tragedians, Dante, Michelangelo, and Milton, or when serious and magnificent as in Beethoven and Van Gogh, art is apparently distinguished from religion chiefly in degree. Yet the artist as such, even in the presence of the holy, knows no inviolable themes or subjects. He may present and illuminate the insignificant aspects of existence or the grotesque and immoral as well as noble and magnificent ideas

[46] A. N. Whitehead, *Religion in the Making*, New York, Putnam, Living Age Books, 1960, p. 15.

and ideals. The demonic no less than the divine may challenge the highest powers of the artist. The judicial functions peculiar to the arts, their typical powers and meanings, are realized whenever a man learns or is taught through them to see any particular qualitative object or complex, to see more clearly and broadly, or to think, act, or create differently by virtue of what he has gained from or through them. In contrast, judgment is specifically religious only insofar as a vision of the holy influences the fundamental structure of personal commitment or of choosing, having, and being. The artist aims primarily to perfect the work or the art object though in doing so he alters his own character and powers; but the religious person seeks the perfection of his own existence and conduct, though his inspiration and guide *may be* the work perfected by the artist. To paraphrase Whitehead, a man *has* artistic powers and *uses* logical and mathematical forms of reason, but he *is* religious. Yet in some instances—perhaps the very best—a man's life is such a balanced complex of interests, powers, and aims that none of his ways of judgment is altogether separable or even distinguishable from the rest.

Precisely because of its profound concern for the perfection of the self, religion prospers in the face of unmitigated adversity, when the world is unfriendly, when the body is threatened by disease and impotence, when the spirit is attracted by incompatible goals, or when man perceives most clearly the utter and incommensurable difference between what is priceless or divine and what is only desired and possible or allowed. The artist qua artist, however, need not always distinguish between the priceless and the allowed, the necessary and the possible. He may view the actual, the possible, the ideal, the hateful, and the priceless with equal care and concern for the distinctive qualities of each. But again his failure to distinguish between the actual and the ideal, for example, does not indicate that the artist has forsaken the pursuit of meaning but rather that he recognizes that the increase of meaning—or the realization, if only in imagination, of a multitude of ways of thinking, acting, being, and creating—is one of the most basic and clearest values of existence.

Through the arts man seeks meanings—qualities, forms, powers, procedures, and possibilities—unhindered by the haunting threat of catastrophe which always pervades the world of religion. In religion and in the religious arts man worships but also rebels and struggles against the severe limits and enormous burdens imposed by the recognition of the holy and the constant danger that all that is worth being, doing, and having may be missed. In the arts man accepts himself and the world, content to see, inform, and delight. The arts speak only to be heard and understood, to clarify and intensify the vision of a specific and limited portion of a constantly surprising world. But religion is a unifying vision, a relentless pursuit of personal, and perhaps unattainable, perfection or a commitment of the self to the stringent discipline implied in a view of the self as inextricably related to the awe-full and the holy. The artist may achieve immortality or undying fame in an early and single work. But the saint can secure saintliness only by vigilance unto death.

It is altogether possible, then, to be religious without deliberate or self-conscious art—in Puritan devotion to duty, in Quaker silence, in acts which signify rather than symbolize the pursuit of excellence. Yet the artistic elements of so many religious traditions are by no means adventitious. And the radical fault of Santayana's view, for example, is not that he valued too highly the poetic or artistic elements of the religions, but rather that he did not understand the necessity of the existential commitment that freely occurs in the religious perspective or see that the artistic portion of religion is more judicial than illusory, even though religious symbols may not be interpreted altogether literally. For the arts too are more judicial than illusory simply because man discovers himself and the world in the light and through the power of artistic perspectives and products. He judges not only in the light of Aristotle, Newton, Darwin, and Marx but also in the light of Aeschylus, Mozart, El Greco, and Isaiah. For whatever he sees, creates, assimilates, or reorganizes may surely become part of the very substance as well as the standards and processes by which he passes judgment on himself and the world. And even as the arts may teach him to see the "infinite variety" of skill and form and quality, he may learn from religion the necessity of choosing one form and quality from among all the rest as the chief guide of his own life. The great and characteristic power of the arts is, by perfecting its methods and objects, to enable us to see, while religion, grounded in the sense of the presence of the holy, may give us the reason and the light to be.

ON RELIGION, ART, AND THE COMMUNITY

The sociability of artists is a paradoxical and pre-caricus thing, and ceases the instant they begin their actual artistic work. But the sociability of religion is part of its fundamental nature.

R. G. COLLINGWOOD

The respective concerns of art for the perfection of the work and of religion for the perfection of life are very often evident in the different relations of each to the community.

In spite of the fact that religion is frequently attributed to extraordinary and supernatural intervention in human affairs, there is neither unambiguous evidence for nor any need to defend the claim that religion is less dependent on the community than are common sense, science, and the arts. In fact the very diversity of belief and practice makes virtually certain the accuracy of the claim that the religions are always closely and inextricably related to the particular insights, joys, fears, knowledge, and aims of specific communities. An individual may nonetheless, by virtue of his own unusual insights, character, and action, reorient a religion even as other individuals, through imagination, interests, and discoveries, may redirect the research and progress of a science or the technical features of a culture. The Buddha, Moses, Jesus, Mohammed, and Luther (in spite of traditions that may now appeal to each of them as an *authority*) are only among the more eminent examples of individuals who, in cooperation with forces already at work and the support of subsequent disciples, succeeded in making more or less radical changes in already established accounts of the nature of the holy or traditions of religious thought and action.

But radical changes in a community may also modify religions. It is indeed in every sense an open question whether the nonreligious changes which provoke basic and novel developments in religion or the secular changes precipitated by new religious insight, criticism, and practice are most fundamental. However, a few examples will make it quite clear that there is really no persuasive reason for accepting either alternative exclusively. There can be little doubt, as the first instance, that the quality of life in the medieval world—its amenities, social structures and problems, and especially its distinctive intellectual questions and achievements—was directly and intimately related to religious conviction and insight. Religion was at the very least one of the most decisive factors in shaping economics, politics, philosophy, and art. On the other hand, however, a very different aspect or possibility of the relation between religion and the other elements of society is suggested by the fact that Max Weber and R. H. Tawney have been able to argue, respectively and also persuasively, that Protestantism created capitalism and that capitalism, "with its deification of the life of snatching to hoard, and hoarding to snatch,"[47] has in turn largely destroyed the traditional Christian ideals and virtues. And finally, the very opposite side of the coin from that presented by the medieval world is plainly evident in the fact that modern scientific developments have clearly and profoundly influenced the religious traditions in the West, forcing them to modify and even abandon certain beliefs, symbols, and practices. So it is now clearly science and not religion that is the more decisive influence on economics, politics, philosophy, and, at least indirectly, the arts. Yet, incredible as it may seem to some, the tide may again turn; for it is almost beyond dispute that the currents of influence may run in every direction between religion and the other major aspects or institutions of civilization.

For the fact that a religion may be modified by economic and scientific conditions and achievements by no means discredits, as some have seemed to think, the fundamental values and judicial character of religion, any more than the fact that international politics may determine in part the direction of scientific inquiry or the fact that science is dependent on biological and social

[47] R. H. Tawney, *Religion and the Rise of Capitalism*, New York, Mentor Books, 1947, p. 235. See also pp. 261-262.

equilibriums discredits science. All that such influences mean is that a religion inevitably bears *in some respects* the indisputable imprint of the economic, scientific, and artistic elements of the culture in which it develops. Yet it is only the character of a religion, and not religion itself, that may be said to be the result of nonreligious factors; and a religion also, just as inevitably, leaves on the culture and on the individual the stamp of its ideals and methods, even if only as something to reject or (as Reinhold Niebuhr has perhaps inadvertently but effectively emphasized) as a sense of sin and failure in the breach of doctrines that are cherished nostalgically as important ideals but dismissed as impractical guides for action.

Indeed, if religion is primarily an attempt to inform and reform the life of man (either oneself or others) by symbolic acts of choosing and cherishing things of immeasurable and inviolable worth, the notion of an absolutely timeless and universal religious symbolism is essentially self-contradictory, at least so long as the capacities, predilections, choices, occupations, and environments of men are so various and so mutable. Universal languages as instruments for carrying on the practical, technical, and scientific enterprises are no doubt possible and perhaps highly desirable. But religion is always concerned with qualitative imponderables: life, love, beauty, hope, hate, misery, despair, and death. And the great variety in these has not been significantly diminished by success in the practical, technical, and scientific areas. Qualitative concerns and decisions can hardly be the same for men whose estate and needs, whose misery and delight, are radically different in kind and degree. Poet and scientist, rich and poor, merchant and farmer, the pain-ridden and the robust must surely speak in different religious accents and symbols. The lamentations of Job can hardly move the person who has never known serious misfortune or whose concerns and intellect are such that Job's questions are merely academic or superfluous.

Only in the community, in the root sense of "those who share," does a specifically religious language arise and perform its characteristic judicial functions. Religions are consequently as diverse as the communities of men. And even so there are on occasion men like Spinoza and Bertrand Russell whose passion for worship, though not atrophied, is outraged or unsatisfied by all the prevailing visions and rituals and who discover a new dimension of splendor and excellence and must worship in their own way. But such men do not so much repudiate the common values as increase them. They forsake the community in order to redeem it.

Religion is then inevitably social to a degree and in a way that art is not. Yet this difference, clear and basic as it is, is by no means absolute and provides no consistently reliable criteria for distinguishing artistic from religious symbols and enterprises. In fact Whitehead has said, not without truth though with obvious oversimplification, that a person's religion is what he does with his solitariness.[48] Although oversimple, this claim is not at all mistaken when construed as Whitehead evidently meant it, and does not in the least contradict the claim that religion is also significantly social. For he emphasized also that the communal features of religion, the shared beliefs, rituals, and moral teachings, are in fact indispensable, although their ultimate worth is derived chiefly from the vision of personal existence, freedom, responsibility, and possibility they evoke or articulate. Thus his emphasis on the solitary only complemented his persistent claim that the individual and the community are in fact inseparable and that neither can be at all adequately conceived or interpreted as only a function of the other. The community transcends the aggregation of individuals, and the individual is an entity (or event) that cannot be wholly accounted for in terms of communal traits and circumstances. The "value of an individual for itself" and the "value of the diverse individuals of the world for each other"[49] are equally irreducible aspects of the world as Whitehead conceived it.

So Whitehead also wrote:

Even for individual intuition outward expression is necessary as a sacrament in which the minister and the recipient are one. But further what is known in secret must be enjoyed in common. . . . The conversion of the Gentiles is both the effect of truth and the test of truth.[50]

[48] A. N. Whitehead, *op. cit.*, p. 16.
[49] *Ibid.*, p. 58.
[50] *Ibid.*, p. 133.

The social character of religion, in slightly different terms, is both the effect and the test, the condition and the consequence, of the personal experience that makes religion possible and necessary. In emphasizing the solitary or deeply personal aspects of the religious life, Whitehead was presumably only pointing up the inescapable fact that *in certain respects* character, thought, conviction, and choice, though surely dependent ultimately on the community, may never be publicly admitted or exhibited because they are the acts and attributes of individuals who in some respects are independent of, or transcend, the community. Communities as such, he recognized, do not deliberate and choose. But some social structures, he also saw, are more conducive to inquiry than others; and in some communities the fact and range of choice are more limited than in others. In any case, however, the communal aspects of a religion must in the end serve the possibilities, needs, problems, and decisions of individual—and in important respects inevitably solitary—persons. But the acts of the individual will surely affect, either directly or indirectly, the choices of persons whose needs and welfare are inseparable from his own; and so the social consequences of his choices and actions will in time influence his own pursuit of things of worth. Religion must sustain the solitary self in its splendid and terrible loneliness. But to do so in a very minimum way requires vision and action that acknowledge and nurture both the necessities and the joys of communal life.

The communal character of religion is in fact so conspicuous and necessary that religion has sometimes been identified with any generalized mode of creating and preserving the social and moral patterns and values on which the existence of a culture seems to depend. And although this is not by any means an adequate conception of religion, it is justified as an acknowledgment that not the solitary self but the social self and not the individual but the community are the most evident and impressive sources and objects of religious judgment and concern. Not soliloquy but dialogue is clearly the most normal and congenial form of religious discourse. The sciences may speak in the accents of omniscient mind addressing no one in particular and expecting no response; but religion must speak out of the depths of the individual's exist-

ential conditions and demands the response of others, the assurance
of God or neighbors that he is not alone. In both origin and effect
the religious life is intrinsically social. Yet nothing other than
life itself is more inviolable than the personal elements of religious
faith and practice.

But if religion is not altogether social, neither is art wholly
an individual or personal matter. It is not without reason or simply
because of his religious commitments that Martin Buber has said:

> All art is from its origin essentially of the nature of dialogue.
> All music calls to an ear not the musician's own, all sculpture
> to an eye not the sculptor's, architecture in addition calls to the
> step as it walks in the building. They all say, to him who receives
> them, something (not a "feeling" but a perceived mystery) that can
> be said only in this one language.[51]

Art is indeed almost always only a variation—an original and
necessary variation, if something new is to be said—in a language
or other medium *common* to a group and also possesses other
communal features and relations comparable to the most social
aspects of religion. Poetry is read and exegesis is carried on in
public. Painting and sculpture are promoted and honored by ex-
hibitions and lectures in galleries and museums and prominently
displayed in public buildings, parks, and squares. The greatest
architectural achievements are temples, churches, museums, and
monuments, or other structures more desired than required by the
community. Clearly no art can prosper without a measure of
community approval or without the enthusiasm of at least some
small group. Yet a painting or a poem is surely not necessarily
or primarily an invitation to communion with others or a mode
of reforming or altering the individual or society or the dynamic
relations between them—even though these may often be a
secondary aim as well as the incidental result of the arts. But
even as the fundamental aim of science is to judge and know—
by searching for and formulating universal relations—so the
primary aim of art is also to judge and know—but by imagining and
making—and not to communicate with or alter other selves. And
although social concerns, commitments, ideals, and possibilities

[51] Martin Buber, *op. cit.,* p. 25.

may of course be the subjects of serious and significant works of art, a work of art may be significantly independent of—or indeed even alien to—the social problems and commitments which characterize the artist, as well as the nonartist, in his day-to-day life.

The artist as such is committed primarily only to seeing and showing, to the craftsmanship by which seeing and showing are possible, to the perceptual values of formal and sensuous qualities, to the relations, harmonies, and conflicts which intensify and clarify ideas and images, and therefore to a radical personal freedom to create and present. In such respects his commitments can hardly be mistaken for a moral, religious, or scientific commitment. But of course the artist shares the interests, the joys, and the woes of mankind. And although he may often be irresponsible in practical affairs, he cannot be wholly indifferent to all moral, scientific, and religious matters. His artistic judgments—his choice of a medium, subjects, style, moods, and techniques of articulation—will depend in part surely on his sensitivity to both the values that are generally accepted and the values that are merely possible. Conversely, the general intellectual and social temper and achievements will also in some measure determine what is possible and impossible both in the arts generally and by any particular artist. Yet granting all the conditions on which he depends, the great artist is nonetheless distinguished precisely by the fact that he stands in his own distinctive relation to the problems and complexes of his world, has his own specific and unusual powers of perception, imagination, and skill, and exercises a high degree of freedom of choice in the use of his own capacities and the influences to which he opens himself. Otherwise his seeing and showing would hardly be highly and artistically significant.

Consequently the work of art is primarily an invitation to others to come and see, not a search for companionship or a critical challenge of the habits and choices of the community; and it may be viewed almost dispassionately as an object or instance of excellence that is at least largely independent of and irrelevant to scientific discoveries, practical necessities, and moral commitments. In spite of all they contribute to man's acquaintance with his own powers and qualities, the arts may presumably be ignored without any immediate peril or assimilated without either threat or aid to the vital and practical activities on which man's existence depends. Even the most speculative theories in religion, philosophy, and science seem often to touch and alter life more deeply than the arts ever do. Indeed it is widely and plausibly assumed that a distinctive, if not the only, value of the arts becomes available only to the extent that one achieves an "aesthetic distance" in which the experience does not touch the deep and efficient currents of belief and commitment by which men live.

But such presumed facts, even if much more certain than they seem, need not commit the arts to any radical illusion or judicial irrelevance. For even apart from any general ontological significance or powers of discovery, which only the most stringent epistemology can deny the arts, the artistic life, drawing its inspiration and choosing its landmarks from one or more of the various arts, is always a distinct and magnificent possibility for the individual person determining the vocation of his spirit. And no form of experience or judgment which thus inspires and guides a life can be altogether illusory. But perhaps more importantly, the sublime independence of artistic judgment by no means prevents or forbids its beneficent influence on the substance and manner of our most practical endeavors.

In contrast to the personal and object-centered character of art, religion is a vision of the self in relation—in relation to the holy, to other persons, to the concrete conditions of existence, and often including presumed personal aspects of the universe on which the existence of the self supposedly depends. Religion is nurtured primarily by and in turn nurtures communal occasions and actions because the community, as the matrix of sustenance and concern, is also the matrix of individual existence, commitment, and destiny.

Yet the respective social and personal aspects of religion and art are never pure. The artist creates out of the depths of his own individual experience and imagination. But his creation—the art object—becomes significantly public, and must be accepted or rejected without approving or violating the personality of the artist. And although the artist and his achievements may no doubt be greatly influenced by the approval or rejection of his work by the public, the art object ceases to be intimately his own and must stand or fall on its own merits. Thus the work of art, and not the communal and moral life of the artist, is judicially or artistically important. Or in the words of André Malraux:

> The only biography of an artist that matters is his life-story *as an artist*, the growth of his faculty of transformation. All that does not tend directly or indirectly to enhance our awareness of his genius, by deepening our knowledge of that faculty, is as futile as it would be to try to write a history in which nothing whatever is left out.[52]

Of course the life of the artist may be interesting and important apart from or even because of his artistic achievements. But the history of art as such, whether the theatre, poetry, music, painting, or architecture, is the history of mediums, styles, techniques, insights, and the influence of these together with particular works of art, and only secondarily, if not altogether incidentally, a history of the social milieu and the practical and moral endeavors or commitments of artists.

On the other hand, religion is sustained, if not demanded, by communal interests, ideas, and actions; and the history of religions is largely inseparable from the biographies of religious men. The religious genius, the prophet, saint, priest, or minister, is a public figure who preaches, teaches, gathers followers, and establishes or sustains a movement or a community of agreement in regard to the nature and requirements of the divine. Yet his inspiration may surely come in moments more solitary even than those of the poet or painter. Moses alone, it is said, received the Commandments from Jehovah on the top of Mount Sinai; but the Commandments were *for* the people. Jesus, it is recorded, fasted alone in the desert and prayed alone in the garden of Gethsemane. But he taught the multitudes as well as his twelve disciples; and his crucifixion—though in one sense surely the most profoundly solitary hours of his life—was both a public spectacle and the climax of his years as a public teacher. And the illumination of the Buddha, it is said, came as he sat alone under the bo tree after seven years of essentially solitary seeking; but there followed forty years of patiently teaching others.

[52] André Malraux, *op. cit.*, p. 420.

Religion speaks for and to the most inward and intimate self to a degree only rarely equalled by the arts. A person's religion is part and parcel of his own being. It is his very own and yet not wholly his own; for it is also a mode of judgment required by the quality which belongs to a common experience of the world. It is a part of the self which others must respect and yet at the same time a vision of existence shared in some measure perhaps with every person who recognizes the holy in any form or manner. Thus the religious person always belongs to the larger community of all who recognize the holy—to all mankind perhaps—though he may identify himself only with those whose symbols and concepts are highly similar to his own. And he will probably belong also, and most intimately, to a smaller community of persons whose lives and commitments are immediately and inevitably involved in the actions demanded by his own envisagement of the sacred.

The arts begin in individual sensitivity, imaginative capacity, and technical skill—the powers of seeing and showing—and result in public or shared objects. But religion is a relation to the other—to the other as holy—and is both the most social and the most personal aspect of existence, the most solitary approach to life, and the most urgent appeal for a sympathetic or comforting response from others. The arts, it may be said, become religious precisely in proportion to their concern and power to identify and articulate the existential problems which require attention to qualities and personal commitment tempered with the acknowledged presence of the holy, rather than knowledge of quantitative relations and powers, for their resolution. A religion, however, is technically an art only to the extent that it emphasizes the formal and sensuous aspects of its symbols and disregards the commitments, debts, and aspirations demanded by a shared vision of the holy. Only worship that is wholly praise—music and song and eulogy and euphony—may approach the joy and perfection of the arts. And indeed the religions never aim primarily to transmute the sadness and tragedy of life into unqualified joy or to exhibit their qualitative form and variety; they seek instead to provide the individual with the strength—the faith and the love—to bear the sad and tragic weight of his life. For man's life is ever open, not only to joy and beauty, but to pain and sorrow and enormous tragedy; and the presence of the holy inspires prayerful petition and preaching as well as thanksgiving and praise and sometimes the intimation that all is well even in the midst of immeasurable and incomprehensible tragedy.

The arts identify, create, and articulate qualitative perspectives, both ideal and actual, through the use of the sensuous, metaphoric, symbolic, and ideological resources of a medium. But the religions identify and articulate existential and qualitative perspectives which include and commit the self to the fulfillment of requirements (ontological, intellectual, and moral) imposed by the sense of the holy. The distinct social features of each, as well as their relations to each other, are implied in the manner in which they respectively serve the completion of man's "wretched but magnificent" life.

ON CONSISTENCY AND CONFLICT IN RELIGION AND ART

Surely no description of what we are can be exact and completely exhaustive of our actual being, and this must be true of any world in which there is a genuine plurality.

MORRIS R. COHEN

The basic dissimilarity between the character and function of religious symbols or activities and artistic products is further evident in the different significance attached to consistency in each or in the fact that each is encouraged to approach the unlimited variety of actuality and possibility in its own distinctive manner. Although perhaps very rarely achieved, religion aims at consistency in attitudes, creeds, and actions. The lives of religious persons, it is claimed, ought not be inconsistent with the principles they profess. A religion or a religious person must not embrace one doctrine today and another tomorrow or teach that what is good for Paul is undesirable for Peter.

The demand for consistency has indeed often threatened or
hindered the development of religious ideas and provoked serious
questions about both the moral sensitivity and the intelligence of
persons who have insisted that religious doctrine and activity must
conform to previous teaching and practice regardless of consequences and irrespective of fundamental conflict with the best
established claims of common sense experience and science. The
concern for complete consistency in religion is of course especially
important in any effort to understand either heresy or the conflict
between scientific inquiry and religious doctrine. The latter will
be discussed in the next chapter. And all that needs to be noted
just now in regard to the former is that the demand for consistency,
in word and act, is at least partially justified by the fact that if
there is to be serious and sustained personal commitment, there
must also be a defined and relatively stable context in which commitment can take place. Otherwise commitment becomes a
terribly vague if not an altogether empty or meaningless concept.
So a religion can contribute to the perfection of life or to the
quality of personal relations and decisions, it may be assumed,
only if there is a fairly well-defined view of requirements and possibilities.

In contrast to the religions, however, the demand for consistency is almost wholly alien to modern artistic traditions. One
must not look, it is often said, for either logical coherence in the
work of art or consistency in the personal life of the artist. In
fact artists notoriously seek variety in experience and are intrigued
and stimulated by the conflict of actions and ideas, including their
own. The great stumbling block to religious peace and harmony—
the conflicting variety of beliefs and practices—constitutes a significant part of the manifold richness of the arts. As R. G. Collingwood has written, "A poet who is disgusted with life to-day, and
says so, is not saying that he undertakes to be still disgusted tomorrow. But it is not any less true that, to-day, life disgusts him."
Disgust, as well as joy, is one of the qualities which the poet may
see and show in its specific manifestations. "And on the poet's behalf," Collingwood continued, "it may be replied, to someone who
argues that a lady cannot be both adorably virtuous and repellently
vicious, or that the world cannot be both a paradise and a dust heap,

that the arguer seems to know more about logic than he does about ladies, or about the world."[53]

The religions also of course often recognize and sometimes even emphasize the irreducible diversity and paradox in experience. Indeed, from Saint Paul's "foolish things of the world" by which God "confounds the wise" and Tertullian's "I believe because it is absurd" through Augustine and Pascal to Kierkegaard, the Christian tradition in particular has often claimed that it is precisely the incomprehensible and paradoxical variety in experience which renders religious faith possible and necessary. Be that as it may, religious inconsistency and diversity are still not self-justifying, and religious moods and symbols remain diverse *in spite of* demands for and persistent efforts to attain agreement in doctrine and practice. Religion attempts to unify and direct the life of both the individual and the community. But the artist, in contrast, may in fact often cultivate various and distinct moods and attitudes in order that objects will apear in different lights and guises. His inconsistency, or diversity, as one prefers, is frequently the source of much of the value and interest of his work. His changing moods and attitudes may indeed be integral parts of his method of seeing and showing; for they may bring to light the "infinite variety" of objects and perspectives. And nothing is more fatal to the arts than the demand for conformity to the standards and precedents set either by the artist himself or by others. For he attempts in each work to catch a new and revealing vision of some portion of the world or to show *what is* in his own inimitable accents and manner. The only consistency demanded of the arts, therefore, is the consistent revelation of fresh perspectives, emphases, and objects.

Consequently, except as an artistic style or content may be related to political and religious or philosophical ideologies, there is no serious conflict between one artistic judgment and another. It is notorious, however, that religious claims not only conflict with one another but have very often been the crucial, if not the dominant, factor in many of the most intense and tragic disagreements and struggles among men. The freedom of religion is indeed a very partial, recent, and still precarious victory of the idea that

[53] R. G. Collingwood, *The Principles of Art*, Oxford, Oxford University Press, 1938, p. 288.

religion is highly personal or that some things, including the freedom to worship in one's own way or indeed not to worship at all, are more sacred and more important to the community than the particular symbols and concepts of any religious tradition. The historic results of variety in religion are of course comparable above all to the conflicts between economic and political systems and doctrines, which presently threaten to become the idolatrous symbols which no man can criticize with impunity and the matrix of catastrophic struggles among men. In other words, historically the variety of religions, like present economic and political differences, has been much too tragic in its effect for any widespread appreciation of the beauty and justness of the fact.

The very genesis of art is plainly, at least in part, the love of the multitudinous facets and possibilities of qualitative experience and order. By its very nature the artistic enterprise must assume that there are varieties of distance and direction from which any object may be viewed, manifold shades of light and infinite nuances in every organ or instrument of perception and expression. The artist and also the lover of art perceives that nothing is gained, and perhaps much lost or missed, by supposing that the perspectives, emphases, and loves of others are either illusory or inconsequential. So one artist can demand of another only that, whatever his medium, purpose, technique, and style, his work be executed with authority and effectiveness. He is required by the freedom he demands for himself to admit that other arts, styles, subjects, and techniques are legitimate, even though he may share no enthusiasm for them.

Yet in spite of the terrible historical record and the genuine necessity of well-defined commitments in religion, both the fact and character of religious conflict may be grossly overemphasized and misinterpreted. And the incompatibility of the various forms of religious judgment need not be nearly as great or as fatal to their meaning and validity as it has often been made to seem, whether by the dogmatic defense of particular religious beliefs and practices or by the equally dogmatic and unperceptive dismissal of all religious symbols and systems of belief as so much superstition or emotive nonsense. The disagreements and conflicts between the religions do not in themselves justify either of these approaches. Even when the conflicts between different religions are not related to political and economic matters, as is so frequently the case, the fundamental issue is only rarely the meaning of the symbol and activities, but rather whether or not a particular complex or act is in fact a religious symbol or can function religiously. And in a genuinely pluralistic world there is of course no reason why two or more incompatible religions (or sciences) should not be equally true since neither exhausts the actualities to be described or the possibilities which may be achieved. So only philosophers with a prejudice in favor of unity find absolute contradiction in the variety of religious judgments or come to believe that religion without impeccable logic can never be genuinely meaningful. The religions themselves do not so much contradict one another as (like biology and physics) ignore or exclude one another. And religious conflicts arise primarily not from the conflict of the religious symbols and meanings themselves, but from the circumstances which prevent one group or community from rightly using or correctly interpreting the symbols and practices of another. Thus the unique interests and capacities of individual persons and the differences between cultural and conceptual traditions, and not the functional meaning of the religious symbols, are the fundamental sources of the religious differences expressed in conflicts. Combined with arrogance and blindness, with lack of respect for personal choice and freedom, or even with only extraordinary enthusiasm for the future of a specific set of religious symbols and practices, such differences may understandably result in disastrous antagonisms between both individuals and groups.

But ultimately the meaning of any symbol, no matter how novel and spontaneous in origin, is surely inseparable from enduring use in particular cultural and judicial contexts. Consequently it seems altogether plausible that if the different symbolisms of the various religions are approached with critical concern and sympathy, comparable to the concern and sympathy which reveal the relevance of the radically different arts and sciences to the meaning and progress—if not the total unity—of these judicial traditions, then religious dogmatisms and the resulting conflicts

may be as ill-founded as complete confidence in current scientific
concepts and methods or as naïve as the conviction that no significant art can still be produced. Indeed the tensions between the
different religious symbolisms may, like the tensions between different philosophical systems and scientific theories, be turned into
creative dialogues which increase both the sense of the holy and
men's understanding and appreciation of one another.

It is then superficial to claim, as Santayana did, that:

> Each religion, so dear to those whose life it sanctifies, and ful-
> filling so necessary a function in the society that has adopted it,
> necessarily contradicts every other religion and probably contradicts
> itself. The sciences are necessarily allies, but religions, like lan-
> guages, are necessarily rivals.[54]

Even apart from the very dubious claim that rivalry is indigenous
to languages but not to the sciences, this statement is a very surprising one. For in the basic terms of his own central thesis,
that religion is poetry become the guide of life and that poetry
is primarily sensuous language and imaginative or ideal vision,
there can surely be nothing mutually exclusive or contradictory in
the diverse religions. But also, even as a mode of existential judgments which commit the self to specific ways of thinking and acting, a religion need not contradict either itself or others. For
apparently a religion could truly and fully contradict itself only
by denying that its symbols and requirements are genuine and
relevant. And one religion could completely contradict another
and different one only if in identical persons and circumstances
two or more exclusive sets of religious symbols and acts claimed
an equal loyalty. But if existence itself—including man—is, as it
seems, pluralistic, indeterminate, and ambivalent, permeated not
only by physical polarities but also by qualitative ones such as love
and hate, joy and sadness, pleasure and pain, then surely no one
should be surprised to find many ambiguities and even contradictions in judgments as spontaneous, comprehensive, and obviously
functional as religious symbols and concepts are. Even philosophy
and the sciences, with their great emphasis on systematic logic and
consistency, have by no means overcome altogether the necessity

[54] George Santayana, *Reason in Religion, op. cit.*, p. 5.

of speaking in paradoxes and contradicting themselves and each other; yet this is hardly grounds for denying that they are genuinely judicial in function.

So finally, one religion can apparently no more contradict another than biology can contradict physics. The holy can appear in quite different religious symbolisms and acts, even as the logical structures of nature may be, and perhaps *must be*, reflected or articulated in different languages and in different conceptual schemes if they are reflected or articulated at all. Religions are enemies of one another, not because they contradict one another, but because the devotees of one can never fully appreciate, for one reason or another, how just and appropriate those that are different are. So Santayana gave evidence of a more genuine, though not wholly accurate, perception when he observed that religions are not true or false but good or bad. But even this claim is not altogether accurate, however, simply because it is by no means obvious that actual goodness is ever less than intimately related to the truth; and in any case goodness is surely neither any less complicated than truth nor more evident in the dim candlelight of human judgment. The diversity in religions need not mean, as Santayana claimed, that none has a standing ground in fact, or, as many others have thought, that all are false save one. A religion, like a science or a philosophy, may surely be relevant in the pursuit of truth even though it has no grasp of the whole truth. But the criteria of its truth may of course be radically different from the criteria of scientific and philosophic truths. Yet if there are aspects of existence which can be articulated only in religious terms (and indeed, as F. J. E. Woodbridge said, "It is difficult to see how these languages could be if there were nothing in existence to support them."[55]), then it is not at all incongruous to speak of their truth. The truth of religion is therefore the theme of the next chapter.

[55] F. J. E. Woodbridge, *Nature and Mind,* New York, Columbia, 1937, p. 482.

SOME SUMMARY REMARKS

. . . the pleasure of the eye is the
beginning of love.

ARISTOTLE

Art and religion have different elements and structures as well as separate functions. Yet they interact and overlap so much that the effectiveness of each seems often to depend on the other. The most primitive as well as the most sophisticated religions have artistic elements: poetic cosmologies, icons, rituals, dances, song, and instrumental music. And these, apparently, are not only sources of important aesthetic values but are also integral elements of the judicial power and function of a religion. Religion often expresses its profoundest insights through the arts. The highest aspiration and the deepest piety or the perfection of life no less than the perfection of the work demand and inspire clear vision and excellence in producing and performing. Yet art is not only the instrument and the mode but also at times the splendid product of the presence of the holy. Recurrently in and through the religious experience or commitment the artist evidently discovers significant qualities and forms or judicial possibilities, and his work becomes mature; thus he apparently sometimes achieves, through a commitment inspired by a vision of the divine, immeasurably more than is possible (great though it is) in the pursuit of seeing for the sake of seeing or in merely formal and sensuous values.

Indeed there is perhaps presently no greater possibility for religion, candidly considered, than that through the arts it may be able to speak again with authority. If current religious beliefs and practices are divisive when they are not half-hearted and are often irrelevant to the desperate needs of man which cannot be filled simply by more and more science and greater economic security, this may be due in significant measure to the fact that the accents and insights, the sensitivity and expressive powers, of the contemporary arts are generally absent from religious themes and enterprises. Whatever beauty and truth the religions still retain, they emphasize too frequently some dreary panacea or a dream-like world on the other side of death which provokes neither a vision of the solid splendor of common things nor the urgency of the decisions and commitments which give shape to the world man must inhabit. Consequently much religion, regardless of its aims and potentialities, is apparently only "another world to live in" and is blandly indifferent to the current perplexity and pain and the genuine possibilities of life itself. If the world wavers perilously between death by fire and death from a supreme lassitude generated by the inability to sustain a vision of anything eminently worth being, doing, or having, the relation of these two great dangers to each other and to the absence of religious vision and commitment may indeed be much closer than anyone imagines.

Science now provides, in both old and new conceptual frameworks, abundant knowledge of quantitative facts and their dynamic relations to each other and to the enormous dangers and possibilities which man now confronts; and the arts have rarely received so much popular and economic support. But the sense of the worth of both and of life itself is evidently vitiated for many by lack of anything ultimate and inviolable, or holy. Indeed it seems to be true that when the sense of the holy declines, man often—if not inevitably—loses the terrible but ennobling burden of responsibility and the sense of destiny which has at least sometimes accompanied the sense of the holy. Neither art nor science is able or even attempts to establish and sustain a community where a vision of the holy or the supreme and inestimable worth of the individual person may be supported by common objectives requiring personal devotion, cooperation, and sacrifice. For the highest excellence of both art and science, though ultimately dependent on the community, is attained chiefly in the lonely commitment of individual persons to the techniques and problems of a discipline and the possibilities within it.

But religious judgment requires that men assume and in assuming discover their common bonds in a divine and inviolable order. No doubt human life and even moral and intellectual distinction are possible without this assumption or without the judicial processes and achievements of either the arts or the religions. Yet there is surely no higher destiny for the arts and no greater function for religion than that they should *sometimes* unite to generate new visions of the awe-full splendor of common things and of the responsibility of each individual in the use of his particular powers and gifts. The arts could then be beautiful without being empty and religion could be articulate and substantive without the superstitions and judicial excesses which may strangle worship in an age of science.

It may be that religion could and should be primarily, not metaphysical claims and speculations about the ground and destiny of man, but a courageous and persistent effort to see and present ever more clearly the overwhelming mixture of joy and tragedy, of beauty and sorrow, of actuality and unfulfilled potential which man's life is. Surely nothing more is necessary to nourish the sense of the presence of the holy, and it may be that nothing more is possible in an age characterized above all perhaps by "the eclipse of God." And by seeing more clearly the qualities of the actual and the possible, as well as the ideal, man might then speculate more wisely about both his foundations and his destiny. At least classical tragedy—probably the greatest of the art forms —was also in part a profound form of religion which developed when a wise and sensitive people faced frankly and boldly the fact that man's being in the world is both awesomely beautiful and unutterably tragic and frightful. And few achievements have cast more light on the complexities and paradoxical qualities which meet in and flow from human decision and action. If we judge our existence through the eyes and accents of the artist, including the tragedian, we shall surely judge it reverently; and though there will always be room for hope and courage, there will be no reason for a sense of irremediable sin and failure when our best efforts do not forestall immense pain and sorrow or even total disaster. For only a world where chance and choice combine to make even the very greatest tragedy possible is also a world where reason, disciplined by sorrow and patiently turning both chance and choice to its own ends, may use the various arts to show both how perplexing and how very luminous existence is and religion— or the articulated sense of the holy—to choose more wisely the future course of mankind.

5

On Religion and Truth

By doubting we are led to inquire,
and by inquiry we perceive the truth.
ABELARD

I count not that as true
which those affirm, who call
each other "fools."—They call
each other so, because
each deems his own view "Truth."
THE BUDDHA

ON THE CONFLICTS AND QUESTIONS

When we consider what religion is for mankind,
and what science is, it is no exaggeration to say
that the future course of history depends upon
the decision of this generation as to the relation
between them.

A. N. WHITEHEAD

The relation of religion to truth—the efforts, claims, and paradoxes so obviously and deeply embodied in religious symbols and practices—has baffled many of the most persistent thinkers. The religions have often claimed to be, if not the only way, then certainly the high and privileged way to truth. Yet the seekers of truth in other areas and by different methods, observing the conflicts between the teachings of the various religions and between the religious claims and the claims of both common sense and modern science, as well as within each religion, have frequently denied, especially in recent centuries, that religion is a way to truth at all. The entire judicial structure and power of the religions have been successfully challenged in the eyes of many and perhaps principally because ancient accounts of the origin and nature of the cosmos and man have turned out to be incompatible with modern scientific discoveries. Yet surely it may be claimed that the religious spirit or the religious modes of discovery and judgment are not any more wedded to its particular claims than the spirit and methods of science are to its own groping and tentative beginnings in Greece and the sixteenth century.

But what now is *truth?* No doubt there are many ways of defining the *term* which simply eliminate the problem of the relation of religion and truth either by denying a priori the possibility of any religious truth or by the presumption that the truth of religion (or rather a particular religion) is sanctioned by a source or authority which is indeed beyond all question. Philosophically, however, both of these methods of avoiding the problems at issue are surely profitless, even though they are not uncommon.

It was suggested earlier that *truth* is the presence or availability, in some form, of the aspects of being or existence which support and guide judgment and thus a quality of the many complex forms and processes through which man successfully recognizes, maintains, and modifies the conditions of his many-faceted existence. Not everyone of course will agree with this concept and description of truth, though presumably no theory of knowledge or judgment can altogether avoid the chief elements or demands of it. In any case, persons interested in religion and truth or in knowledge and the methods by which knowledge is possibly discovered, achieved, and expressed face difficult and complex problems which cannot be wholly determined or denied by any definition. The fundamental questions seem to be: Is religion only one phenomenon among many others that may be examined and understood through the methods of scientific inquiry? Or is religion itself, even as the various sciences, a fundamental way of knowing? Is religion, as religious persons have consistently claimed, an approach to existence or reality that is essentially different from the approach of common sense and science, but nonetheless true? Does religion discover or disclose dimensions or aspects of existence which are utterly inaccessible through the methods of the sciences and ordinary experience? Or is it perhaps the case that religious languages and experiences are, as some have insisted, only expressions of blind impulse and emotion or the phantasies of the neurotic human psyche?

The preceding chapters have of course already suggested implicit, if only probable, answers to some if not all of these questions. But it is now necessary to deal more directly and more fully with these and related problems. Definitive answers are no doubt improbable, if not impossible and even undesirable, but several types of answers may be examined and some possible and plausible conclusions suggested.

ON EMPIRICISM AND THE TRUTH OF RELIGION

Intelligent practice is not a step-child of theory. On the contrary theorizing is one practice amongst others and is itself intelligently or stupidly conducted.

GILBERT RYLE

The most radical and serious challenge to the claim that religion is a mode of veridical judgment has come during the last three centuries from the philosophical position generally called *empiricism* and more recently known as *logical positivism* or alternatively as *logical empiricism*. The roots of this position, with its sceptical approach to religion, are deep in the empiricism of modern science —an empiricism that began even with Copernicus, Kepler, and Galileo as an emphasis on sensory experience plus the formal attributes of language (logic and mathematics) as the only necessary and truly reliable elements of scientific knowledge and with a corresponding distrust of introspective and qualitative experiences

and the nonformal, or artistic, uses of language and other mediums
as signs or symbols of anything primary or genuinely real. David
Hume was the first to use the principles of empiricism in a truly
critical analysis of religious belief. Persuaded that "All the objects
of human reason or enquiry may naturally be divided into two
kinds, to wit, *relations of ideas,* and *matters of fact,*"[1] and that all
matters of fact are knowable only from impressions, or from
"our more lively perceptions, when we hear, or see, or feel, or love,
or hate, or will,"[2] Hume proceeded to demonstrate that such
religious phenomena as belief in the existence of God, immortality
of the soul, and miracles have absolutely no standing ground in
experience or in fact. And reasoning, or the manipulation of abstract ideas, he claimed, can prove the existence of nothing beyond
the ideas themselves.

Hume's most forthright conclusion about the claims to religious knowledge, as distinct from the *value* of religious *faith* and
activity, is most succinctly stated at the end of An *Enquiry Concerning Human Understanding:*

> If we take in our hand any volume; of divinity or school meta-
> physics, for instance; let us ask, *Does it contain any abstract rea-
> soning concerning quantity or number?* No. *Does it contain any
> experimental reasoning concerning matter of fact and existence?*
> No. Commit it then to the flames: for it can contain nothing but
> sophistry and illusion.

The contemporary logical positivists or empiricists have essentially only deepened and intensified the original antipathy between
the quantitative and relational languages of the sciences on the
one hand and the qualitative or imaginative languages of the arts
and religions on the other, or the distinction between *relations of
ideas* and *matters of fact* emphasized by Hume. Consequently the
unadmitted and often denied metaphysics of empiricism includes,
at least implicitly, the account by Thomas Hobbes of language
as essentially a "supernatural" or independent addition to man's

---

[1] David Hume, *An Enquiry Concerning Human Understanding,* Sec. IV,
Pt. I. First published in 1748, there are many editions of this work.
[2] *Ibid.,* Sec. II.

natural powers, the distinction (made by Galileo and Locke among others) between primary and secondary qualities, and Hume's account of the impossibility of any nonempirical knowledge.

Accordingly, the empiricist must claim, with more or less rigor, that only two types of linguistic usage (the only form of judgment or experience which he thinks may be appropriately called *true*) may be said to have cognitive or intellectual meaning. The first is *analytical* or *tautological*, or the use of statements which either simply record accepted definitions or express ultimately arbitrary decisions to employ particular words in specific ways. "All bachelors are unmarried men" is a frequently used example of a tautology, or of a statement in which (in Kantian terms) the predicate merely *unpacks* what is already included in the concept of the subject, or (in terms often preferred by the logical empiricists) simply a *linguistic rule*. Such statements, according to the empiricist, neither assert nor imply anything whatever about existential conditions. So the statement above only prescribes or describes, and so determines arbitrarily, how the word "bachelor" is to be used. And thus the meaning or truth of such statements, the empiricist claims, is either purely conventional or based wholly on their use; and all logical principles and mathematical axioms are said to belong to this class.

The second cognitive use of language is called *empirical* and is said to consist of assertions which, instead of describing or prescribing the use of language itself, describe the observable, quantifiable, and presumably existential attributes of things themselves. "Most bachelors are bald" may serve as an example. And the only way to determine the truth or falsity of any claim with cognitive and existential content, according to the empiricist, is to observe the objects or the effects of the objects to which they refer. Now clearly nothing is more a matter of experience than qualities, sensory and nonsensory. But because qualitative experience is presumably infinitely various, subjective, and derivative, statements about qualities or qualitative statements can be included in cognitive language, the most rigorous of the contemporary empiricists claim, only insofar as, in the words of Rudolf Carnap, "Rules are set up for translating all such statements into quantitative statements so that *e.g.* the statement 'It is rather cool here' might be translated into the statement, 'The temperature here is between 5 and 10 degrees centigrade.' "[3]

In effect, then, the general approach of the empiricist to religion rests upon the assumption that no statement, product, or activity can be intellectually or judicially meaningful except linguistic assertions which make no existential claims and existential assertions which may be either proved or disproved or rendered more or less probable by direct or indirect sensory experience. In other words, there is no logical or mathematical truth except by convention, and a claim such as "There is a red book on a five-legged table in the next room" derives *both* its cognitive meaning and its truth from the fact that rooms, tables, and books are observable, or, at the minimum, from their observable consequences. If a sentence refers to such observables (or to observable consequences) it is *meaningful,* and if the sensory experience corresponds to the meaning, the statement may be called *true.* But language that is neither tautological nor subject to sensory verification is emotive, poetic, and noncognitive or nonsensical. Such instances of linguistic usage (as well as artistic products and religious symbols) are then neither true nor false but meaningless. The empiricist might of course agree that such language may be beautiful or useful or profoundly symptomatic of other important matters but not that it is in any sense a true, relevant, or cognitive judgment of existential matters.

Empiricists are not, however, necessarily or in every respect opposed to religion. Indeed, George Berkeley, in some ways the most perceptive and consistent of the empiricists, was convinced that the fundamental categories of religion are as fully a matter of experience as are the basic categories of science or common sense. Even as the experience of an inanimate object is inseparable from and limited to the experience of color, size, figure, and motion, so the closest observation, said Berkeley, yields nothing more than "the color, size, figure, and motion of a man," or only certain sensations or ideas excited in our own minds.

[3] Rudolf Carnap, "The Physical Language as the Universal Language of Science," in *Readings in Twentieth-Century Philosophy,* William P. Alston and George Nakhnikian, eds., New York, Free Press, 1963, p. 405.

Hence it is plain we do not see a man—if by *man* is meant that which lives, moves, perceives, and thinks as we do—but only such a certain collection of ideas as directs us to think there is a distinct principle of thought and motion, like to ourselves, accompanying and represented by it. And after the same manner we see God; all the difference is that, whereas some one finite and narrow assemblage of ideas denotes a particular human mind, whithersoever we direct our view, we do in all times and all places perceive manifest tokens of the Divinity: everything we see, hear, feel, or in anywise perceive by sense being a sign or effect of the power of God; as is our perception of those very motions which are produced by men.[4]

In spite of all the conceptual and questionable reconstruction necessary to enable Berkeley to make these claims, there is a candid logic about them which is not always characteristic of the empiricist. Nothing comparable is heard from a similar perspective until John Wisdom (who is basically an analyst rather than a traditional empiricist, of course), in his relatively recent article called "Gods," observes, as Berkeley did, that "We are as if there were hidden within us powers, persons, not ourselves and stronger than ourselves," that, "What is so isn't merely a matter of 'the facts,' "[5] and that the divine, or God or gods, apparently shine out of nature for some, as that which "watches in the hills and manages the stars,"[6] even as beauty or reality shows itself to others in a Manet or Van Gogh or in the face of the beloved.

Even David Hume recognized the appeal, though he denied the intellectual cogency, of *faith* in religious doctrines; and he was much more clearly opposed to so-called rational religion or to "those dangerous friends or disguised enemies to the *Christian Religion*, who have undertaken to defend it by the principles of human reason," than to the view that religion is a matter of faith. He in fact wrote, though not without ambiguity, that "Our

---

[4] George Berkeley, A *Treatise Concerning the Principles of Human Knowledge*, Sec. 148. This work, first published in 1710 (2d ed. 1734), is available in several different editions.

[5] John Wisdom, "Gods," in *Logic and Language*, Antony Flew, ed., New York, Philosophical Library, 1951, p. 192.

[6] *Ibid.*, p. 202.

most holy religion is founded on faith, not on reason; and it is
a sure method of exposing it to put it to such a trial as it is, by
no means, fitted to endure."[7] And in the nineteenth century John
Stuart Mill, one of the most uncompromising of the empiricists,
suggested that "It is . . . perfectly conceivable that religion may be
morally useful without being intellectually sustainable,"[8] and proceeded to defend religious belief as both "an instrument of social
good"[9] and the "source of personal satisfaction and elevated feelings"[10] for many individuals.

More recently R. B. Braithwaite, in *An Empiricist's View of
the Nature of Religious Belief*, although accepting the empirical
principles that the meaning of an assertion is determined by
its use, and truth only by sensory observation, has dissented from the
view of the more rigorous positivists to claim that religious assertions, instead of being nonsensical or merely expressing or
evincing "feelings" or "emotions," are *conative*, or "declarations
of commitment to a way of life." This he regards as equivalent to
saying that religious beliefs are essentially a form of moral principle or decision since otherwise "it makes no sense to speak of
putting them into practice."[11] But they are different from moral
principles in so far as they concern internal as well as external
behavior and are expressed concretely, rather than abstractly, by
"stories" ("parables," "tales," "myths"), which need not be believed and which belong to a particular religious system.[12] Thus
one becomes religious not by intellectual persuasion or conviction,
but by "a reorientation of the will"[13] which is supported by
particular stories. And the only difference between the Buddhist
and the Christian, unless there are differences in moral behavior,
is that the one defends his behavior by an appeal to the Buddhist
stories and the other to the Christian stories. According to Braith-

[7] David Hume, *op. cit.*, Sec. X, Pt. II.
[8] J. S. Mill, *Nature and Utility of Religion*, New York, Liberal Arts,
1958, p. 48.
[9] *Ibid.*, p. 50.
[10] *Ibid.*, p. 84.
[11] R. B. Braithwaite, "An Empiricist's View of the Nature of Religious
Belief," in *Classical and Contemporary Readings in Philosophy of Religion*,
John Hick, ed., Englewood Cliffs, N.J., Prentice-Hall, 1964, pp. 431-432.
[12] *Ibid.*, pp. 435-436.
[13] *Ibid.*, p. 433.

waite, the support provided by the stories is of course "psychological and causal"[14] rather than logical. For a moral decision, though by no means arbitrary, cannot really be either logically or empirically justified.

For the philosophy of religion (or a religious philosophy), the most important characteristic of empiricism, with the exception of Berkeley's unusual version, is that both cognitive meaning and truth, in being limited to tautologies and claims that can be verified by sense experience, are denied to all the traditional forms of religious symbolism and language. Even if Hume may be interpreted as a defender of religion "founded on faith," he leads to a dead end insofar as there is absolutely no criteria for choosing one faith rather than another or by which a faith may be critically examined and modified. Mill and Braithwaite are equally open to all the objections to identifying religion with morality. They ignore both the fact that the religious categories and the moral categories are apparently incommensurable and that even if religious claims could be translated into moral terms, by strict empirical criteria they would still be unintelligible.

Consequently it must be admitted that the treatment of religion and morals most consistent with the basic principles of empiricism is that of Alfred J. Ayer, who, in *Language, Truth and Logic*, dismissed all religious assertions as "metaphysical" or "emotive" and "literally senseless." Ayer claimed in effect that all such word combinations as "God exists," "The Lord is my shepherd," "Lying is wrong," and "Man is a free moral agent," or all theological, metaphorical, ethical, and metaphysical statements are neither tautologies nor empirically verifiable and are therefore neither true nor false but meaningless. There is no reason to discuss in detail the arguments which supposedly justify the claim that all these various types of linguistic usage have no cognitive meaning. But religious language generally, he clearly believes, depends for its cogency on the existence of God. But the claim that "God exists" is meaningless, he asserts, because it is a "metaphysical utterance"[15] which follows "grammar beyond the bound-

---

[14] *Ibid.*, p. 437.
[15] A. J. Ayer, *Language, Truth and Logic*, rev. ed., New York, Dover, 1946, p. 115.

aries of sense."[16] He disregards not only any possible connections between claims about the existence of God and the immediate experience of supreme worth, the divine, or the holy which might provide important phenomenological content, but also the difficulties involved in the analysis of certain fundamental problems and aspects of existence which give the theistic claim some plausibility as a hypothesis, at least to certain and not always unintelligent people. Simply on the basis of a general theory of language he proceeded to the conclusion that theology cannot possibly be logically other than a completely mistaken use of purely linguistic categories—plus the psychological comfort sometimes derived therefrom. Discourse about the power and wisdom of God is as unintelligible or as fanciful and foolish as discourse concerning the diet, weight, mating habits, and birthrate of unicorns.

It is therefore futile to attempt to make sense of religion. Not consisting of genuine claims at all, religious "utterances . . . cannot stand in any logical relation to the propositions of science." The only notable relation is that by bringing men to believe it possible "to understand and anticipate" the course of nature science destroys the "feeling of awe" and thus "takes away one of the motives which make men religious." And observing that it "has recently become fashionable for physicists themselves to be sympathetic towards religion," Ayer argues that this supports his hypothesis. The physicists turn to religion because they "lack confidence in the validity of their hypotheses, which is a reaction on their part from the anti-religious dogmatism of nineteenth-century scientists, and a natural outcome of the crisis through which physics has just passed."[17]

Unlike Braithwaite, Ayer does not suppose either that religious claims can be translated into moral claims or that moral assertions are in some sense empirically meaningful. Although statements about right and wrong, good and bad, may seem to make specific claims about existential matters, in fact, according to Ayer, they state nothing or express only the emotions of the speaker. Because no sensory experience can confirm or disconfirm them, moral judgments have no intellectual content and may be compared only to

[16] *Ibid.*, p. 43.
[17] *Ibid.*, p. 117.

sighs, groans, and exclamations. Thus religion, theology, meta-physics, and ethics, traditionally the heart of much serious philos-ophy, are not properly subjects for philosophical inquiry at all except to the extent that philosophical analysis may reveal that their characteristic claims are neither tautological nor empirical and so must be disregarded in the search for truth or genuine knowledge.

The empirical theory of meaning and truth, even in its most rigorous form, may seem fair enough at first blush or to the cautious man of the world who prefers not to take any but the absolutely necessary risks. And the procedures the empiricists recommend do in fact describe precisely and cogently the manner in which many questions of meaning and truth, particularly in regard to practical affairs and physical processes, are decided. No doubt the meanings of numerous words are partly, if not com-pletely, established by use or convention and some even by quite arbitrary decision. Also normal eyesight is admittedly a pre-requisite for determining the truth and even the meaning of most statements about colors. And no reasonable person would ever attempt to describe the precise attributes of living creatures, if any, on distant or unobservable planets. The procedures and criteria adopted by the empiricists for determining the meaning and truth of *all* statements are no doubt in *some* instances quite necessary, appropriate, and effective.

But are such procedures ever actually as simple and as straight-forward as the empiricist suggests? Or, perhaps more importantly, are these actually the only methods of discovering or determining meaning and truth or the only proper uses of the words *meaning-ful* and *true*? The present essay is of course based on the premise that anything (word, object, complex, or quality) may be *mean-ingful* if its presence, or the manipulation or assimilation of it, may subsequently modify deliberate acts, procedures, or products of judgment; and such judgments may be *true* (or indicative of what is) insofar as the judicial modes and processes are thereby sus-tained or promoted. Seeing and hearing may then be no less verid-ical or no less misleading than stating. But even apart from a theory of meaning and truth as broad as this, the process of verifying such claims as that "There is a red book on a five-legged table in the next room" can be thoroughly analyzed and accurately described, if at all, only in enormously complicated terms. The meaning of the statement, it is clear, must be grasped before not after the verifying process; for this achievement is obviously the complex and necessary condition, rather than the result, of either decision or empirical investigation. The several crucial elements of the claim must be retained in memory while the verifying process goes on; and memory is notoriously complex and baffling to the epistemologist. The observer must also be able to distinguish five-legged from four-legged and six-legged tables. He must not mistake books for tables or tables for chairs. And his memory and sense of color must be such that he will not identify green or yellow books as red books. Such features of even the simplest judgments are apparently not wholly or even primarily a matter of combining sensory events and conventional linguistic categories. So any instance of so-called sensory verification, whether a critical and methodical process or simply spontaneous, is evidently dependent on both previous and simultaneous judgments which assume or recognize the reliability of reason no less than linguistic cogency and sense experience itself.

Indeed judgment seems always to depend much less on sensory equipment and experience and the conventions of language, necessary as these are, than on specific interests, needs, and moods or on the entire capacity or total configuration of an individual in relation to a total situation which provokes and sustains or frustrates and rebukes specific decisions. In any case judgment is never obviously or simply a function of individual sensory discriminations but of the individual in a context of particular quantitative and qualitative attributes, powers, and demands. To make meaning and truth completely dependent on sense experience and linguistic convention is in fact to suppose that all judgment is utterly and inescapably subjective, the product of the fortuitous powers of a particular organism or of inexplicable and ultimately arbitrary decision, rather than the very substance of man's existence in an intelligible, if not wholly rational, world.

The logical empiricists admit in fact that their definitions of *meaning* and *truth*, on which their theory rests, are essentially only decisions to use these words in a specific and consistent way. They justify this decision in turn by the claim that all linguistic usage is ultimately based on such arbitrary determinations. But oddly enough they do not attempt to verify this claim, which seems to be a factual claim, and ignore the apparent necessity of having a language in order to make any decisions at all concerning language. Thus language is treated as the extraordinary nonnatural miracle which enables man to transcend the world he judges, and introduces logical order or intelligibility into an existential flux that is otherwise unintelligible. Important and amazing as language no doubt is, this seems to exaggerate its importance. Also, the claim that meaning and truth belong only to tautologies and to statements which can be verified directly or indirectly by sense experience is neither itself a plausible tautology nor verifiable by sense experience. For if a tautology must be either self-evidently so or established by a widespread convention, the claim is clearly not a tautology. Neither *truth* nor *meaning* is either self-evidently or widely identified with *a tautology* or *verifiable by sense experience*. And not even the empiricists themselves suggest that these basic premises can in fact be verified by sense experience.

Critical thought has of course long recognized that tautology is one—though surely a limited—form of meaning and truth and that sense experience, though often trustworthy, may also be illusory. But it is by no means clear that the tautological use of language can be wholly separated from the empirical use or that use always determines meaning rather than meaning the use. Here too the currents of influence apparently run in both directions and independence is always a matter of degree. In any case, the meanings of *meaning* and *truth* are no more evident to the senses alone and no more subject to determination by fiat than the meaning of *God*, *right*, *love*, or *blue*. If intellectual cogency requires that we no longer talk about God or right because they are nonempirical notions, then it also requires that we speak of neither meaning nor truth. For in spite of the empiricists' assertions to the contrary, the fact that their claims about *meaning* and *truth* are neither meaningful nor true when judged by their own criteria is a serious if not altogether fatal flaw.

It is plain, then, that empiricism, no matter what its form, can claim that the languages of the religions, arts, and morals are cognitively meaningless only because of particular and highly questionable decisions about the nature of existence, especially the nature and functions of language. In spite of their appeal to the empiricism of the natural sciences, the empiricists' views of language, truth, and meaning are clearly not similarly empirical. There is perhaps a sense in which the use of a single word, such as *bachelor,* may be correctly described as the result of a more or less arbitrary decision or that its use determines its meaning. But the existence of language itself—or the total configuration of articulated intelligibility within which a word may be arbitrarily given a meaning—is not at all the result of decision. So whether or not a particular tautology has meaning is basically and ultimately not any more subject to arbitrary decision than whether or not there are in fact bachelors or unicorns.

Consequently the description of truth by Julian Huxley, for example, though certainly vague, is conceptually more adequate and better justified by experience as a whole than the approach of the empiricists. "Truth includes," says Huxley, "not only all the true propositions . . . and their individual if partial trueness, but also the ideal of complete and absolute truth by which every proposition must be judged as to its individual truth."[18] In other words, and as Saint Augustine put the matter, if anything at all is, then truth may surely be said to be or to be potentially, though no one apprehends it. And cast into similar terms of an ideal and complete truth, the concept employed in this essay is that *truth* is the *availability,* at least theoretically, *of all that is,* including qualities and relations (whether past, present, or future and whether ideal or actual) to the judicial capacities, powers, processes, and interests of a creature radically open to the world. And the claim that *all that is* (which must, no matter how paradoxically, include the linguistic accounts of nonlinguistic existence) can be observed through the senses, simply and naïvely begs many of the most crucial questions to which inquiry must still seek answers.

It would be a mistake nonetheless to dismiss the claims of even the logical empiricists or positivists as completely untrue or mean-

---

[18] Julian Huxley, *Religion Without Revelation,* New York, Mentor Books, 1958, p. 38.

ingless. They apparently strive above all else not to speak nonsense, though apparently they do sometimes commit the sin they despise. But their close attention to the character of the language of science and philosophy, though they have neglected equally important matters, has in fact resulted in important insights and in a deepened appreciation of the necessity of rigorous discipline and care in the philosophical enterprise. Yet the most important philosophical task is apparently not simply a rigorous analysis of linguistic forms and functions, particularly if such analysis must assume that language is strictly a secondary rather than a primary form of existence or that the basis of language is arbitrary decision about the use and meaning of words. The severe limits of empiricism may be suggested by simply observing that *man* may be arbitrarily defined as *a two-legged, food-cooking animal* and much that is both true and important said in the conceptual framework so established. But the dimensions of man not included in this definition will not therewith miraculously cease to be or to trouble the perplexed students of man and his existential powers and problems. And indeed the modes of judgment, as well as the dimensions of existence, neglected or denounced by the empiricists suffer much less from this fact than does empirical inquiry itself.

In summary, the empiricists' theory of meaning and truth, though applicable and reliable within limits, neglects certain important matters and distorts others. Their rigorous methods and careful attention to language, in spite of serious limits and faults, are exemplary for any systematic inquiry. They have also rightly emphasized the tremendous, even incommensurable, differences between the languages and methods of the sciences on the one hand and the languages and methods of the religions and arts on the other, though they have by no means rightly understood or evaluated these differences. They are apparently correct in suggesting that religious symbols and claims cannot be validated or justified in the same manner as scientific claims. Yet they are presumably no less mistaken in the claim that religious symbols are therefore judicially or cognitively meaningless. Those who regard the religions and arts as modes of serious, revelatory, and effective judgment, or as significant methods of apprehending and communicating meaning and truth, need not be greatly disturbed by either the attempts of the more generous empiricists to translate religious claims into moral or psychological terms or the positivists' cries of "Nonsense!" and "Meaningless!" For if the positivists' own theory is true, such judgments express nothing more than their own preferences, emotions, and attitudes. And in both cases the most extravagant claims are called into very serious question, if not thoroughly refuted, by the persuasiveness of other theories of truth and accounts of experience and especially by the inescapable cogency of the artistic, moral, and religious enterprises themselves.

ON RELIGION AND THE COHERENCE THEORY OF TRUTH

Prima facie the world is a pluralism.
                                        WILLIAM JAMES

Religious philosophers have traditionally relied greatly, though not ever completely, on the coherence theory of truth. This theory is as ancient as Plato, who insisted that "heaven and earth, gods and men, are held together by the principle of sharing, by friendship and order, by self-control and justice" (*Gorgias*). The presupposition of the coherence theory is of course that all existence forms a rational whole, that the order of thought is also the order of existence, or as the seventeenth-century philosopher Gottfried Leibnitz expressed it, that

> not only is the order of the universe the most perfect possible, but also that each living mirror representing the universe in accordance with its point of view, that is to say, that each *monad*, each substantial centre, must have its perceptions and its desires as well regulated as is compatible with all the rest. . . . For everything in things is regulated once for all with as much order and harmony as is possible, supreme wisdom not being able to act except with perfect harmony. The present is big with the future, the future could be read in the past, the distant is expressed in the near. One could become acquainted with the beauty of the universe in each soul, if one could unfold all its folds, which only develop visibly in time. . . .

As in walking on the sea-shore and hearing the great noise which it makes, I hear the individual sounds of each wave, of which the total sound is composed, but without distinguishing them; so our confused perceptions are the result of the impressions which the whole universe makes upon us.[19]

More recently the coherence theory has perhaps been most ably and explicitly defended without reference to theological, moral, or religious principles by Brand Blanshard, who has written in *The Nature of Thought:*

Truth is the approximation of thought to reality. It is thought on its way home. Its measure is the distance thought has traveled, under guidance of its inner compass, toward that intelligible system which unites its ultimate object with its ultimate end. Hence at any given time the degree of truth in our experience as a whole is the degree of system it has achieved. The degree of truth of a particular proposition is to be judged in the first instance by its coherence with experience as a whole, ultimately by its coherence with that further whole, all-comprehensive and fully articulated, in which thought can come to rest.[20]

Thus the coherence theory claims that not sense experience alone or any single event or appearance but rational consistency among all the various judgments derived from and supported by extensive experience and thought or reason is the only conclusive evidence of truth. No single claim, observation, or experience, it is said, is such that it may be confidently called *true*. For the quality of truth belongs to parts only insofar as they are related to and determine or signify the quality of the whole—or Truth. So only when several instances or avenues of experience, both rational and sensory, point to the same conclusion or lead to the same result can there be a justified claim that truth has been approached. Even a claim based on direct observation, if inconsistent with the burden of experience and reason or with other known facts, may have to be rejected as false; for sensory experience is notoriously fallible. On the other hand, the hypothesis which is con-

---

[19] *The Philosophical Works of Leibnitz,* trans. by G. M. Duncan, New Haven, Tuttle, Morehouse & Taylor, 1890, No. XXXII, p. 215.

[20] Brand Blanshard, *The Nature of Thought,* London and New York, Allen & Unwin and The Humanities Press, 1964, Vol. II, p. 264.

sistent with the known facts may have to be regarded as true, even though there is absolutely no immediate or even possible sensory experience to confirm it. Each of us, for example, must consider it true that other people suffer unhappiness and pains similar to our own, even though no sensory experience can of itself ever confirm or disconfirm this belief.

The strictest advocates of the coherence theory insist in fact that the laws of thought, exemplified in the consistency of logic and mathematics, are altogether true independently of any empirical facts, and that sense experience must be considered illusory insofar as it is incompatible with the logical or rational. And when the logical empiricists insist in turn that systems of logic and mathematics are true only by definition or convention and thus assert nothing that is either true or false about existential matters, the reply is that this is clearly not so and that existence itself is obviously such that a language in which it is false that nothing is both red and yellow all over or true that sometimes $4 + 3 = 8$ is inconceivable and therefore apparently impossible. At least the terms of such a language, the rationalists claim, would not mean the same as the corresponding terms in prevailing languages, and consequently identical terms would assert entirely different claims. The defenders of the coherence theory point out that truth is a function of meanings, not of particular linguistic sounds or signs; they insist that anything can have meaning only as a part of a complex rational whole. Furthermore, they argue, sense experience can never verify historical claims or theoretical interpretations of past events or any system of inclusive laws or hypotheses about the general order of events. The assurance of truth in such matters, and therefore cogency in science and life itself, can then come only from coherence within and between the multitude of facts seen in the light of the general and consistent theories which are used to account for them. Or in other words, a trustworthy approach to truth is indicated, according to the coherence theory, only when the fragments of experience begin to fit reasonably, if not neatly, together like the pieces in a jigsaw puzzle.

Apart from the enormous difficulty of determining which of various consistent systems best describe existence, the most obvious and devastating criticism of the coherence theory, if it is taken to be an altogether adequate account of the nature of all truth and existence, is that conclusive evidence is completely lacking for the claim that things and events do in fact generally exhibit anything approaching the harmony, regularity, and coherence required by the theory. That thought should expect, in Blanshard's words, to "come to rest," attractive as rest may seem to human weariness, appears almost wholly alien to the restless spontaneity that actually characterizes especially—but not only—the living forms of existence. But more specifically, the predictability of events in nature, which should be very precise and reliable if rational consistency prevails, is in fact only statistical and highly precarious. Particularly in human affairs, almost nothing can be predicted with certainty concerning the behavior of the individual; and even in the physical world every prediction must be made within a margin of error. The coherence theory utterly fails to account for such irregularities or for the fact that existence which is presumably rational always deviates more or less from what complete rationality would seem to require. The partisans of coherence have of course sometimes suggested that the apparent irrationality or incongruity in nature is not at all surprising in the light of man's limited knowledge, and that complete consistency and accurate description in terms of rational principles will be possible and predictability will improve only when knowledge has vastly increased. But this seems to beg the current and fundamental questions almost as much as the positivists' claim that all reliable evidence is revealed through the senses.

Yet whether one is concerned about discovering the structure of the atom or determining the "facts" in a court of law, the appeal to coherence is clearly inevitable and presumably reliable. At the very least the demand for consistency in the search for judicial reliability or knowledge seems as fruitful and inescapable as a criterion of success as the demand for diligent and careful use of the senses. Certainly no philosophy sympathetic to religious experience, symbols, and claims can ignore the plausibility of the rationalist's approach to many of the baffling problems raised by religious activity and ideas. A classic and perennial defense of the cognitive significance of both moral and religious ideals is that the demand for rationality or coherence in

the universe as a whole can be satisfied only if the universe is in
fact such that experience does not generate demands and expectations that are not ultimately fulfilled. In a rational universe,
it is said, the things that seem most important—or perfect and
divine—to reflective thought must indeed turn out to be the most
real and enduring. And one of the most venerable and persistent
arguments for the existence of God is that only God, as the Alpha
and Omega of being, can complete the harmony and intelligibility
of the universe. This argument has recurred again and again,
from Plato and Aristotle to Aquinas, Kant, and Whitehead. Even
the great pragmatist William James was compelled to argue
that God is "the normal object of the mind's belief, inasmuch as
any conception that falls short of God is irrational, if the word
'rational' be taken in its fullest sense; while any conception that
goes beyond God is impossible. . . ."[21] Persuasive and inevitable as
such arguments often appear, the evidence for complete harmony
or coherence is nonetheless so meager and inconclusive that no
scrupulous religious philosophy, or philosophy of religion, can rest
its case solely on the assurance of ultimate rationality in the
universe.

ON RELIGION AND PRAGMATISM

Knowledge does not copy anything presented; it
proceeds from something given toward some-
thing else. When it finds that something else,
the perception is verified. When it fails, or to
the extent that it fails, we have error or illusion.
                                             C. I. LEWIS

Since the last decades of the nineteenth century many religious persons, convinced that religious claims cannot be verified
by either sensory experience or rational arguments or by the more

---

[21] William James, "Reflex Action and Theism," in *Essays on Faith and
Morals*, New York, Meridian Books, 1962, p. 132.

complex methods of scientific inquiry, have often appealed to the pragmatic theory of truth as the most promising philosophical method of justifying religious practices and ideas.

Insofar as there is any notable unity in this diverse movement of thought, pragmatism may be said to be based on the conviction or discovery that an appeal to neither sense experience nor to rational consistency is an altogether satisfactory method of establishing the beliefs and defending the actions and values which are humanly most significant. Accordingly, the pragmatists point out that traditional empiricism, which may now be said to include positivism, rests ultimately on the uncritical assumption that sensory perception is necessary, reliable, self-correcting, and sufficient in every truthseeking enterprise, while rationalism or the coherence theory of truth is based on the unprovable, and in many respects unjustified and superfluous, claim that a pervasive and unitary harmony prevails among the apparently pluralistic and quite often mutually antagonistic aspects of existence. But the most crucial problems, the pragmatists insist, are neither related directly to sense perception nor are they questions of logical coherence or rationality. Man is fundamentally a very complex organism that must above all adjust to the various demands of a particular but diverse and ever-changing environment or solve problems that are immediate, many-sided, ever-present, and momentous so far as his own personal existence is concerned. Consequently the pragmatists claim that through the ages, regardless of sophisticated and impressive proposals to the contrary, *truth* has meant primarily an idea or theory or process that leads to desirable or predictable results. So the true and the useful, when the useful is broadly and humanly conceived, are presumably closely related; and a statement or theory may be rightfully called *true* only when repeatedly and successfully tested by the activities which promote the complex processes of adjusting to and manipulating the environment or meeting the sundry demands of life. The "true belief" can be distinguished from "false belief," according to the pragmatists, only by considering the total and practical results of each in the complex conditions of man's life.

Pragmatism was originally a logical theory designed to aid the philosopher and the scientist in the attempt to clarify ideas.

Charles Sanders Peirce, who gave pragmatism its name (but later preferred to call his own philosophy *pragmaticism* in order to distinguish his own theory from what pragmatism had become under the influence of what he regarded as more literary and less rigorous thinkers), was not only a logician, however, but also a metaphysician and deeply concerned, not primarily with the so-called practical issues which are so often thought to characterize pragmatism, but with both scientific and highly speculative questions. Unlike his younger contemporary, George Santayana, he never succumbed to the scientific materialism popular in his day and was appalled by the very idea that "consciousness in general" is "a mere illusory aspect of a material system."[22] But he regarded the then current forms of idealism or rationalism as equally mistaken in claiming that the universe is a harmonious or coherent whole. The conviction that chance and genuine spontaneity are objective aspects of existence and provide the necessary conditions for both personal freedom and the genuine efficacy of intelligence pervades Peirce's metaphysical writings. He accordingly argued that the theory that causal necessity prevails in nature is based on nothing in experience. "Try to verify any law of nature," he wrote, "and you will find that the more precise your observations, the more certain they will be to show irregular departures from law."[23] He of course admitted that no ultimate explanation can ever be given of any fact, much less of ubiquitous necessity or of spontaneity and chance. But he was also convinced that much that is inexplicable in terms of mechanics and law can be understood if one begins with spontaneity and chance. For experience, he observed, is filled with indisputable examples of variety, diversity, and apparent novelty, none of which is compatible with a thoroughly rational or mechanical order. He suggested that:

> The endless variety in the world has not been created by law. It is not of the nature of uniformity to originate variation, nor of law to begat circumstance. When we gaze upon the multifariousness of

---

[22] Charles Sanders Peirce, *Collected Papers*, C. Hartshorne and P. Weiss, eds., Cambridge, Belknap Press, Harvard University Press, 1934-1935, 6.61. In accordance with the practice of the editors, all references to Peirce's writings are by numbers which indicate volume and paragraph.

[23] *Ibid.*, 6.46.

nature we are looking straight into the face of a living spontaneity. A day's ramble in the country ought to bring that home to us.[24]

If the universe is indeed the sort of universe that Peirce conceived it to be, significant and reliable judgment must necessarily include more than sensory and rationalistic or deductive elements and processes, though both observation and reason will be nonetheless important. Knowledge must grow out of the complex experience of living, acting, and thinking. The function of inquiry, Peirce said, is to settle doubt and produce beliefs. Beliefs, however, are by no means purely mental but are rather habits of action, including of course habits of language and thought, since "My language is the sum total of myself; for man is the thought."[25] And genuine differences in thought and belief can be distinguished only by the different results they produce. In Peirce's best known example, the only evidence that a person believes that a given object is hard is the action—the uses of the object— which bears witness to the belief. If a supposed theory or belief has no distinctive consequences for action, according to Peirce, it is indeed a theory or belief in name only. So true belief is a recognition in action—but by no means excluding the various forms of linguistic activity—of the character of existence. Truth may be verified only by action and its results. But of course not all activity is evidence of truth; illusion and falsehood as well as truth may inspire action. But activity (even speech and thought) based on illusion or falsehood, Peirce suggested, will never stand the test of extensive use or inquiry and are in the long run self-defeating.

The pragmatism of Peirce was then essentially logical— rigorous, realistic, and experimental. He regarded pragmatism as a generalization of the systematic procedures employed by the scientist in the laboratory; and this method, tolerantly and patiently employed, he thought, could solve the most difficult and disparate problems—the problem of a future life (as distinguished from the immortality of the soul) as well as the problem of the structure of matter.

But Peirce's view of religion was hardly pragmatic in the

[24] *Ibid.*, 6.553.
[25] *Ibid.*, 5.314.

general sense of that term, largely perhaps because he did not wholly identify religion with belief—not even with belief evidenced in action. He wrote that it is "absurd to say that religion is a mere belief. You might as well call society a belief, or politics a belief, or civilization a belief. Religion is a life, and can be identified with a belief only provided that belief be a living belief—a thing to be lived rather than said or thought."[26] Religion, he said again, "is a sort of sentiment, or obscure perception, a deep recognition of a something in the circumambient All," an affair of the community, "welding all its members together in one organic, systemic perception of the Glory of the Highest—an idea having a growth from generation to generation and claiming a supremacy in the determination of all conduct, private and public."[27] Instead of being a mere belief, he suggested, the religious experience provides a man with "as good reason—putting aside metaphysical subtilties—to believe in the living personality of God as he has to believe in his own. Indeed, *belief* is a word inappropriate to such direct perception."[28]

Therefore, far from suggesting that religious perceptions, ideas, and activities are generated or justified pragmatically, or in terms of their usefulness, Peirce insisted rather that "religion, in the proper sense of the term, can arise from nothing but the religious sensibility,"[29] and can be appreciated chiefly through Musement. And Musement, he said, is "Pure Play . . . a lively exercise of one's powers." The religious thinker, precisely because personal and crucial matters are at stake, can never pursue his ideas in "singleness of heart, and must always suspect himself of reasoning unfairly. . . . But let religious meditation be allowed to grow up spontaneously out of Pure Play without any breach of continuity, and the Muser will retain the perfect candor proper to Musement."[30] And in this "Pure Play of Musement" or in complete detachment from practical or pragmatic problems, "The idea of God's Reality will be sure sooner or later to be found an attractive fancy, which the Muser will develop in various ways.

[26] *Ibid.*, 6.439.
[27] *Ibid.*, 6.429.
[28] *Ibid.*, 6.436.
[29] *Ibid.*, 6.433.
[30] *Ibid.*, 6.458.

The more he ponders it, the more it will find response in every part of his mind, for its beauty, for its supplying an ideal of life, and for its thoroughly satisfactory explanation of his whole three-fold environment."[31] (This threefold environment is constituted of the *internal world* of ideas, musings, and emotions; the *external world* of existing and interacting objects; and the *logical world* of ideas which are related to one another.) So Peirce was really neither pragmatist nor rationalist in religion. He suggests in fact that it is no more appropriate to demand a justification of religion as such than to demand a justification of reason as such. Or if reason may be said to bear its own credentials, so does religion. Religion is one of the ways in which man responds to the "signs" around him—a way, form, or quality of life which is no more reducible to other things than is red or triangularity. Religion is a basic element of experience, or to use Peirce's own term religion is *instinctive* belief in "the reality of God."[32]

Yet perhaps a pragmatic note is sounded when he concludes that:

> Any normal man who considers the three Universes in the light of the hypothesis of God's Reality ... will come to be stirred to the depths of his nature by the beauty of the idea and by its august practicality, even to the point of earnestly loving and adoring his strictly hypothetical God, and to that of desiring above all things to shape the whole conduct of his life and all the springs of action into conformity with that hypothesis.[33]

But the credit or the responsibility for the wide use of pragmatic arguments in the defense of religious ideas must be given to William James. James was philosophically, though perhaps not personally, more individualistic than Peirce. He was also less rigorous but not any more imaginative in his inquiries and was surely less confident of the success of the established methods of scientific inquiry in the attempt to solve certain problems. Consequently in the hands of James, whether for better or worse, pragmatism became a more amorphous and personal philosophy and more literary than Peirce had ever intended

---

[31] *Ibid.*, 6.465.
[32] *Ibid.*, 6.496 f.
[33] *Ibid.*, 6.467.

pragmatism should be. Experience and truth, said James, are inevitably and equally individualistic and private, not public. So where Peirce had insisted that the real (and thus the truth) has a specific character, an "external permanency," independent of what anyone happens to think and is conceivably unknown to anyone, James claimed that "True ideas are those that we can assimilate, validate, corroborate, and verify."[34] Peirce wrote that "Philosophy . . . must not care, or must not seem to care, whether her conclusions be wholesome or dangerous."[35] But James insisted that true ideas must be practical and beneficent or act as guides to the solution of problems that are personal, immediate, inescapable, and momentous.

James was of course radically opposed to all forms of religious authoritarianism, to all claims of infallibility and revealed truth. James was, like Peirce, a pluralist, and his theory of truth reflects his pluralism. All truth, he thought, like all experience is private and plural; and reality—since experience is reality—is radically discontinuous and many-faceted, an "aboriginal sensible muchness."[36] Each person must consequently discover his own truth—the truth of his own existential situation, needs, and possibilities—for himself, though this does not mean that there are no general principles which seem to be true for everyone. Apart from his ambiguous and unfortunate emphasis on the "usefulness" and the "cash value" of truth—since James recognized as well as anyone that the actual character of the world is often and in many respects alien to human needs and hopes—he conceived *truth* as that which guides man in any of his enterprises, interests, and activities. But interests, needs, and necessities (or the truth) depend on choices already made, roads taken, enterprises under way. Therefore, "Truth is *made,* just as health, wealth, and strength are made, in the course of experience."[37]

This is not of course the scientist's view of *truth.* The scientist seeks above all for the unchanging laws which describe ma-

---

[34] William James, "Pragmatism's Conception of Truth," in *Pragmatism,* New York, Meridian Books, 1955, p. 133.

[35] C. S. Peirce, *op. cit.,* 6.434.

[36] William James, *Some Problems of Philosophy,* New York, Longmans, 1931, p. 50.

[37] William James, "Pragmatism's Conception of Truth," *op. cit.,* p. 133.

terials that are neither created nor destroyed, neither increased nor diminished, an "external permanency" unaffected by his thought of it. For the scientist truth is discovered, not made. But for James the truth that the philosopher seeks must include the scientist in the laboratory, the saint among the sinners, discovering, reforming, in some respects increasing and in others decreasing the various powers and conditions which sustain and limit the life of man. The world in which man has created new instruments, discovered the law of gravity, and split the atom is a radically different world from the world in which these events have not occurred. Such a world, James thought, is surely a world in which the truth is made and not only discovered.

> So the whole coil and ball of truth, as it rolls up, is the product of a double influence. Truths emerge from facts; but they dip forward into facts again and add to them; which facts again create or reveal new truth (the word is indifferent) and so on indefinitely. The "facts" themselves meanwhile are not *true*. They simply *are*. Truth is the function of the beliefs that start and terminate among them.[38]

So truth, according to James, is what guides us. Consequently, the truth may refer to an external permanency unaffected by our thought about it. But it may also be an expression of our needs and desires, our own character, aspirations, and possibilities. On the other hand, there may be no external permanency whatever. Perhaps all is flux. The truth still is. In any case the truth will include man, his needs, and the instruments by which he discovers and knows. No doubt the world may be discovered, at least in part, by the methods of the sciences or by being in the world as if one were in the laboratory. But we are guided—as Peirce also recognized when he was not defining *truth*—by things other than the scientific method of discovery and proof. We may be guided, according to James, by artistic qualities, religious experience and hypotheses, by economic and social needs. The world is pluralistic and truth comes in many forms. Or in other words, there are many different ways of being guided through "the aboriginal sensible muchness," or the welter of qualities, quantities, and relations which make up the world experienced by man.

[38] *Ibid.*, p. 147.

James was by temperament a profoundly religious man and especially sensitive to the language and ideals of the Judeo-Christian tradition, though he was intellectually an agnostic and never identified himself with any tradition. He defined religion as *"The feelings, acts, and experiences of individual men in their solitude, so far as they apprehend themselves to stand in relation to whatever they may consider divine."*[39] Religion, he says, also declares that the best things are eternal, and that "the so-called order of nature . . . is only one portion of the total universe, and that there stretches beyond this visible world an unseen world of which we now know nothing positive, but in its relation to which the true significance of our present mundane life consists."[40] Therefore, the central claims of religion, he suggests time and again, concern such matters as the existence and nature of God, a "spiritual" and "higher" universe, the immortality of the soul, "private personal destiny," or in other words, the classic problems of metaphysics.

But even though the central and essential claims of religion are metaphysical, according to James, he thought the sole test of the truth of religious beliefs is nonetheless thoroughly practical. He was of course convinced that man is basically a *practical* creature and not primarily a *cognitive* or *theoretical* being. And on this assumption he concluded that where practical and theoretical claims come into conflict, it is the theoretical rather than the practical aspects of life that are put into question thereby. Indeed, perhaps the most fundamental premise of James' pragmatism is that when the demands of reason are opposed to the demands of practice, it is the demands of practice that must be trusted. Consequently it is necessary, he insisted, "to use human standards to help us to decide how far the religious life commends itself as the ideal kind of human activity. If it commends itself, then *any theological beliefs* that may inspire it, insofar forth will stand accredited. If not, they will be discredited, and all without reference to anything but human working principles."[41]

[39] William James, *The Varieties of Religious Experience*, New York, Longmans, 1928, p. 31. The original is in italics.
[40] William James, "Is Life Worth Living?" in *Essays on Faith and Morals, op. cit.*, p. 20.
[41] William James, *The Varieties of Religious Experience, op. cit.*, p. 331.

In other instances he said simply that if theological ideas have value for human life, they are also, insofar, true.[42] After all, he claimed, metaphysical or theological questions and conflicts cannot be settled either positively or negatively by rational and empirical methods of inquiry. The practical or pragmatic test is then not only the most relevant but in fact the only test possible.

Should one then believe in the existence of God and the immortality of the soul? One has the right to believe, James said, in any live option or in the truth of any claim that is not clearly false and which satisfies the urgent or inescapable demands of life. And religious questions, he also thought, are clearly among those about which it is impossible to be "indifferent and neutral."[43] "To bid the man's subjective interests be passive till truth express itself from out the environment, is to bid the sculptor's chisel be passive till the statue express itself from out the stone."[44] Quoting Fitz James Stephan, he compared the person seeking answers to traditional religious questions to a person lost on a mountain peak in blinding snow. If he sits still he will most surely perish. If he tries to find his way through the storm, he may lose his way and plunge over a cliff to his death. But he may also find a path to shelter. In any case, James suggested, action offers more hope than inaction, and faith more hope than scepticism.[45] Similarly, he implies, faith in the traditional religious claims is validated in part by the fact that the clearest alternatives to them offer nothing but inevitable doom. The person who stands on the side of faith in the existence of God and immortality has his own life in eternity to gain and nothing at all to lose. But also, James thought, within the context of life here and now, belief may help greatly to create the very fact or experience sought. Particularly in times of crisis, he suggested:

> The part of wisdom as well as of courage is to *believe what is in the line of your needs*, for only by such belief is the need fulfilled. Refuse to believe, and you shall indeed be right, for you shall ir-

[42] William James, "What Pragmatism Means," in *Pragmatism, op. cit.,* p. 133.
[43] William James, "Pragmatism and Religion," in *ibid.,* p. 184.
[44] William James, "Reflex Action and Theism," in *Essays on Faith and Morals, op. cit.,* p. 130.
[45] William James, "The Will to Believe," in *ibid.,* p. 62.

retrievably perish. But believe, and again you shall be right, for you shall save yourself.[46]

Pragmatically, James was convinced, religion asserts only that the best things are eternal and that we are better off for believing this here and now. Yet he also claimed that *any* religious claim or belief which cannot be disproved empirically or rationally may be regarded as true, if the results of believing it are more desirable than the results of disbelief or if belief enables one to live more confidently and happily. "On pragmatistic principles," he wrote, "if the hypothesis of God works satisfactorily in the widest sense of the word, it is true."[47] And such hypotheses *work*, he suggested, when by acting on them, we achieve the ends we seek or find our way through this "aboriginal sensible muchness" without serious mishap and so live to think and act another day. "The will to believe," in the context of James' empiricism, pluralism, and pragmatism, is thus not so much a state of the psyche as a method of discovery. For we live, he thought, always by faith—by faith in this or that. "The will to believe" is essentially a claim that we might as well live boldly as timidly, that we might as well bet on the best rather than the worst, since "Dupery for dupery, what proof is there that dupery through hope is so much worse than dupery through fear?"[48]

Human need or the conviction that ultimately existence must conform to personal demands and hopes has never been more frankly asserted as the basis of religious faith and judgment. And much of the recent emphasis on the psychological basis and the practical value of religion, both of which are dubious foundations, is no doubt due to the extraordinary influence of this version of pragmatism. But whatever the faults and limits of James' philosophy, it must be said, if we may use his own words, that his careful attempt to articulate religion pragmatically is also among the "most sustained efforts man's intellect has ever made to keep still living on that subtle edge of things where speech and thought expire."[49]

[46] William James, "Is Life Worth Living?" in *ibid.*, p. 28.
[47] William James, "Pragmatism and Religion," *op. cit.*, p. 192.
[48] William James, "The Will to Believe," in *op. cit.*, p. 58.
[49] William James, "Reflex Action and Theism," in *ibid.*, p. 122.

Yet a fundamental fault in identifying religion with metaphysical beliefs and then attempting to verify these beliefs pragmatically or through their practical import is surely evident in the thoroughly contradictory results the method produced in the philosophies of James and John Dewey. By James' pragmatic standards it was possible for him to vindicate at least the major concepts as well as the spirit of the religious traditions in the West. In effect he even affirmed the pragmatic truth of the doctrine of original sin by claiming that a uniform and genuine perception of all religions is "that there is *something wrong about us*" from which we may be saved "by making proper connection with the higher powers."[50] But Dewey, as we have already noted, who was no less a pragmatist than James, dismissed practically all traditional religious beliefs and practices as stumbling blocks to intelligence and freedom or scientific and social progress. Many of the very ideas that James regarded as "live options" Dewey castigated as "superstitions." And while James enthusiastically accepted the functional, if not the literal, validity (or truth) of many traditional religious doctrines, Dewey insisted that these doctrines, especially the doctrine of original sin and the traditional view of the existence of God, have prevented men from using their own powers in the solution of their problems.

This disagreement between James and Dewey concerning the value of religion makes all too evident the severe limits of pragmatic criteria alone in the solution of metaphysical or ontological problems, particularly when powerful psychological and utilitarian factors may be involved. Perhaps both James and Dewey had altogether too little of Peirce's respect and capacity for "Musement" and thus often lacked the severe detachment which certain speculative questions apparently demand. Even though the useful is no doubt often related to the true, if one's perspective is unusually broad or narrow in some respect, almost any belief or action may be defended by the pragmatic criteria. Propaganda to create enthusiasm for carrying on a war, for example, may be or seem to be useful. But such usefulness cannot render the propaganda *true* in any critical sense. Another fundamental difficulty for the pragmatic theory is that *the useful* is, at least in

[50] William James, *The Varieties of Religious Experience, op. cit.*, p. 508.

many instances, no less indeterminate and ambivalent than *the true*. Indeed the subjective connotations are probably always greater. For the useful is obviously and inseparably dependent on the particular ends men seek. Yet the most naïve and unthoughtful person must occasionally recognize that the truth is sometimes radically unfavorable to man's apparent purposes and needs, and that even the clearest recognition of the truth may bear no practical fruits at all. So to measure the truth by its usefulness may surely encourage the neglect of the austere but nonetheless liberating visions of objective truth, including the aspects of the universe that are apparently indifferent or even alien to the goals that men set. And the great philosophical achievements of both James and Dewey, including as they did such austere visions, were surely in part independent of their professed pragmatic theories of truth.

Traditionally the useful and the true—that which produces the desired results and that which reveals essential characteristics —have been definitely, though not always sharply, distinguished. The practice of numerous men, both wise and good, affirms that certain truths are to be contemplated—or assimilated so as to become integral parts of what the self is—rather than used. Yet there can be little doubt that the pragmatic test is often appropriate and reliable, especially where social and personal problems must be solved. The pragmatic test is in fact frequently the only one possible in both scientific and practical matters, for example, in the treatment of disease or the development of skills. And the theory that produces useful results is called *true* with indisputable, though no doubt often insufficient, evidence. But religion at least does not deliberately seek to be primarily useful until after it has lost all hope of being true in the most radical sense of the term. And by then it has usually ceased to be genuine religion and has become an apology for the status quo in moral and social institutions and traditions.

ON THE PROPRIETY OF CALLING RELIGION "TRUE"

Things are revealed to us not only by the scientists with microscopes, but also by the poets, the prophets, and the painters.

JOHN WISDOM

Religious beliefs and practices, it must apparently be admitted, are not significantly validated by either sense experience, by their consistency with one another and with other discoveries about existence, or by their pragmatic functions. Few religious or nonreligious persons, however, are very greatly impressed or affected by the failure of such methods in the attempt to justify religion. But few also would completely deny the relevance of such methods and criteria in conducting inquiries *into* or *about* the character, conditions, and consequences of religious claims and practices. To find a correspondence between religious claims and the observable world (whatever this may mean), or to discover that the ideals and actions of the various religions are ultimately coherent and harmonious with each other and with other aspects of experience, or to determine that religious activities do in fact favorably affect mental health, emotional security, and even the "cash value" of experience, is perhaps not clearly impossible no matter how improbable and certainly not insignificant if possible. Indeed the efforts to apply observational, rational, and pragmatic tests to the religions need not be altogether vain, even if the precise kinds of results sought are very meager or even lacking completely. For such efforts may at least reveal, if nothing more, the unique and important features and effects of particular religious symbols and practices. And presumably the more that is known *about* religion, the more reasonable and just the judgments of it (though perhaps not the religious judgments themselves) will be.

But all knowledge gained by inquiry *into* religion, although

religious claims and practices may surely sometimes be radically
influenced by it, is clearly *about* religion and not itself religious
knowledge. And of course no one seriously concerned with the *truth
of religion* is willing to equate judgments *about* religion with religious judgments or religious knowledge. *To know about
Buddhism,* for example, important as this may be, is without doubt
fundamentally different from *being and judging as a Buddhist.*
And as William James wrote, "If religion be a function by which
either God's cause or man's cause is to be really advanced, then he
who lives the life of it, however narrowly, is a better servant than
he who merely knows about it, however much."[51] For even though
the origin, basis, and function of any judgment are quite legitimate
objects of scientific or philosophic inquiry, every judgment—
whether scientific, artistic, religious, or moral—is presumably also
in some measure an irreducible and "situational" recognition or
revelation of some limited portion of the universe or an account in
a particular mode of what an individual has encountered from a
specific perspective. And although inquiry into the origin and functions of a judgment may reveal its so-called "necessary and sufficient" conditions as well as the factors which made it more or less
compelling, such inquiry cannot itself ever perform the specific
functions of the judgments which it thus articulates. In other
words, every honest judgment is partially validated or justified by
its mere occurrence and inquiry into its conditions, character, and
functions can hardly do other than suggest more or less forcefully
that from different perspectives, which may include more or less,
the judgment is more or less revelant and compelling. And of
course the most urgent question is always not whether a judgment
was justified in the past by its original form and function, but
whether a present form and function are necessary and reliable
in the continuing processes of judgment.

The fact that religious judgments are not significantly validated by the methods current (and presumably reliable though
surely not altogether infallible) in the sciences and philosophy has
persuaded some who acknowledge that religious beliefs and symbols are meaningful to deny nonetheless that it is ever proper or
necessary to call religious judgments *true* or *false.*

[51] *Ibid.,* p. 489.

A special case in this connection are those who presently regard linguistic analysis as the most promising approach in philosophy. Although such analysts very frankly deny the positivistic assertion that religious claims are meaningless as well as the more moderate attempt to translate religious beliefs into moral policies, there is among them hardly a single candid spokesman for the general reliability or truth of religion. They speak rather of *meaning* or *significance* or sometimes *validity* but very infrequently of *truth*. The analysts' neglect of *truth* in favor of what may generally be called *meaning* is based, however, not on any denial of the possibility of religious truth but on very dubious assumptions about the nature of truth and philosophic inquiry.

First of all, in common with the secular practitioners of the method, who reject the truth of religion on essentially the same basis as the positivists reject its meaning, the religious analysts assume that religious language, like the language of morals or science, possesses a logic and meaning of its own. This meaning, they suggest, is essentially independent of both its existential context and other uses of language but can be helpfully articulated and made clear by a careful and analytical scrutiny of its structure and use. I. M. Crombie expresses this by claiming that "All that is necessary for an utterance to be a meaningful statement is that it should be governed by rules which specify what it is about, and what it asserts about it."[52] And John Hick, in order to show what he takes to be the complete autonomy of language and the irrelevance of philosophic reason to any form of knowledge, asserts in *Faith and Knowledge*:

> The reason why it is impossible that we should ever find a five and a seven which do not add up to twelve is simply that twelve is our name for the result of adding together five and seven. Thus definitions create, rather than state, necessity; and the necessity which they create holds sway not in the world which we inhabit but in the language in terms of which we inhabit it.[53]

Neither of these claims bears any evidence of the sensitivity to language characteristic of the greatest of the analysts, Ludwig

[52] I. M. Crombie, "The Possibility of Theological Statements," in *Faith and Logic*, Basil Mitchell, ed., London, Allen & Unwin, 1957, p. 35.
[53] John Hick, *Faith and Knowledge*, Ithaca, Cornell, 1957, p. 10.

Wittgenstein, who observed that "a great deal of stage setting is presupposed if the mere act of naming is to make sense."[54] And of course one of the chief concerns of the present work has been to call into question this essentially Hobbesian and positivistic approach to language as an exception to the general order of nature. At best this approach is arbitrary and implausible. But it seems particularly and strikingly out of place, as well as uncritical, in those who confess a faith in which persons are presumably of primary importance and includes a major document which claims that "In the beginning was the Word." For this view simply ignores how intimate and apparently inevitable the relation is between language and personality or between language and all the characteristically human forms of experience and judgment. But even more serious and surprising is the utter failure on the part of Hick particularly to recognize that necessity can never be demonstratively verbal, except to the extent that there is also a necessity that is ontological or existential or due to the very nature of thought rather than merely conventional.

Language as both a primary instrument and a basic object of knowledge or as both a means of knowing and a significant dimension of the existence we seek to know should, it seems, be taken seriously in any attempt to construct a general and dynamic religious philosophy or ontology. And Paul Tillich's treatment of religious language is at least, though perhaps not more than, a beginning. Tillich also, in spite of his genuine contributions, has approached language or religious symbols largely as a secondary form of knowing or as a way of pointing to something beyond rather than as a basic form of experience in which the knower, the known, and the knowing are at least in many respects inseparable. The analysts, however, are apparently convinced that Tillich puts entirely too much confidence in reason (or theology) and not enough in an experience which is assumed to be somehow independent of language. In other words, the analysts insist, in the terms of Crombie, that the function of religion is to "proclaim a mystery" and not to "propound a cosmological hypothesis."[55] The

[54] Ludwig Wittgenstein, *Philosophical Investigations*, trans. by G. Anscombe, New York, Macmillan, 1953, p. 92e.
[55] I. M. Crombie, *op. cit.*, p. 82.

philosopher, it is suggested, insofar as he properly respects the religious appeal to faith in a mystery, will refrain from constructing a systematic theology which purports to prove what can only be believed.

The second questionable assumption of the analysts, not altogether consistent with the first, is that a religious language always presupposes "God." This assertion takes several forms, including "To 'know God' or to be confronted with God's 'personal Presence' means, of necessity, having certain sorts of emotions and feelings" (C. B. Martin),[56] " 'I worship God' amounts to 'I worship what I worship' " (S. Coval),[57] religion is "the assertion and veneration of some absolute authority" (Austin Farrer),[58] and the professed faith that God is "the unique infinite personal Spirit, 'holy, righteous, wise and loving,' who created the existing universe and who is fashioning human personalities for eternal fellowship with himself through their own free responses to the environmental challenges and opportunities which he appoints" (John Hick).[59] Now apart from their disregard for the results of studies in primitive and comparative religions, and other difficulties already discussed, it is in fact both odd and inconsistent for the religious analysts to claim that "God" is the *sine qua non* of religious language, even though He may be the *sine qua non* of *true* religious language. For they are saying, at least when orthodox, that the meaning of religious language is inseparable from the "God" or the "absolute authority" or the "Supernatural" to which it supposedly points, instead of taking seriously the presumably more basic principle, which, in the words of Austin Farrer, is that "Philosophical analysis tries to show how any sort of talk goes, and what it does."[60] Thus they begin by assuming with G. E. Moore that philosophers have spent too much time "endeavoring to prove that 'Yes' or 'No' will answer questions, to which neither answer is

[56] C. B. Martin, "A Religious Way of Knowing," in *New Essays in Philosophical Theology*, Antony Flew and Alasdair MacIntyre, eds., London, SCM Press, 1955, p. 93.

[57] S. Coval, "Worship, Superlatives and Concept Confusion," *Mind*, Vol. LXVII, April 1959, p. 219.

[58] Austin Farrer, "A Starting-point for the Philosophical Examination of Theological Belief," in *Faith and Logic*, p. 14.

[59] John Hick, *op. cit.*, p. xi.

[60] Austin Farrer, *op. cit.*, p. 9.

correct."[61] But where Moore obviously suspected that there is something logically odd and unphilosophical in both the questions and the claims concerning such matters as the existence of God and the immortality of the soul, the religious analysts clearly want to keep all the traditional religious questions or at least the claims which presumably answer them, in spite of the inconsistency with the basic principles of the method they employ. In this manner they "make room for faith" wholly apart from reason or for the use of traditional theistic language without the disturbing possibility that subsequent developments in logic, science, philosophy, or religion itself might demand fundamental shifts in religious beliefs and practices.

And this leads directly to their third questionable assumption. Again in common with the secular practitioners of philosophy as simply linguistic analysis, the religious analysts assume that it is never any part of the philosopher's task to make judgments concerning the *truth* or *falsity* of specific claims. The philosopher, then, can never legitimately affirm or deny the truth of any religious assertion or belief on the basis of philosophical inquiry. The only legitimate concern of the philosopher, as one who talks only about talk, is with meaning. And so where the secular analysts insist that truth can be determined only by the empirical investigations of the sciences, the religious analysts claim that religious knowledge is wholly a matter of faith in certain metaphysical propositions or mysteries, or, in the words of Hick, that "faith takes on the quality of absolute certainty, which is knowledge."[62] So, strange as it may seem, the philosophical analyst, although he cannot affirm that religious claims are true, apparently can assert (particularly if he happens to share the faith about which he speaks) that the religious person (whether himself or another) speaks truly when he claims by faith, for example, that God is his refuge and strength. And in so doing, the analyst apparently supposes, he does not in the least violate the principle that the philosopher talks only about talk!

Now of course philosophy cannot and need not make ab-

---

[61] G. E. Moore, *Principia Ethica*, Cambridge, Cambridge University Press, 1960, p. vii.
[62] John Hick, *op. cit.*, p. 217.

solute judgments about the truth or falsity of either the empirical claims of the sciences or the specific intimations which may accompany the increased depth and quality in understanding or judicial power which may flow from religious experience, belief, and activity. But this by no means implies that philosophy is merely talk about talk or cannot ever speak truly from its own perspective and in its own terms about the substance, the logical character, the presuppositions, and certain apparent functions and limits of any specific system of scientific inquiry or scheme of religious belief and activity. Furthermore, philosophy, no less than art, science, and religion, has in certain respects its own objects and aims, standards of cogency, and criteria of excellence none of which is either altogether separable from or merely a matter of linguistic cogency. To claim otherwise is to make the assumption, contrary to all reflective experience, that there are absolutely privileged perspectives and methods or that the structures and qualities revealed in certain approaches are clearly and in every respect secondary or illusory while others are just as clearly fundamental and reliable —which in turn rests on a metaphysics that is neither self-evident nor articulated.

So finally, the philosophical analysts, although they have sometimes effectively called attention to profoundly important and neglected aspects of language and meaning, have by no means demonstrated that philosophy has no right to inquire into the truth of religion or that the sole knowledge (or truth) which religion can claim is exclusively or even primarily a matter of faith in certain metaphysical propositions or mysteries.

Others have claimed that the religions are important for characteristics and achievements which are quite distinct from contributions to what is properly called understanding or truth. Truth, it is said, is an attribute of straightforward statements or declarative sentences which assert that something is or is not the case and that significant religious, as well as artistic, symbols are not and do not suggest straightforward claims that something is or is not the case. Their meaning, the argument generally holds, is not in stating what is true but in doing what is impressive or expressive and valuable. So even though the religions and the arts may express man's profoundest feelings and aspirations or even represent and disclose important powers and features of the objective world, they should not be called *true*.

Now except for the derogatory implications for religious judgments and the complimentary overtones for scientific and philosophical modes of judgment, there is surely no compelling reason why *truth* should not apply exclusively to science and perhaps the claims of common sense. Surely the profound differences between scientific claims and religious claims, in both form and substance, suggest that it would be convenient and at least in some respects more accurate to describe their judicial qualities with distinct terminology. But words—especially when old and honorable—do not obey the arbitrary rules made for their use, and the terms employed inevitably reflect some degree of worth attached to their object. So the question of whether religious judgments should be called true is not simply a question of terminology but involves a whole series of questions concerning the total, though relative, worth and significance of scientific and religious methods and judgments. Are religious perspectives illusory in the sense that nothing gained from them ever increases either man's awareness of the existential complex or his own capacity for further discovery and reliable decision? Is scientific method unquestionably the paragon of all judicial thought and action? Are the religions and the arts irrelevant to the recognition of any "facts" as such? The claim that only the straightforward statements of the sciences and common sense are to be called *true* should assume a positive answer to each of these questions.

In fact, however, one of the most persuasive arguments against calling religious and artistic judgments *true* is that of J. H. Randall, Jr., who does not deny that they may "reveal," "express," and "teach" that which is available in no other way. Instead, his thesis, which deserves to be examined at some length, is that the religions and the arts, in contrast to the sciences, belong fundamentally to "the world *for* knowledge" or "to the subject matter to be understood"[63] and not, or at least not significantly, to the instruments by or through which the world may be understood.

[63] John H. Randall, Jr., *Nature and Historical Experience*, New York, Columbia, 1958, pp. 303 ff.

Religion, according to Randall, is most fruitfully regarded "as one art among many others."[64] And the most general function of the arts, he suggests, is to create "impressive symbols." But these symbols are not merely formal or empty. Lyric or dramatic poetry, for example, "grasps and conveys . . . feelings and reactions, the qualities of . . . private experience, in the interest of communicating 'feelings,' sharing 'experience,' 'appreciations,' and sensitivities. It tries to express and convey and thus to 'reveal' the values . . . of the situation, the 'immediate values' and qualities of the human interaction."[65] In a similar manner the painter qualifies "not merely his canvas, and not merely our experience, but the visible world itself with new qualities hitherto unsuspected."[66] The arts, then, are generally means of "expressing and sharing"[67] experience. But they may also "teach us how to see selected aspects of the world more adequately than we could without their assistance."[68]

The specific function of religion is of course different from that of the arts. Using the terms which John Dewey applied primarily to the arts, Randall suggests that religion transforms our ordinary knowledge "in emotional and imaginative vision."[69] But where the painter shows "us how to see the visible world," "the prophet and the saint teach us how to see the divine better—how to see God."[70] But in spite of these descriptions of their functions, he insists that the arts and religions do not provide "understanding" or "knowledge" in any usual sense and that they should be called "noncognitive" rather than "true" or "false." What the arts and religions teach is not *that* something is so but *how to do something better.* The prophet and the saint "teach us how to see

[64] John H. Randall, Jr., *The Role of Knowledge in Western Religion,* Boston, Starr King Press, 1958, p. 124.

[65] John H. Randall, Jr., "The Art of Language and the Linguistic Situation: A Naturalistic Analysis," *The Journal of Philosophy,* Vol. LX, January 17, 1963, p. 42.

[66] John H. Randall, Jr., "Symposium: Are Religious Dogmas Cognitive and Meaningful?" *The Journal of Philosophy,* Vol. LI, March 4, 1954, p. 161.

[67] John H. Randall, Jr., "The Art of Language and the Linguistic Situation: A Naturalistic Analysis," *op. cit.,* p. 30.

[68] John H. Randall, Jr., *The Role of Knowledge in Western Religion, op. cit.,* p. 103.

[69] *Ibid.,* p. 126.

[70] John H. Randall, Jr., "Symposium: Are Religious Dogmas Cognitive and Meaningful?" *op. cit.,* p. 161.

what man's life in the world is, and what it might be. They teach us how to discern what human nature can make out of its natural conditions and materials. They reveal latent powers and possibilities not previously noticed."[71] But in spite of such powers of revelation, religion provides no knowledge properly so-called because it "offers no descriptions and no explanations. . . . Religion is rather itself a human activity that demands careful observation and description, explanation, reflective understanding, and intelligent criticism."[72] Even more pointedly, religious symbols and claims are not cognitive because religious experiences "do not proclaim by their mere occurrence how they are related to other experiences, or, what is crucial, how their supposed 'objects' are connected with other experienced objects. They do not come to us uttering clearly their causes, conditions, and consequences. All these matters are obviously occasions for the kind of critical intellectual inquiry we call 'scientific.' "[73]

So although it may be said that religion "reveals" certain aspects of existence and may be said to provide "knowledge" in the sense of a "know-how" when this is very carefully distinguished from the propositional knowledge of science, Randall writes, "It is well to keep 'truth' for the knowledge that is science, with all its complex procedures and criteria for verifying propositions that can be stated in words."[74]

But are there in fact any sound or inescapable reasons for distinguishing sharply between the cognitive status and content of "knowing that" and "knowing how?" At least every deliberate judgment appears to involve in some measure the knowledge both *that* and *how* things are as they are; consequently, the distinction between them in different areas, although justified in certain respects, seems too much a matter of degree to be an important or decisive factor in determining the cognitive content or function of science, art, or religion. For surely, as Randall himself somewhere suggests, all *knowledge that* something is the case is finally dependent to some extent on *knowing how* to discover it, *how* to

[71] John H. Randall, Jr., *The Role of Knowledge in Western Religion*, *op. cit.*, pp. 128-129.
[72] *Ibid.*, pp. 103-104.
[73] *Ibid.*, p. 95.
[74] *Ibid.*, p. 133.

demonstrate it, or *how* to verify it. Evidently no genuine knowledge *that* something is the case, whether the presence of cancer cells in the lungs or the name of the current Premier of Russia, is at all possible apart from some cognizance of the method by which it may be discovered or demonstrated. And it is equally true that "knowing how" is not possible without "knowing that," although it is plainly possible to learn how or to know how to do many things without knowing all that is involved in doing them. Television repairmen may know quite well *how* to make the set function again without any knowledge of the electronic facts and principles involved. But surely something very similar is significantly the case in every instance of knowing and doing; the very same distinction can be drawn, for example, between the artist as technician using specific materials and the artist as one who *knows* and can articulate artistic traditions, the cultural tendencies, the potentialities of mediums, and the depth of insight required to make any particular work of art possible and significant. It might of course be replied that the latter is really scientific knowledge. But this claim would beg the question insofar as such judgments are presumably possible only through distinctly artistic sensitivities and discriminatory powers. Whatever analytical powers the artist possesses in such matters are clearly derived chiefly from his artistic perception and experience rather than from his acquaintance with the established categories of scientific analysis and explanation. In a very fundamental sense, only the poet can "explain" a poem.

"Knowing that" and "knowing how" are, then, no doubt analytically distinguishable. But both are apparently present in any process of inquiry, action, or production. If "knowing how" is dominant in the arts and religions and "knowing that" in the sciences, this should not obscure the importance of conceptual elements (knowing that) in artistic and religious concern for the qualitative aspects of life or of the techniques of production (knowing how) in the scientific discovery of structures and relations.

But the "noncognitive" label might still be justified for the arts and religions if it is true that to know or understand involves "both description and explanation," and science can in fact provide explanations which are fundamentally different and more revealing than anything which occurs in the religions and arts. Presumably no one would seriously question the claim that the arts—especially poetry, the theatre, the novel, and even in some sense, painting, music, and the dance—may function descriptively, even though they do not necessarily or always do so. Perhaps then the crucial question concerning the cognitive powers of the religions turns on the concept of *explanation*. At least Randall implies that if the religions and arts are not cognitive, it is primarily because they are themselves subject to explanation instead of being modes of explanation.

But what does it mean to "explain" a complex or event? Is there a paradigmatic guide to the meaning of this term? Is the assumption justified that through the religions and arts we can only "express" or "present" or "show," while the sciences "explain" or enable us to "know" or "understand?" Surely one need not wish to deny the fundamental and impressive differences between the religions and arts on the one hand and the sciences on the other in order to question these particular and popular characterizations.

Etymologically, *explain* (*ex* "out" plus *planere* "to make level or plain") suggests that the *explained* is simply *spread out* before us, making plain that which was hidden or that obstructions are removed and we can see what formerly we could not see. But surely the arts at least are notoriously expert, as Randall himself has emphasized, at enabling men to see—to discriminate, recognize, and articulate—many things which they could not see before. According to some, of course, the arts are in fact best at making men see what is not there at all. Be that as it may, and surely no pluralistic account of existence need subscribe to it, anyone who has read Shakespeare or Landor or looked at a landscape by Van Gogh has surely had things—if only the illusive creations of others— made plain to him. He has seen things which presumably he did not and indeed could not see before.

It is frequently claimed that scientists use the word "explain" to mean "brought under a law."[75] This usage is probably observed at least as often in the breach as otherwise, however, since biologists, to say nothing of sociologists and psychologists, can hardly

[75] John Hospers, *An Introduction to Philosophical Analysis*, New York, Prentice-Hall, 1953, p. 179.

be said to "explain" phenomena in terms of general laws. But even if scientists were strictly consistent in this usage, Wittgenstein would be no less justified in saying that it is an "illusion that the so-called laws of nature are the explanations of natural phenomena."[76] Why is this an illusion? Simply because the laws of nature, no matter how effectively they organize our thoughts or how precisely they describe and anticipate certain aspects of experience and existence, do not ultimately make anything at all plain. Particular events and facts still puzzle and bewilder, and explanation in terms of general laws often satisfies neither the intellect nor the emotions. Such explanation may be, as the scientific philosophers are generally ready to insist, all that anyone has any *right* to demand. But the laws, when considered by either the ordinary sensitive person or the scientific genius, may nonetheless demand explanation no less insistently than do the "facts." And higher-level laws are apparently no more satisfactory in this respect than the lower-level laws. Whatever epistemological victory the philosophers of science intend to win over the religions and arts by defining "explanation" in terms of law is in many respects empty. For only to the extent that one prefers very general descriptions or theoretical systems from which the descriptions can be derived because of their scope or usefulness, can one justify a preference for the so-called laws of science over the artistic descriptions of impressive particulars as ways of "knowing" existence. The cognitive power—if this relates to a revelation of the actual traits of the real—of neither is clearly superior to the other.

So apart from the debatable cognitive value of predictive powers, there is apparently little to justify the thought that scientific descriptions are more penetrating or more cognizant of the actual than artistic descriptions. Who knows and can describe a man? The physicist who measures action and reaction? Or the chemist who discovers the constituents of flesh and blood? Or the biologist who anticipates the general process and forms of maturation? Or the painter and the poet who accentuate and in accentuating portray or reveal the extraordinary qualities of a particular man? Or the saint who expresses his longing for per-

[76] Ludwig Wittgenstein, *Tractatus Logico-Philosophicus*, London, Kegan Paul, 1922, 6.371.

fection and strives to embody qualities of infinite sympathy and tenderness? To say that the one "knows" and the other does not seems an altogether unjustified stringency in the use of a word or else a completely unnecessary austerity in the conception of knowledge, although knowledge is perhaps always severely limited. Of course the chemist and the poet know different things, even as the astronomer and the biologist do. And if they do not ultimately know what they know in basically different ways, at least their methods of demonstration and persuasion are incommensurably different. But surely this does not mean that they are not equally knowers.

Probably the most candid use of the word "explain" is by the late P. W. Bridgman who confessed that scientific explanation "consists in reducing a situation to elements with which we are so familiar that we accept them as a matter of course, so that our curiosity rests."[77] And in this sense perhaps the religions and the arts can hardly be said to explain anything at all, though Aristotle did not clearly err in claiming that a function of the tragic drama is to render intelligible (explain?) the demise of a great and honorable man and that consequently tragedy is more philosophic (explanatory?) than history. But by and large the arts, including Greek tragedy, do not so much satisfy our curiosity as whet our wonder. Our perplexity is perhaps not increased but we are nonetheless amazed, not so much by what we do not know as by the fact that one aspect of existence becomes so clear and luminous. Surely the arts and religions allow nothing to be accepted simply as a matter of course; for it may be said that their very aim is in part to make the world astonishing in its expressive beauty and presence.

Shall we call this knowledge or truth? Surely neither the artist nor the scientist nor the philosopher is altogether dispassionate in the use of such words. But at least the poet (Robert Graves) is no less honest in claiming that "the scientist concentrates on analysis and classification of external fact" while "the poet concentrates on discovery of internal truth"[78] than the

[77] P. W. Bridgman, *The Logic of Modern Physics*, New York, Macmillan, 1927, p. 37.
[78] Robert Graves, "A Poet's Investigation of Science," *Saturday Review*, December 7, 1963, p. 82.

scientist or philosopher (Rudolf Carnap) who insists that the poem merely expresses "certain feelings of the poet" and "has no assertional sense" while the sciences do contain knowledge.[79] No doubt many—artists, scientists, philosophers, and prophets alike— often aspire to the discovery of a truth more comprehensive than all together in fact now possess. But few stay for an answer when the nature of truth or especially their own version of it is in question. Although it may often seem justified or practically and even morally necessary to suppose that the truth possessed is unqualified, in our candid moments we must know that the light of consciousness and the articulation of its objects, bright and priceless in each of its forms, leave not only most of the past and the future but also much of the present, including especially our understanding of the forms of knowledge, in outer darkness. If it is by our cognitive powers, however, that we identify and deliberately maintain or alter the conditions—the activities, moods, and judicial premises as well as certain physical necessities—on which a particular form and quality of existence depend, then surely the arts and religions must be included among them and may sometimes and in some respects be judged true or false.

Indeed, if we take seriously Randall's own functional theory of language, which seems admirably sound, we must admit with him that it is "impossible for any 'sentence' to 'mirror' or literally 'describe' existence,"[80] and that it is not possible "to make more than a distinction of degree between what is commonly called a 'literal' and a 'symbolic' statement."[81] Within such a theory of language, where it is also claimed that such connectives as " 'but,' 'and,' 'hence' refer as much to factors in the objective structure of the situation as do any other terms,"[82] it seems both unnecessary and inconsistent to suggest that there is some "ordinary sense" in which scientific propositions may be true or false and that in this "ordinary sense" artistic and religious claims and symbols are not "knowledge" at all. Is it in some identically

[79] Rudolf Carnap, "The Rejection of Metaphysics," in *The Age of Analysis*, Morton White, ed., New York, Mentor Books, 1955, p. 209.

[80] John H. Randall, Jr., "The Art of Language and the Linguistic Situation: A Naturalistic Analysis," *op. cit.*, p. 34.

[81] *Ibid.*, p. 55.

[82] *Ibid.*, p. 56.

"ordinary sense" that both common sense claims and scientific accounts of the nature of matter are said to be *true?* Is there an "ordinary sense" of "truth" which applies unequivocally to both chemical analysis and the theory of evolution or to both the descriptions of sense experience and to philosophical analysis?

Surely if the exact meaning of *truth* is due in each instance, as it seems to be, in some measure to the distinct aims and methods of discovery or to the processes of verification, then there is little specific, even though there is a general, meaning common to the various forms of judgment. In the most general sense truth in science apparently refers primarily to that complex of ideas and operations which, at any given stage of development, sustains and promotes the processes of scientific inquiry. Ultimately there is evidently no other test. And at least historically the arts and religions, no less than the sciences, have been among man's most distinctive and substantive forms of perceptual, creative, and judicial powers or among the methods by which he has utilized materials, instruments, and meanings to discover, articulate, preserve, and transform the features, both quantitative and qualitative, of the world he must inhabit. And it is evidently impossible to be just to the artistic and religious enterprises with any label which suggests that at their best they have less ontological and epistemic significance than do common sense and science. For it is not at all clear that the methods and complexes of meaning and value which constitute artistic and religious claims and activities are either less indicative of the enduring character of existence or less revelatory and necessary to the career of man than are the characteristic procedures, conclusions, and values of the sciences.

It is also highly questionable whether the religions or the arts provide "material for knowledge" in any sense radically different from the way in which the sciences do. Or in slightly different terms, it is by no means evident that instead of being forms of apprehending or understanding existence, the religions and arts are primarily in need of being understood scientifically. Apart from the very relevant question of whether any experiences or claims "proclaim by their mere occurrence how they are related to other experiences" or "come to us uttering clearly their causes, conditions, and consequences," the scientists are not after all the arbiters of either language or truth. As Randall himself somewhere suggests, truth sustains the scientist, and not vice versa. And the merest possibilities, no matter how inconsequential, apparently belong somehow in "the realm of truth" no matter how they are discovered or revealed.

There is no doubt much to be learned *about* religion and the arts from scientific observation and analysis. But it is equally true that much can also be learned *about* the various sciences, their conditions and relations to each other and to other aspects of existence, by studying them scientifically. Yet such scientific studies of science may often cast no additional light at all on the validity of the specific claims or functions of chemistry, physics, biology, or psychology. To discover the conditions that apparently make a science (or science) possible or to discover the influence of a science on politics and religion, interesting as this may be, by no means necessarily illuminates or puts into question the cognitive or judicial character of the science itself. Likewise the fact that the religions and arts are in need of "careful observation and description, explanation, reflective understanding, and intelligent criticism" does not necessarily imply that they themselves never provide, in their own terms, the partial descriptions, reflective understanding, and intelligent criticism of which man is capable. In other words, although the religions and arts may be "scientifically explained," or understood in any of a number of ways, none of such "explanations," it may be plausibly argued, touches the heart of the matter: that the aspects of the world "revealed" through them are no less "real" or important and influential than any others in the selective or judicial processes by which men deliberately choose the objects and values to nourish and those to neglect or condemn.

No doubt the sciences of nature and man must be used to shed whatever light they can (and it may be very great) on the religious and artistic enterprises. But this need not imply that it is not also relevant and revealing for the prophet and the artist to bring their own special sensitivities, interests, techniques, and skills to bear in reflective criticism of the methods, aims, and achievements of the sciences. And surely there is no reason a priori why, if this is done, we may not expect to learn equally as much *about* the sciences from the prophets and the artists as we do *about* the religions and arts from the sciences—though to be sure we shall learn nothing scientific from religion or art and nothing religious or artistic from the sciences. Understanding, knowing, passing judgment, and sustaining the vital and cognitive processes of the life of man are surely complex matters. But it seems altogether dubious that any of the ways of apprehending and deliberately altering or qualifying either one's own perceptive powers or the objective structure and quality of existence is less than indicative of *what is*, or cognitive and capable in some sense and measure of *truth*.

Surely no one can deny the profound reliability or the necessity of scientific methods and conclusions in particular domains and within limits—and the limits themselves are perhaps always indeterminate. Yet almost no one is more aware than the more candid scientists that many aspects of life—the objects and qualities of delight, love, and devotion as well as sorrow and sadness—are fundamentally exempt from scientific judgment and control. Does this mean that the sense of worth—one of the most effective elements, if not the very substance, of man's existence—is blind, noncognitive or nonjudicial? Or does it mean rather that veridical judgments (judgments that in one respect or another reveal the actual) must occur in other modes also?

In any case the whole of *what is* is obviously not amenable to expression and communication in the languages of the sciences. For the sciences do not speak of worth at all except as devotion to scientific inquiry is itself unimpeachable evidence that the judicial activities of the scientist have a high intrinsic as well as a utilitarian value. In fact the splendid order of nature is perhaps nowhere better evident than in the sciences. Yet one cannot speak scientifically of this splendor. Religion, however, is essentially an acknowledgment of things of splendor and worth. Thus if the search for truth must embrace all aspects of existence, religious judgments, even though they may in part create the reality they recognize and celebrate, are not altogether wide of the mark. For ultimately the experience of worth, its ontological status and implications aside, is not less a matter of fact than the motions of the atoms and the planets. And even though it may be the case that all matters of worth are existentially inseparable from the blind movements of atoms and planets, the language which describes the one is still essentially irrelevant to the description, if not the experience, of the other.

Furthermore, if a person speaks of truth at all he must do so within the limits and fallibility of all judgment, recognizing that he may well be mistaken and that what he has seen or thought and said is not all that is. Honesty requires him—not indeed to be silent—but only to recognize the limited functions and powers of his judgments. And it should be noted that John H. Randall, Jr., who is clearly more profoundly aware than most men of both the great importance of religion and the immense and irreducible difference between science and religion, added to his claim that religious judgments should not be called true the quite different suggestion that "Perhaps the scientists themselves are abandoning 'truth' as the name for the test of their knowledge, for some other property like 'confirmability' or 'warranted assertibility.'"[83] And indeed if these latter terms, which are certainly more modest and probably more accurate, were generally adopted to describe and evaluate the best established conceptual schemes in the sciences, then it would no doubt be altogether appropriate or even necessary to adopt similarly modest, although different, terms for describing and evaluating the revelatory functions and achievements of the religions. Insofar as "truth" suggests a kind of finality and completeness in judgment, there can be little doubt that "confirmability" and "warranted assertibility" are more honest labels for the transitory forms in which judgments so often, if not always, occur and knowledge is achieved. However, even if it is clearly more honest and humble to speak only of "meaning," "confirmability," and "warranted assertibility," and never of "truth" in either science or religion, the worth of each and personal preferences may nonetheless compel the most unpretentious to assert the truth of one or both with a conviction that is stronger than the evidence. But in any case, if religion is a mode—even though a very limited one—of guiding and sustaining the judicial

[83] John H. Randall, Jr., *The Role of Knowledge in Western Religion*, op. cit., pp. 133-134.

career of man or of communicating and qualifying the splendors and tragedies of existence, there need be no singular apology for speaking of *religious truth*.

ON RELIGIOUS TRUTH AND REVELATION

If an angel comes to me, what proof is there that it's an angel? And if I hear voices, what proof is there that they come from heaven and not from hell, or from the sub-conscious, or a pathological condition?

JEAN-PAUL SARTRE

One of the most serious hindrances to honest and sympathetic inquiry into the validity of religious judgment and the wisdom of religious men is the widespread assumption that religious experience and claims are inspired or provoked only by the most unusual events or circumstances such as special revelation, extraordinary visions, mystical trance, or direct encounters between God and the individual person. A frequent corollary of such premises is that religious judgments are absolutely beyond the reach or need of validating inquiries or justifying procedures.

But surely unless there is some way of distinguishing true from false revelation or pretenders from genuine prophets, all claims of revealed truth must be logically regarded as equally dubious. At least the arguments against special revelation are more cogent than arguments for it, considered either rationally or pragmatically. Rationally considered, the claim that religious judgment is based on or derived from some special revelation has by its own admission no support at all in reason. For a claim to revelation is precisely the claim that reasonable support is neither possible nor necessary. And pragmatically considered, the argument for special revelation is completely self-defeating. For if a person should accept even a small proportion of the different claims which are purportedly based on revelation, he undoubtedly would find himself committed to utterly contradictory beliefs and actions. No instance of so-called special revelation is either self-evidently so or subject to proof that it is so.

Yet it should also be noted that when taken as serious and responsible judgment, the appeal to revelation, far from being—as many suppose—simply arbitrary and arrogant, may be a profound and humble recognition of the dark origins and status of all man's knowledge. Indeed all knowledge is or may be regarded as a gift from the unknown. As Socrates and Plato suggested in the theory of reminiscence, or that knowing is remembering what the soul experienced in a previous existence, the ultimate origins of our most ordinary ideas is finally dark and inexplicable. So as C. S. Peirce observed, "Faiths lay claim to divine authorship; and it is true that men have no more *invented* them, than birds have invented their songs."[84] Or as Einstein reputedly said, the most incomprehensible aspect of the universe is the very fact that it is comprehensible. It is of course often possible to discover or reconstruct in retrospect the apparent sources and elements of the most creative or original and complex thought. But such discoveries and reconstructions clearly do not *explain* how or why an idea occurred in the first place and provide no rules for the direction of the mind in the pursuit of further ideas. Indeed freedom of thought and speech is justified in part precisely by the occurrence of original and important ideas in unexpected quarters and in ways past finding out.

But the mystery of the origin of ideas, if it should be called that, does not distinguish the winged words of the prophet from the sheerest sort of poetry or even from the formulae that guide men in their scientific and most practical endeavors. No matter how much one strives for novel and effective ideas, their occurrence is always largely gratuitous, their form unanticipated and often surprising, and their results largely unpredictable. Copernicus, Newton, Hume, and Darwin might have claimed the sanction of revelation for their theories or Shakespeare and Shelley for their poetry, and no one could have offered decisive evidence to the contrary. But what would any one of them have gained by the claim? Perhaps a greater momentary popularity attained perhaps at

[84] Charles Sanders Peirce, *op. cit.*, footnote to 5.380.

the cost of critical examination and appreciation of their own efforts and the intrinsic and functional excellence of their achievements.

Ideas, or judgment in its many forms, must be evaluated finally not by their origin, but by their truth or by their relevance to the interests, questions, and problems of men. If all origins are dark and deep, there is little profit or distinction in the claim that certain ideas originated in some *deus abscondus*. When all ideas are recognized as wonderful there is no point in seeking an extraordinary origin for a select few, even though they may have extraordinary functions in our lives. If the worth of an idea is dependent on special revelation, the content is in effect nullified. Or if the idea is intrinsically and functionally important, the claim that it is justified by revelation is superfluous apart from genuine evidence that the powers which produce the most common ideas are not also sufficient to generate the most extraordinary.

Consequently religious judgments cannot be validated, even though they may be made more persuasive to some, by an appeal to revelation. There is no sound reason to suppose that a thoroughly critical approach to religious judgment is less necessary than the use of rigorous logical and empirical tests in science and philosophy. Furthermore there is also no reason to suppose that religious judgment or knowledge is any less tentative, temporal, functional, and circumstantial than the claims of current physics and epistemology. Yet this does not necessarily imply that there is no enduring or eternal reality against which truth claims can sometimes be measured or which supports our conceptual and symbolic systems and processes. It means rather only that, luminous and impressive as the discoveries and creations of man are, there may still be many more astounding things to come than all our sciences, arts, philosophies, and religions have yet revealed, discovered, created, or even suspected.

Indeed to deny the necessity of continuous critical evaluation of religious perspectives is to surrender the mansions of religion to the indiscriminate practices of every nomadic visionary who mistakes his fears, hopes, and illusions for the most substantial reality. And such practices will surely offend the sensibilities of the serious truth-seekers who wish to dwell there but who may, out of respect for themselves and the truth, leave the house to be totally ruined by the lack of discipline. For the person who lives in the house of religion is no less in need of credentials and discipline than he who lives in the house of science or philosophy. Yet the demand for more than partial and provisional credentials, which are all anyone can offer, or for disciplines that frustrate new developments and growth, excludes not only the visionaries whose motives are dubious but also the most honest and responsible pilgrims.

ON RELIGION AS ONLY SYMPTOMATIC

Religious truth must be developed from knowledge acquired when our ordinary senses and intellectual operations are at their highest pitch of discipline. To move one step from this position towards the dark recesses of abnormal psychology is to surrender finally any hope of a solid foundation for religious doctrine.

A. N. WHITEHEAD

As symbolic and conceptual systems informed by feelings, perceptions, imagination, and communal concern, religions are at least prima facie no less eligible for judicial functions and veridical quality than the sciences and philosophy. Yet much, if not all, religion has often been regarded, especially in recent centuries, as essentially the by-product of forces or conditions which overwhelm and frustrate the cognitive powers of man. And indeed songs of despair and desperate hope, prayers of anxious petition, and disenchanted curses are apparently often and simply evoked *from* man by the terribly alien and destructive powers which surround him. And on this level religion may seem and in fact sometimes be very largely symptomatic—a product, as many Marxists, Freudians, and other social philosophers and scientists have sometimes claimed, of particular economic, neurotic, cultural, or social conditions but in no sense a judicial form or cognitive power by which man's awareness of himself and the world is genuinely increased or favorably modified. And certainly there seems little reason to doubt that even the most genuine and genial powers and values of even the highest forms of religion may be destroyed by various circumstances while the vestiges of religion remain.

But if all religion were simply a by-product or a symptom of nonreligious conditions and forces, there could be only two senses in which one might speak of its truth neither of which is comparable to the truth claimed for the sciences and philosophy. In the first place one might claim that such religion is *true to* the needs of a people, an inevitable expression of or a satisfying release from painful stresses and strains or perhaps a reflection of joys and hopes which have biological and economic explanations. On this level, then, religion might be regarded as a *true symptom,* in much the same sense that a certain rash and a fever are *true symptoms* of a particular disease. But such symptomatic religion would be related to genuine judgment and knowledge only in the sense that it provides the anthropologist, sociologist, or psychologist with clues which might be used to interpret or understand and provide therapy for the problems and failures of a culture or an individual.

Secondly, one might claim that such symptomatic religion provides knowledge in the sense of immediate acquaintance or in the sense that one knows *truly* what a disease is by having it. Religion so conceived is simply a subjective experience which occurs in certain circumstances; and one knows what it means to be religious, but nothing more, only by being in or passing through the circumstances and the experience. But again such symptomatic religion is neither true nor a judicial action nor a cognitive pronouncement in any fundamental sense. It is rather an experience comparable to the ephemeral effect produced by liquor, drugs, or disease. Being truly religious, if this is in fact an accurate account of religion, can only be compared to such conditions as being truly intoxicated, truly sick at one's stomach, or truly neurotic— or in any case, an instance of having something done to one, something that one suffers, rather than a mode of active and purposive judgment. The matters of fundamental importance are then the *causes* of religion and not the *meaning* of religious symbols and claims. Such analyses of religion in spite of their utter inadequacy have sometimes led the less critical sociologists and psychologists to suppose that they understand the religious person much better than the religious person can ever understand himself.

Yet the inadequacy of the claim that religion is basically only symptomatic is of course not clearly self-evident. However, no such analysis has ever made at all clear the criteria by which genuine judicial activity or knowledge is distinguished from merely symptomatic claims and behavior. It is certainly not very helpful to say simply that science and philosophy provide more adequate descriptions and explanations of all that is; for at their very best science and philosophy can describe and explain only certain kinds of events or entities and then only in terms of very special categories; their adequacy depends altogether on what is demanded or sought and on their basic premises rather than on some self-evident and unqualified sufficiency. So although religion, at least in some respects, can perhaps be "explained" in the categories of any number of sciences or inquiries—in terms of the physics and chemistry of sight and sound; in terms of the physical instruments, processes, and mediums that make its concepts and symbols possible; in terms of biological processes and needs; or in historical, semantic, or psychological, and sociological terms—this by no means entails the symptomatic or secondary character of religion itself. For even as one type of "explanation" does not preclude the others, all together need not preclude the more fundamental possibility that religion also "reveals" or "discovers" and is therefore a mode of deliberately assimilating and radically qualifying selected aspects of the existential complex which includes man.

The claim that religion is only symptomatic also clearly fails to account adequately for the apparently profound influence of religion on the character of both individuals and cultures. The influence of religious beliefs and practices on economic, social, and intellectual events, though plainly not always for the better, is apparently an inseparable part of man's most deliberate actions, and therefore of his most impressive judicial history, even if thoroughly consistent patterns of influence and evidence of necessary connections are lacking. The inescapable presence of churches, temples, sectarian schools, and religious books is the obvious, but perhaps not the most important, evidence of the effect religion has on the entire range of modern man's thought and activity. That all this is essentially symptomatic and not genuinely judicial is of course a metaphysical possibility; but if this is in fact the case, then it is at least equally possible that all the arts and the sciences are only symptomatic of dark and intricate involvement in powers and processes about which man has absolutely no genuine knowledge and over which he has no control. But in such reasoning, reason can of course ultimately only affirm its own futility.

Furthermore, the view that religious activities are only symptomatic of the stresses and strains in the various areas of experience cannot at all account for either the universality of religious practices or the great diversity of religious symbols and beliefs. For only as a fundamental form of experience and judgment but related to all the existential, imaginative, and conceptual powers of man, can the magnificent diversity in religious symbols and beliefs be in some measure accounted for or understood. And nothing less than a judicious, if only implicit, recognition of its relevance in dealing with certain crucial problems would seem to justify and sustain religion, with its characteristic assumptions and activities, so universally and in every sort of culture and circumstance. No doubt religion begins spontaneously, as do the arts and sciences, in the interaction of specifically human powers with the objective elements of existence. But religions are also plainly developed, along with the arts, sciences, and social and economic practices, with deliberate concern for personal and communal welfare and in the support of the dynamic order supposedly required by man's qualitative interests and needs.

As Whitehead suggests, to regard religion as a psychological or sociological symptom is to dismiss the possibility of its truth. Yet a defense of religion as true or as an effective mode of judgment must insist not necessarily that any specific religious doctrine is eternally relevant, but only that man in fact recognizes and modifies certain crucial aspects of existence by acting and speaking religiously. Religious ideals, actions, and claims—if the truth of religion is to be defended at all—must function not as symptomatic evidence of stress or joy but as effective discoveries or recognitions of existential conditions and possibilities.

And indeed when a religious object or an object possessing religious quality is identified by consciousness, there is no more apparent reason to assume that this quality is reducible to some neurological condition or sociological complex or that its ontological and judicial significance is thereby nullified if it is so reducible than there is to assume that the quality of inductive and deductive reasoning is primarily neurological or sociological in origin and function. The religious judgment, far from clearly reflecting only the predilection of subjective sensibility and emotion or the consensus of social opinion and trends, seems often to flow from and to affect the conclusions of both observation and strictly logical argument or to be essentially both objective and highly individualistic in their origins and social chiefly in important consequences and functions. At least no account of the religions can ignore either the manner in which they reflect the influence of such objective phenomena as the starry sky, the changing seasons, and "all the furniture of the earth" or their apparent influence on social structures and events. Surely if psychological or sociological explanation of logic and the sciences is ultimately impossible or at least possible only in ways largely irrelevant to their judicial power and validity, the same may also be claimed in regard to religious experience and judgment. In fact to suggest that logic and the sciences are essentially immune to reductive psychological and sociological analysis but that the religions and the arts are fair game for such reductive approaches is to exhibit an unreasonable and arbitrary faith in one method and subject matter while denying that similar faiths are ever justified in other domains and different methods.

ON THE WORLD REQUIRED FOR RELIGIOUS JUDGMENT

> *There is a dark*
> *Inscrutable workmanship that reconciles*
> *Discordant elements, makes them cling together*
> *In one society.*
>
> William Wordsworth

If religious judgments are generally more or less trustworthy, what does this imply about the general nature of the world? Or in different but similar terms, in what kind of world can religion claim to be a necessary, appropriate, and effective mode of judgment? And is there any substantial evidence that the world is this kind of world?

First of all, it must be admitted that if the world can be known only spectatorially, religion cannot be said to be a possible way of knowing the world. If existence were knowable only spectatorially, the appeal of the logical empiricists to sensory criteria would be plainly the last word in validating all forms of judgment; and all claims not based on sensory experience would be either more or less than knowledge. For, as already admitted, the empiricists are clearly correct in denying that religious judgments can be validated by sensory experience. The truth or significance of religious judgment is then inconceivable in the world envisaged by thoroughgoing empiricists or positivists. On the other hand, both the rationalists and the pragmatists conceive a universe in which religious judgments might be both possible and judicially significant or true. The evidence, however, is quite insufficient to justify completely either the claim that existence possesses the harmony required by the coherence theory of truth or that there is the general affinity between the useful and the actual envisaged by the pragmatists. The experience of man is finally witness to neither pervasive harmony nor a cosmos designed primarily to satisfy his needs and desires. Nonetheless men may of course often judge truly and effectively by seeking coherent evidence for hypotheses and elaborate theories or by claims and actions based on insights into their own needs and desires. Coherence and usefulness, no less than careful observation, may bear witness to the truth.

But judgment is more diverse in form and more precariously based than conventional forms of rationalism can allow and also sometimes more objective and disinterested than pragmatism apparently supposes. For there is evidently only a flexible or loose continuity and a mutual sensitivity between the manifold events and features of existence. Yet even the stars and planets, if modern theories of physics are to be trusted, are not altogether "blind" to their existential situation and are at least in some primitive sense "moved" by each other. An object, whether characterized by subjectivity or not, is therefore largely what its contextual relations make it; and the question of just what an entity or creature is wholly independent of its environment is apparently unanswerable precisely because there is in fact no such thing. This seems most clearly and intensely the case with living organisms. But of course each distinguishable and enduring thing, whether animate or inanimate, must also be envisaged as a more or less unique structure which reacts to or assimilates and manipulates the environment in its own ways. But the difference between highly similar structures in discrete environments soon becomes significantly more than mere differences of spatial location and external relations. Consequently judgment may presumably reflect, not only the generic modes of choosing and acting and unique forms or degrees of independence, but also the specific existential involvement and relations of the individual.

Now if it is the case that man's symbol-making capacities and conceptual powers are rooted in, though they may also transcend, the mutual sensitivities of the diverse elements of existence to each other, there is certainly no reason why sense experience is the only or chief or even an indispensable source of judgment or knowledge as such. In fact Whitehead seems to be eminently right; the senses are ultimately superficial and misleading insofar as they suggest the complete independence of the organs of perception and the perceived objects. Indeed the senses do not witness at all the complex involvement and interaction of things and events with each other.[85] Only deliberate experiment and reasonable inference, made possible primarily by symbolic and conceptual schemes, ever reveal the vast and intricate web of interdependence pervading the manifold elements of existence. In other words, judgment, which presumably requires *both* the sensitivity or "openness" of one individual to another and some degree of independence, is apparently guided by conceptual schemes and symbols which are subject to every imaginable form of influence, including reflective critical analysis and rejection, and is both directed and sustained by a persistent sense for matters of importance. So standards of judgment are never set simply, if at all, by precise and arbitrary labelings of matters of fact discriminated by sight and hearing. Indeed, as suggested earlier, it is altogether dubious that there are any such simple facts. In any case it is hardly an exaggeration to say that the sense of worth is infinitely less dispensable in the pursuit of judicial cogency than the sense of either sight or hearing. For the existence of man qua man is clearly not most distinctively a matter of discriminable quantitative facts, but a unified and dynamic direction of energies and susceptibilities (or openness) guided by a sense for the important and a constant demand for the invention of concepts and symbols "for meanings as yet unexpressed."

All judgment is then plainly and certainly the product of experience but of an experience that is an intricate embrace of individuals who are valuable both for themselves and for each other, and who do not exist independently of one another, rather than the experience of a completely detached spectator. David Hume was no doubt verbally right, "Our ideas reach no farther than our experience."[86] But the reach of experience is evidently sometimes surprisingly vast if judged by the resulting ideas and theories which not only unify seemingly discrete phenomena, but also lead to the discovery of unsuspected facts and relations. Experience reaches into the deepest and darkest recesses of exist-

---

[85] A. N. Whitehead, *Modes of Thought*, New York, Putnam, Capricorn Books, 1958, pp. 41 and 181.

[86] David Hume, *Dialogues Concerning Natural Religion*, New York, Hafner, 1948, p. 16.

ence, into the past and future, and is often consummated in judgments that surprise men—when they are at all modest and self-conscious—with their own wisdom. Or as Whitehead has said: "In being ourselves we are more than ourselves" and "our experience, dim and fragmentary as it is, yet sounds the utmost depths of reality."[87] The problem of knowledge, perhaps ultimately as insoluble as it is fascinating, is clearly not wholly distinct from the problem of existence: man knows that he is and that he knows but not how he came to be or how he knows. But in experience man and the elements of the world he knows are not independent one of another. They are wedded, however, not by a superficial or legal ceremony, but by an awesome and inviolable community of being.

And in this community—composed of earth and air and sky and sea and all that is in them—man seeks with a desperate delight for perspectives that will reveal the character and relations to one another of its many and diverse elements. And not only the powers and delight of the senses but also the unseen objects of love and the longings of the heart are apparently among the most primitive and inescapable data of experience or the beginning and the indispensable support of judgment and knowledge. Philosophical and scientific speculations, as well as religious vision and social reform, seem indeed to begin often, not in any obvious incongruity between conceptual claims and sense experience, but with only a poorly articulated feeling or hunch that a theory or situation is wrong, inadequate, or discordant. Discovery and creative judgment occur when there is an awareness of—perhaps only a feeling for—a deficiency and an actual or ideal possibility. Witnesses to the fact and importance of such feelings are specific and impressive. Wrote Henri Poincaré:

> It may be surprising to see emotional sensibility invoked *a propos* of mathematical demonstrations which, it would seem, can interest only the intellect. This would be to forget the *feeling* of mathematical beauty, of the harmony of number and forms, of geometric elegance. This is a true esthetic feeling that all mathematicians know, and surely it belongs to emotional sensibility.... This har-

[87] A. N. Whitehead, *Science and the Modern World*, New York, Mentor Books, 1948, p. 20.

mony is at once a satisfaction of our esthetic needs and an aid to the mind, *sustaining* and *guiding*.[88]

Albert Einstein wrote movingly of the religious feelings of admiration and awe which inform and are informed by "the faith in the possibility that the regulations valid for the world of existence are rational, that is comprehensible to reason."[89] Robert Oppenheimer has passionately insisted that the world of the scientist is such that:

> Each of us, knowing his limitations, knowing the evils of superficiality and the terrors of fatigue, will have to cling to what is close to him, to what he knows, to what he can do, to his friends and his tradition and his love, lest he be dissolved in a universal confusion and can know and love nothing.[90]

And on the basis of such testimony by those who have devoted their lives to the pursuit of knowledge, combined with his own experience, Whitehead has suggested that nature contains "within itself a tendency to be in tune, an Eros urging towards perfection,"[91] that "progress is founded upon the experience of discordant feelings,"[92] and that the greatest adventure and the most impressive characteristic of life is "the search for new perfections."[93]

Existence, this surely suggests, must be envisaged as systems of interrelated entities which generally neither frustrate nor leave unsupported the efforts and purposes of the independent individual. Man is in the world as a flower is in the soil and air, nourished by its substance, tossed by its storms, gilded by its sunlight and shadows, and sensitive to every manner of change and quality. He is infinitely open to the world in many ways and

[88] Henri Poincaré, "Mathematical Creation," in *The Creative Process*, Brewster Ghiselin, ed., New York, Mentor Books, 1955, p. 40.

[89] Albert Einstein, "Science, Philosophy and Religion," in *Readings in Philosophy of Science*, Philip P. Weiner, ed., New York, Scribner, 1953, pp. 604-605.

[90] Robert Oppenheimer, "Art and Science in the Atomic Age," The Concluding Address of the Columbia University Bicentennial Celebration, 1954. Reprinted in *Gadfly*, Chicago, University of Chicago, March, 1955.

[91] A. N. Whitehead, *Adventures of Ideas*, New York, Macmillan, 1933, p. 323.

[92] *Ibid.*, p. 330.

[93] *Ibid.*, p. 332.

directions, even though much always remains hidden from him. Man is indeed apparently, as Martin Heidegger has called him, "the openness of Being" to the world.[94] And so only rarely are his judgments altogether illusory—though perhaps equally rare are the instances when he discovers truths that are universally and eternally significant. His judicial existence is rooted in and witness to complex structures and processes. Thus even when he seems most detached and dispassionate he speaks, acts, and creates (or in another word, judges) with the whole of his being involved in a world that supports, embraces, and informs without strangling or warping.

The world in which religious judgments are possible, relevant, and reliable is, then, a world in which the qualitative aspects of things, events, and persons are often reflected in each other, where individual choice determines in part the methods and objects of manipulation as well as the qualities which will be assimilated, and where the presence and urge of the divine or the holy, whether actual or ideal, broods over the whole and unites elements of it in the pursuit of perfections that are possible and momentous.

ON THE FORMS OF RELIGIOUS TRUTH

... there might be diversity in two symbols, supplied by two different organs of sense or two different grammars of thought, without either of the two being, in its own mode, a false symbol....

GEORGE SANTAYANA

Much of the recent difficulty in talking about the truth, if not the meaning, of religion has plainly been due to the fact that scientific propositions, conceived as ultimately and logically

---

[94] Martin Heidegger, "The Way Back Into the Ground of Metaphysics," in *Existentialism from Dostoevsky to Sartre*, Walter Kaufmann, ed., New York, Meridian Books, 1956, pp. 214-215.

coherent with each other as well as testable by sensory experience, have been so widely regarded as the paradigmatic form, if
not the very *sine qua non*, of truth. But surely the truth, conceived
as the presence or availability to a judging creature of the aspects
of being or existence which support specific activities or sustain
judicial forms, products, and processes, need be no less various,
in either form or content, than the relations between the world as
the object of judgment and the many ways through which the world
is assimilated and manipulated or judged. The truth may then
both *be* and also *signify* a part of the existential complex which
sustains a life of deliberation and choice and may include recognitions of good and evil, the contingent and the necessary, the
dangerous and the indifferent. The various forms of judgment,
within and without the religions, may also be true in radically
different ways or senses, though all forms of truth may be rightly
described as revelatory, trustworthy, or reliable modes or instances
of speaking, acting, or making. Religious ritual need not be cognitively meaningless, although it must be judged in different terms
than religious doctrine.

One traditional form of presumed religious as well as artistic
truth is that of the *ideal* and the actions and claims consistent
with it, whether the ideal is conceived as a moral possibility or an
ontological form. Aristotle, as already noted, suggested (and many
others have agreed with him) that every existing thing has an
ideal development or implicit perfection which might in favorable
circumstances be more thoroughly, if not completely, actualized.
This account of the ideal as an element of both existence and
knowledge of existence (or truth) seems altogether defensible in
many respects and is at the very least one of the most effective
forms of interpreting the demands of personal moral standards
and social justice. And the apparent power of the ideal to inspire,
here and there, its own achievement is indeed one of the most
extraordinary aspects of man's history.

Presumably, then, the religious ideals, produced as they so
very often are by sensitive, informed, and critical persons, may
appropriately claim to be *at least* ways and instances of apprehending and inspiring efforts to achieve the possibilities implicit

in the actual. (Of course, the value of apprehending the ideal need not depend altogether on achieving it. Contemplation or vision for its own sake is not always or necessarily less important or less justifiable in religion than in the arts and sciences.) And such religious ideals may be not only *true to* experience as evidence or symptoms of hopes and affections but also *true about* the existential situation insofar as they may reflect as well as be significant elements in the comprehension of the total character of actuality and possibility or insofar as they may in fact sustain the effort necessary to make the possible into the actual. And it has been often and plausibly, if not conclusively, argued that religious sensibility, reflecting on the aspects of the world that render it worshipful, first apprehended and articulated such moral ideals and possibilities as the intrinsic worth and dignity of each person, human equality, the inviolability of the right to life, and the right to counsel in a court of law as well as the purely logical concept of a universe thoroughly comprehensible to reason. And surely few "discoveries" about the nature of existence have done more to sustain and enhance the extraordinary career of man as a judging or knowing creature.

Indeed the religious ideal seems often as decisive and effective in guiding qualitative decision, though not altogether as universal or as predictable in its results, as the knowledge of physical fact and relation so obviously is in determining quantitative issues. And like scientific formulae and hypotheses or the categories of practical logic, such ideals, instead of being absolute and unchanging—though they may seem so to many who hold them—may be partial, tentative, and subject to change or even abandonment as persons and circumstances develop or alter. Yet the objective reference, relevance, and reliability of such ideals, regarded as judicial guides and instruments, need be no more put into question by their provisional character than is contemporary physics by the possibility that its particular claims may one day be superceded. Man lives by groping, by finding now one place and then another to stand while seeking directions and methods for further discovery and adventure. Even if there is no single good, no mark to be missed or no direction that can be rationally or pragmatically defended above all others, one cannot, like the proverbial cowboy, ride off in all directions at once. For to live at all it is necessary to live with some consistency of habit in choice and behavior or with the sense that greater worth lies in one direction rather than another. So a religious ideal, finely articulated and defined, may provide the necessary purpose and direction for choice and action, even if all modes of life and all decisions are ultimately arbitrary. And religious ideals may even in such cases be regarded as no less functional and true than the ruling or guiding principles of science, even though their diversity be greater and their efficacy less obvious.

Another sense in which religion may be considered true is suggested by Whitehead when he observes that "The best rendering of integral experience, expressing its general form divested of irrelevant details, is often to be found in the utterances of religious aspiration.... Accordingly we find in the first two lines of a famous hymn a full expression of the union of two notions in one integral experience:

> Abide with me
> Fast falls the even tide

Here the first line expresses the permanences, 'abide,' 'me,' and the 'Being' addressed; and the second line sets these permanences amid the inseparable flux." A sentence omitted as indicated declares that "One of the reasons of the thinness of so much modern metaphysics is its neglect of this wealth of expression of ultimate feeling."[95]

When the qualitative is not summarily dismissed as derivative or secondary but admitted as a basic category of the judicial process, Whitehead is plainly right. The search for and expression of metaphysical truth or a satisfactory articulation of the generic traits of the existential integration of fact and value or the quantitative and the qualitative in experience can hardly or wholly succeed without the singular union of form, content, and quality found in religious language. And many of the persistent paradoxes in religious claims—the emphasis on both rigorous

[95] A. N. Whitehead, *Process and Reality*, New York, Macmillan, 1929, p. 318.

discipline and unlimited aspiration, on both the sinfulness of man and the grace of God, on both the mercy and the justness of God, on vanity and splendor, on the incomparable glory and the utter misery of man's condition—seem clearly to belong to the effort to express *the truth* about man's total and unified experience. Thus the poignant Negro spiritual which declares:

> Nobody knows the trouble I've seen
> Glory Hallelujah

may also be said to express truly, if ever so briefly, a common if not universal experience: the sense of both infinite weariness and immeasurable joy which are so often inseparable and the most obvious elements in the structure of man's splendid but tragic life. His troubles are indeed so great they cannot be told; yet in the midst of them the joys of being and seeing are almost overwhelming.

Some of the profoundest aspects of experience can apparently be expressed only in religious language. Religion may then be said to be *true* to the extent that crucial aspects of "integral experience" or qualitative, and sometimes paradoxical, elements of man's total life are adequately articulated and made more generally available and subject to contemplative control through religious symbols, concepts, and activities.

Finally and perhaps most fundamentally, religious judgments may be said to be true when they identify, create, or illuminate objects of inviolable and intrinsic worth. Or in other words, religious judgments are true when what they reveal is divine or holy, or when they create, clarify, or intensify a vision which actually and consistently inspires and sustains the passion for worship.

For example, the religious vision of the Negro slave, as expressed in spirituals and in his own simple but inspired interpretation of the Bible, no doubt provided an ideal of his eventual freedom; it also reconciled him to his lot or enabled him to make decisions which the immediate circumstances demanded; and it truly expressed the integral quality of his suffering and hope. Yet it did more. In the most spontaneous song the modern world has witnessed, he not only portrayed but also transcended the com-

munity of suffering to which he belonged. The slave did not
choose the community in which he suffered—and in this respect
he may be profoundly symbolic of all mankind. But he transformed the imposed community of sorrow into a free spiritual
community of joy, at least occasionally, by assimilating and adapt-
ing to his own condition a vision of existence which had already
a long history of revealing the sacred and making worship possible
to the spirit caught in circumstances impossible to reconcile with
human dignity and temporal hopes. His judgment was not essentially a search or petition for superhuman comfort and aid
but a creative transformation of the self and the community. In
his religious vision he escaped slavery and dwelt, at least for the
moment, in the order of splendor that is revealed when, by choice
or necessity, the spirit regards the world *sub specie aeternitas*.
When there is no hope in time, eternity butts in. When small
ambitions and pleasures are denied, a man may lift his eyes
and catch a vision of the splendor which no man has made and
which no man can altogether deny another. Such vision is the
mysterious womb and the unmerited fruit of the passion for worship; and the religion which consistently reveals or creates
such a vision of the world may be called true, regardless of whether
it is shared by few or many and even though it may be an inconclusive sign of the enduring order of existence.

The great visions of the Psalmist, the Buddha, Jesus,
Augustine, and even the tentative cosmology of Socrates—where
all things are ordered as is best—belong primarily to this genre
of religious truth and bear the same general relation to religious
life and judgment as the extraordinary theoretical achievements
of a Newton, Darwin, or Einstein do to the ongoing careers of
the sciences and scientists. Without such men, religion (or, as the
case may be, science) of a low order would of course still inform
and guide the lives of many if not most men; but great vision
and achievement are generally possible to all but the genius only
in the presence of luminous symbols and concepts which already
point the way.

If the religions may claim to be true *at least* in the three
ways indicated above—by being the source and expression of

ideals which may be actualized or which may guide various activities, by being the only effective modes of articulating certain qualities of integral experience, and by creating visions or providing revelations of the world which inspire and sustain worship— what about the so-called *literal truth* of claims, so important to many individuals and religious perspectives, concerning the existence of a personal God, the immortality of the soul, and the cosmic significance of righteousness?

The very notion of literal truth involves serious difficulties which are not often recognized or admitted. In the strictest sense of the term nothing is *literally true* except the word-for-word repetition of what has previously been said. But of course the phrase has come to be largely synonymous with "verifiable fact," as opposed to "mere symbol," "metaphor," "figurative language," "myth," "parable," etc. But surely it is now generally clear that existence is much too complex, judgment much too diverse in form and function, and verification much too complicated and dependent on particular interests or purposes to suppose that there is some "open sesame" by which we enter and leave the realms of literal and symbolic truths. In any case claims about the existence of God and immortality are not *symbolic* in any weak sense of the term, though they may be called *fictional*, since they are neither verifiable nor falsifiable, *if* as Moses Maimonides claimed in commenting on the story of Job, it may be said that fiction sometimes "includes profound ideas and great mysteries, removes great doubt, and reveals the most important truths."[96] The concepts of God and immortality are at least ideals which may function in the same manner and be considered true in the same sense as any ideal which may reveal more clearly the character of the actual. Furthermore, although from the perspective of man the light of the divine shining out of creation and not a personal Divine Creator is the primary datum, the concept of God is not only as satisfactory as any way yet devised to account for certain aspects of existence, including the religious experience, but also casts into sharp relief man's frailty—intellectual, artistic, moral, and physical—against the presumed handiwork of beneficent

[96] Moses Maimonides, *The Guide for the Perplexed*, New York, Dover, 1956, p. 296.

omnipotence. Also the stark mortality of man is, to all appearances, inescapable. Yet even mortality acquires much of its specifically human character—sharply tragic and ever present, an absurd limitation—in the light of the concept of the possibility of immortality.

Belief in the existence of a personal God and immortality are religiously important, however, only to the extent that the significance or efficacy of religious symbols and activities may be said to depend upon the existence of God or to the extent that it may be plausibly argued that the fact or quality of a future life is dependent on aspects of life here and now which are directly related to religious symbols and activities. Certainly religion as such requires neither of these beliefs in order to survive or to be true in the ways indicated above; and presumably the truth of both claims would be less than reliable indication that religion is either required by God or effective in attaining a desirable form of immortality. A personal God may conceivably exist but disapprove of all the characteristically religious beliefs and activities while existence may, without a personal God, be such that the religious forms of judgment are the only effective ways of apprehending and communicating certain aspects of it. Or immortality might indeed be the case and religion the most ineffective way of securing a desirable form of it.

Basically, then, claims and questions concerning the existence of God and immortality, which have of course appeared widely and often in experience and reason, are philosophical rather than religious or require a speculative and logical rather than a symbolic and devotional articulation. Speculative and logical capacities, however, are rarely among the conspicuous features of the profoundly religious mind. And a theology is at best only a backhanded justification of religion since it seeks to account for and validate immediate qualities of experience, which are intrinsically valuable, by an appeal to abstract argument. Consequently the question of the truth of religion is, in certain basic respects, completely different from the question of the truth of a theology. For a religion is not primarily a form of argument—even though an argument may occasionally be one of the most effective forms of worship or of articulating that which is presumably holy or inviolable, as in the case of Saint Anselm's ontological argument for God's existence and especially in Saint Augustine's eulogistic but nonetheless analytical demonstration of the amazing powers of the soul.

However, insofar as claims concerning the existence of God and immortality are integral parts of a particular religious perspective and commitment, as they may surely be, they must of course be articulated religiously. And this may involve but is never only a theological or a philosophical and logical enterprise. A religion is bound to confront and worship the holy as it appears here and now, without undue speculation about its source and the future. And no particular envisagement of the origin of the divine, the destiny of the soul, and the cosmic significance of righteousness can be made the *sine qua non* of religious truth. It must, nonetheless, be humbly admitted that the wide appeal of such claims to informed and critical minds, in both religious and philosophical contexts, is a notable, though by no means an unquestionable or decisive, factor in their favor. No argument can in fact ever be conclusive in such matters, regardless of how persuasive it may be. Consciousness, for example, can never be sure—no matter how perfect the world that presumably sustains it—that it will endure.

And so every person who is tempted by right and unselfish reason to believe in the existence of a personal God and the immortality of the soul will also say with Socrates that his case is based ultimately on the faith that "All things are ordered as is best" and that "A man of sense will not insist that these things are exactly as I have described them. But I think that he will believe that something of the kind is true . . . and that it is worth his while to stake everything on this belief."[97] For in the end every account of the way the world is, no matter how detailed and comprehensive, must, like the description of an image within an image ad infinitum, always stop short and leave the rest to fancy or to faith.

[97] Plato, *The Phaedo*, trans. by F. J. Church, New York, Liberal Arts, 1951, p. 70.

ON THE WAYS OF VALIDATING RELIGIOUS JUDGMENTS

But the dogmas, however true, are only bits of the truth, expressed in terms which in some ways are over-assertive and in other ways lose the essence of truth.

A. N. WHITEHEAD

How are religious judgments—symbols, ideals, claims, and actions—justified or validated? The first important word on this matter is that complete or final validation is neither necessary nor possible. On the one hand, as a spontaneous event recognizing and expressing the holy, the religious symbol, activity, or claim is validated simply by being created, performed, or made. On the other hand, as Justus Buchler has said, "The incompletion within life is perpetual," and only continuous query (including of course invention and artistic creation as well as practical and moral activities and scientific investigation) can prevent "stagnation and ruin."[98] This is singularly true of the intellectual and spiritual life. A completely static or dogmatic religion may of course serve as a stabilizing factor in an unchanging community. But if a religion belongs to the progressive life of discovery and creativity, to the most significant forms of judicial power, validation of one sort or another must be somehow and continuously possible.

One, and perhaps the most familiar, way of validating religious judgments is to explore and articulate their immediate relations to the claims and activities which are primarily moral and scientific. Yet religious judgments are, as we have already argued, notably unique and autonomous; consequently, there is of course little or no reason to suppose that they must or will be altogether consonant with either moral or scientific judgments.

---

[98] Justus Buchler, *Towards a General Theory of Human Judgment*, New York, Columbia, 1951, p. 169.

If radical incompatibilities and incongruities cannot be eliminated *within* the moral and scientific perspectives themselves, it is certainly unrealistic to expect that religious judgments should conform to either the logic or the substance of science and morals. For in scope, religious judgments are in certain respects more comprehensive and their form and content are even more intractable than either scientific or moral judgments. Science attempts chiefly to understand, to anticipate and control, quantitative facts and relations in the light of experimental evidence and general laws; and purely rational morality seeks excellence as well as security in a compromise between ideal goods and actual dangers. In the strictest sense scientific judgment as such must ignore qualitative factors, including the intrinsic worth and apparent causal efficacy of the qualitative aspects of certain experiences as well as the regulative functions of ideals; and any purely rational system of morality, based on the logic of social interaction and the search for relative security, must emphasize the dangers which perennially threaten to wreck or destroy the individual or the community, rather than the radiance and splendor that move men to worship. On the other hand, though there is surely no justification of the claim that any and every world view or integrating philosophy which envisions a ground and destiny for man is a religion, every religion is a specific envisagement of the divine and may affect many, if not all, of the dimensions of life.

Religious symbols, claims, and actions cannot then be comprehended in the logic of science and morals; and religion must always guard jealously its right and obligation to speak in *critical* and *informed* disagreement with current scientific theories and ethical ideals, particularly when the scientific and moral enterprises suppose that their own modes of judgment are exhaustive or completely sufficient. The person in whom the sense of the holy is profound or highly developed and informed, no less than the person whose logical powers are acute and highly cultivated, may presumably speak with authority in his own terms. And there is no necessity and apparently no possibility or even desirability of completely accommodating religious vision and judgment to scientific and moral perspectives.

Yet religion is at best only one among several modes of

judgment and can never assume that science and moral philosophy are irrelevant or dispensable. If religion is not simply morality or a pseudoscience which becomes extinct or irrelevant as conceptual knowledge increases in scope and power, neither are science and morals merely the handmaidens of religion. Religion must for the most part transcend or complement and not contradict scientific and philosophic judgment. In other words, that religion is truest which, admitting the genuine relevance of the best established perspectives in science and morals, can speak most cogently in its own terms and without apology about the existential nature and needs of man. If a religious vision reveals clearly the need for moral reform or suggests that current scientific accounts of nature and man neglect matters of critical importance, religious persons *ought* to speak boldly and unequivocally in behalf of their insights and convictions. If on the other hand scientific and moral developments clearly imply, as they may, the falsity or immorality of some particular religious belief or practice, revision can (if religion is actually a fundamental mode of judgment) be undertaken with confidence that every specious loss will be compensated by a genuine gain.

Indeed only the religions that are able to adjust to the requirements of critical, comprehensive, and constantly changing knowledge and experience can expect to maintain and augment perspectives and traditions which command the respect and support the values of an age dedicated to—and indeed radically dependent upon—the constant increase of scientific knowledge and greatly in need of moral sensitivity and ethical concepts relevant to its own peculiar predicaments. A religion is then partially justified when its voice is neither silenced nor intimidated by the scientific and social changes which require adjustments in its own teachings and practices—even though the religion that endures without significant adjustments in times of revolutionary changes in science and society may very well be simply blind and dogmatic rather than true and relevant. So this method of validating religious judgments is of course very limited and essentially negative or indicates not so much the significant and enduring truth of a religious mode of judgment as that other modes do not nullify its claims. The method is nonetheless important, and a religion that cannot meet this test is rarely of unmixed value—and may be a positive danger—to the community.

A second method by which religious judgments may be justified or validated is by examining and articulating their relations to historical events and processes.

But this must not be interpreted to mean that to verify the historicity of an event is to establish its religious truth or significance. Even as, in the words of Albert Camus, "History explains neither the natural universe that existed before it nor the beauty that exists above it,"[99] so even the most etxraordinary historical events as such have no religious value. Aside from all the methodological difficulties and existential conditions which make every conclusion about historical facts partial and dubious, the historicity of a religion is not in itself of profound significance. Supposing, for instance, it could be established beyond a reasonable doubt that Moses in fact came face to face with Jehovah on Mount Sinai or that Jesus lived, said, and did all that is recorded, was crucified, and left his tomb on the third day, the religious truth (as distinct from the historical truth) of the Bible and these exceptional events would be validated only if such literal truth is clearly and inevitably related to the power of inspiring and informing religious movements and sustaining in men a sense of the presence of the holy. And although historical truth is by no means altogether and always religiously unimportant, in many instances the obviously fictional event or entity, the parable, the myth, or the dramatic tragedy may speak most effectively about the sacred or about what is required and forbidden by the presence of the divine. Even as the history of physics is not and does not validate physics, so the history of a religion (whether of Christianity, Judaism, or Buddhism) is not and does not justify the current forms of religious judgment. Yet this does not deny that the substance, power, and significance of both religious perspectives and physical theories may be more thoroughly understood by way of historical inquiry and analysis.

But important as history may be to a fuller understanding

[99] Albert Camus, The Myth of Sisyphus, trans. by J. O'Brien, New York, Knopf, Vintage Books, 1959, p. 136.

of the existence of anything which involves particular historical events or temporal developments, no religion can be significantly validated by an appeal to historical events simply as such. The critical intellect is bound to demand, not primarily that the mottled history of the religions be spread before it as evidence of their grounding in fact, but that the religions prove themselves, by their judicial and qualitative cogency or by their total effects in the lives of men, to be revelatory and beneficent modes of articulating current and existential perplexities. Clearly the crucial question is, not whether ancient prophets articulated the demands of the holy in a particular situation, but whether their words and deeds have also consistently guided men in their continuing search for the divine.

Therefore, the historical validation of religion which is important, and perhaps in some, though surely limited, measure possible, involves discriminating the apparent effects of religious thought and action in significant historical achievements or in the processes of historical development to determine whether or not particular instances, as well as the general modes, of religious judgment have also been ways of effectively guiding and sustaining the contexts of beneficent decision or revelatory creation and action. The manifold threads of history are of course infinitely complex and never completely separable. To trace the effects of any single factor is invariably difficult and perhaps always dubious. This is particularly true in the case of religion. For religious concern about the qualitative · character of life is itself inseparable from social, political, economic, artistic, and scientific interests and achievements. So while there is, as noted earlier, a sense in which the history of art or science may be written without extensive reference to other elements of culture, a history of religion is clearly impossible without continuous attention to other areas and modes of experience and judgment. A history of religion without such attention would touch only the aesthetic surface and articulate nothing of the qualitative or regulative effects of religious vision and commitment on existential problems. Thus the very conditions which render the historical validation of religion possible and necessary also by their great complexity make such validation exceedingly problematical.

Many historical accounts have of course claimed that the religions have had the most decisive roles—by default if not by some positive influence—in determining the character and direction of civilization. Although all such accounts are perhaps far from definitive, much of the burden of proof, nonetheless, obviously seems to rest with those who claim either that religion is wholly an effect rather than an influential part of the total culture or that religion has always hindered rather than promoted cultural and intellectual progress. No doubt the claims of religious historians have frequently been grossly exaggerated, partly because their aim has so often been to exonerate religion or a particular religious tradition of all blame for catastrophe and tragedy. But judgment is of course rarely justified by apologetics; and any significant validation of religion in terms of history must, like a similar approach to social problems and the sciences, discriminate the narrow alleys and dead ends from the ways of creative discovery and adventure.

Yet to distinguish clearly between what has happened because of religion and what would have happened anyway, we have in effect admitted, is perhaps always impossible. However, this need not suggest that it is therefore completely impossible to determine the approximate direction in which religious ideals and commitments have moved men and events if they have moved them at all. For example, as long as there is no decisive evidence to the contrary, the argument remains cogent that the idea of the inestimable worth of the individual and the unparalleled effectiveness of the relations and actions based on this idea, including the growth of democracy and personal rights, have been intimately, if not inevitably, related to religious ideals, insights, no quantitative factors or social analysis can discover or arouse and teaching. Obviously no merely sensory or logical processes and and support the conviction that each individual is of singular and inestimable worth.

It seems also to be of more than merely incidental significance that important scientific inquiry and discovery have sometimes evidently derived their original inspiration and direction at least in part from the attempt to justify the ways of God to man or from the effort to show that religious doctrines are altogether compatible with, or even required by, the nature of existence and intelligence. More interesting and relevant, however, is the apparently more direct influence of religious concepts on the very origin and logic of certain scientific movements. In this connection John Herman Randall, Jr. has recently noted in *The Career of Philosophy* that although "In general it seems fairly clear that Newton's theological ideas were determined by his scientific concepts," it is also true that "The more famous of Newton's assumptions—like those of absolute time and absolute space, which awakened vigorous criticism in his own generation—were made more plausible by the theological background of his natural philosophy."[100] But they were not for that reason any more dispensable:

> Absolute time and space are God's sensorium: by existing God constitutes them, as the container wherein all motions take place. This Divine Sensorium or Mind sustains the entire world of physics. . . . The consequences of the necessity of such a constitutive mind have been momentous for the subsequent philosophy of physical science. . . . Despite all the drive towards positivism, such a mind, whether taken as God or reason, has persisted in some form as an ultimate physical concept. Where such a constitutive mind has been wholly lacking, as in the empirical tradition, natural science has had little structure or permanence; and empiricists have been always committed to trying to persuade physicists that their science ought to be a far different kind of thing, and ought to have a far different kind of structure, from what it in fact is and has.[101]

And other notable scholars have argued that religious assumptions and ideals influenced decisively the beginnings, if not also the development, of modern science. With an obvious exaggeration that ignores the other side of the coin, D. M. MacKinnon has claimed, "By clearing away all sorts of false and frightening views of the way the universe worked, Paul helped later generations to explore its secrets without fear of malign forces. And with confidence of success too; for its processes were no longer regarded

[100] John H. Randall, Jr., *The Career of Philosophy*, New York, Columbia, 1962, pp. 582-583.
[101] *Ibid.*, pp. 591-592.

as governed by their caprice."[102] The same vision and trust that sustained Paul's passion for worship, MacKinnon in effect claims, also helped to prepare the way for scientific inquiry and discovery. But Whitehead has made a more creditable case for a similar view with the argument that the great confidence which the earliest modern scientists had in their inquiries and which supported their "incredible labours" was based on the "inexpungable belief that every detailed occurrence can be correlated with its antecedents in a perfectly definite manner, exemplifying general principles," and that this idea in turn originated in "the medieval insistence on the rationality of God, conceived as with the personal energy of Jehovah and with the rationality of a Greek philosopher."[103] Again, the argument is that a religiously conceived universe or the ideal which justified worship and sustained the view that existence is essentially holy was also the immediate source of the guiding principles of the measurable universe of science.

Yet granting that MacKinnon and Whitehead are perfectly correct about the great influence of religious ideas on the beginnings of modern science, the fact is surely less than proof that Paul's or the medieval concept of the universe is either sufficient or necessary for the appearance and development of either scientific or religious ideas. But the correctness of the claim, could it be established as highly probable, would be powerful support for the view that religious beliefs, attitudes, and actions may be among the most decisive—if not the most revelatory—in the total direction and quality of a civilization. Indeed if religion has only a fraction of the influence suggested by its apparent effects on ideas and practices which recognize the worth of individual persons or on the beginnings of modern science as proposed by MacKinnon and Whitehead, it is clearly important both practically and intellectually and ought surely to receive the most critical attention and care. Nor does the truth of Whitehead's hypothesis by any means imply that religion is simply an earlier and necessary but less rigorous and dispensable method of constructing and adopting

[102] D. M. MacKinnon and Antony Flew, "Creation," in *New Essays in Philosophical Theology, op. cit.,* p. 176.
[103] A. N. Whitehead, *Science and the Modern World, op. cit.,* p. 13.

theories about the nature of the cosmos and man. As a fundamental form of judgment religion has little in common with
science, and cannot—except in an age of credulity toward the
supposedly unlimited powers of the one or the other to reveal
or manipulate the conditions of existence—come into conflict
with it. Even though science may have been made possible by
ideals and methods which originated in religious faith and vision
—at least to the extent that such factors might have been the
decisive influence—science is nonetheless a different form of
thought, a judicial mode in which the canons of adequacy or truth
are altogether and inevitably different from the requirements of
effective religious judgment. Religion and science, even as politics
and technology or biology and microscopy, may influence each
other decisively without the one being in any sense reducible to
the terms of the other. And such mutual influence, whether for
better or worse, can at least sometimes be best discovered and
articulated through historical inquiries.

And although no historical inquiry can possibly show that
religious claims are eternally true, the historical discovery that
religious symbols and ideals are significant elements in the deliberate decisions and effective actions which determine the course and
quality of culture would surely indicate that being religious is
no less important existentially than other forms of possessing and
exhibiting intelligence or other ways of revealing and qualifying
both the judicial capacity of man and the world as an object of
judgment. Religious enthusiasts must remember, however, that
if religious judgments may be justified by historical inquiries, they
may also be condemned. If one looks to history for support of the
religious modes of judgment, he must not close his eyes to the
evidence that contradicts his claims and hopes.

The third and final method of validating religious judgments is
by the continuous process of judging religiously. Religion for religion's sake is not obviously or intrinsically any less defensible
than art for art's sake or science for the sake of science. And if it
may be said with some reason that man actualizes his uniquely
human character and capacities in scientific and artistic enterprises,
it may also be said with similar reasons that religion is as distinc-

tively human as the search for so-called explanatory laws and relations or the creation of beautiful and illuminating objects. Thus if scientific theory and discoveries are largely validated, as they seem to be, not by their practical and technical uses or sensory experience, but by what they contribute to the total and ongoing processes of scientific inquiry or by the further discoveries they make possible and if works of art may be said to be validated (insofar as the term is applicable to them) by their subsequent and undeniable influence on further artistic creativity, aesthetic perception, and appreciation, then surely religious judgments may be said to be most significantly validated or justified by their consequences upon and within the complex processes of judging religiously. In other words, there need be no more apology for or question about the experience of the world or some dimension thereof as holy or divine than for the experience of the world as exemplifying logical or moral or aesthetic qualities and relations. Each mode of experience may be equally and uniquely revealing and perform functions that are both intrinsically valuable and indispensable. And if we must judge the world logically not merely because it contains logical orders and possibilities but also to keep certain parts of it logical and morally in order to preserve our moral capacities and artistically to increase both the beauty of the world and our own sensitivities, then surely it may be said with equal cogency that we must judge the world religiously in order to keep it holy and ourselves aware of the divine. If the sense of the presence of the holy is not altogether illusory, this is indeed of all the ways of justification the most weighty and urgent.

This method of validating religious judgment may be further illustrated chiefly by example. And any of a number of examples might be chosen: the moral universe of the ancient Hebrews; the aesthetic and anthropomorphic pantheon of the Greeks; or the infinite possibilities of being and knowing as articulated by the Hindus. But surely one of the most obvious and instructive examples is that of the Augustinian vision of man in the world. For the world in which Saint Augustine lived was hardly prima facie one to arouse or sustain a profound sense of being in the presence or under the jurisdiction of the holy. His achievement is therefore perhaps unusually indicative of the possibilities continually open to religious sensitivity and judgment. In a way Christianity had of course triumphed in the world in which Augustine lived; but the world in which it triumphed was in many respects a world of terrible ruins and dreadful conflicts. Before and during his life the Roman world was weakened from within and without, ravaged by political instability, afflicted by the ghastly rites of desperate religious cults, sacked by the barbarians, and debauched by the love of pleasures that required extraordinary suffering on the part of the innocent and unfortunate.

How could anyone in the midst of such decay, inequity, and ugliness construct a vision of man as a rational and noble creature at home in the world or regard existence as divine and the earth a temple? Certainly experience would justify nothing either sentimental or altogether hopeful. Order and reason had practically vanished from the earth; and justice and mercy, when they appeared, seemed almost wholly gratuitous. The sense of the divine had either to be dismissed as irrelevant or justified by an interpretation or vision which, without wholly ignoring or distorting the facts, would make worship possible in a world largely alien to both intelligence and the insistent sense of supreme and inviolable worth. And Augustine's choice of the latter alternative has been religiously validated by certain men ever since, including Luther and Calvin and their distinguished disciples, who have turned to him for a vision that moves men to worship even in the face of their own infamy, fallibility, and tragedy.

An unusually sensitive and brilliant man, subject apparently to extraordinary passion and excess, Augustine was long tormented by the search for a perspective which would make worship possible in his terribly ambivalent world. Inspired by beauty and crushed by ugliness, he was obviously often overwhelmed by the "awful and wonderful excellence" of nature and by delight in his own keen senses and intellect. Along with profound sensitivity and intellectual curiosity he had also an intense—if sometimes wavering—conviction of being in the immediate presence of the holy, or an insatiable passion for worship. He possessed or was possessed by a terrifying love of life (or perhaps a profound dread of non-being) and a parallel insight that personal existence—the joy of seeing and knowing—is an incomparably precious gift which no man can deserve and which might at any moment be snatched away or snuffed out. The only proper and sufficiently accurate mode of judging this ambivalent but nonetheless splendid order of being, he finally concluded, is through worship. And he found in Christianity, after he had tried Manichaeism and Neo-Platonism, the concepts and symbols that seemed to justify worship in spite of the tragic ambivalence of existence.

Oversimplified, the vision that made worship possible for Augustine was this: In the beginning a perfect, omnipotent, and omniscient God created the world out of nothing. He created the world perfectly good but with the possibility that evil would appear in it. And evil did appear when Adam chose by disobeying the perfect law of God to destroy both himself and his freedom. And by Adam's sin all men were corrupted; for mankind as a whole was generated out of the sinful body of Adam. Consequently all men deserve, if they receive justice, to be punished. But God, being merciful as well as just, elects some to be saved—to know not only the pleasures of the senses and the pain and terror of death but to discover also the unspeakable order and beauty of existence and to gain eternal felicity. Man is therefore utterly dependent upon God; and God's severe justice, beyond the comprehension of any man, may condemn to hell the fairest of children —whose apparent goodness is only their impotence—along with the most hardened reprobates.

It is gross oversimplification, in spite of the very obvious—if not fatal—difficulty in the doctrine that an omnipotent God who is the cause of all things is not also the cause of sin and evil, to suppose that Augustine innocently and creduously accepted simply as literal truth the account of creation in Genesis and Saint Paul's doctrine that man is by nature a corrupt and incorrigible sinner. The original and agonizing inconsistencies in his teachings are weighty—if not conclusive—evidence to the contrary. Rather, as an unusually intelligent, sophisticated, informed, and critical philosopher, Augustine thought he had, in his own experience and the travail of the world in which he lived, unquestionable evidence of the symbolic but inescapable and agonizing truth of this vision of existence. In himself and others he observed a longing for what is perfect in form, a vision of perfection, holy, immutable, and unthreatened by any catastrophe. As a Platonist he interpreted this as an innate memory of a time when man had in fact possessed this indescribable perfection. Why all the ideals and utopias and aspirations unless there is in man a recollection of that which is infinitely superior to both what the senses perceive and to what men are in fact able to choose or achieve in the conduct of their lives? Augustine was almost tragically aware, not only of the utter failure of governments to establish justice, but also of his own personal and absolute failure to achieve wisdom and righteousness. Both faith and reason declare, it seemed to him, that only the completely incomprehensible justice and mercy of God can account for the "wretched but magnificent" career of man in the world.

Of course many modern thinkers, theists as well as atheists, find Augustine's vision fantastic, reprehensible, and even terrifying. That a thoroughly civilized, sensitive, and informed man, who also believed in the goodness of God, could express such barbarous sentiments is indeed difficult to accept. But if his judgments seem severe, uncompromising, and sometimes even self-contradictory, they were by no means false to the world that produced them. And Augustine was clearly seeking not merely for comfort and salvation but for a true—if terrible—vision of *what is* or of the world and man's place in it. His vision was the result of a diligent if passionate search for truth or for a comprehensive vision which would make sense of the world, including his own diverse and conflicting needs and desires—a view that would fulfill his need to know worshipfully in a world where much, if not all, that was precious seemed to common sense so obviously and irrevocably doomed to wreck and ruin. The Christian perspective fulfilled simultaneously his need to inquire and to worship; and subsequently he insisted that reason is never less important than faith in religious matters and that faith is equally as important as reason in philosophy and science. He accepted Christianity, not as the completed answer to all human problems and needs, but as a perspective within which a worshipful inquiry into a perplexing but nonetheless splendid world could go on. He of course affirmed the complete adequacy of the Christian faith. Yet his faith must quite obviously be compared to the contemporary scientist's faith in inquiry—tempered to be sure by intense love instead of the desire for objectivity, predictability, and control—rather than to what so often passes for the essence of religion or a faith that denies the necessity of inquiry and sanctifies ignorance by dogma.

Yet that the Augustinian vision has not been wholly replaced by a more benevolent and realistic perspective may indeed seem truly regrettable. But a symbol, once generated, puts down deep roots, like a living thing, and lives in part on what it destroys. But no matter what religious vision one prefers, if any or none, little is gained by castigating the Augustinians for judging the world as it is given to them. The sense of the presence of the holy or the need and the capacity for judging the world religiously is apparently a radical requirement generated by the manner in which man finds himself in the world. And the Augustinian vision has made worship possible, or sustained man's sense of being in the presence of the holy, among the meek and world-weary as well as among the courageous reformers who have sought to hasten the coming of the Kingdom of Heaven upon earth.

And considered religiously any judgment, whether an intellectual or imaginative vision, a didactic poem, a program of social reform, or a Negro spiritual, is justified by increasing the scope, depth, and duration of the sense of the presence of the holy. Yet religion is only one, and at best a limited and sometimes distracting, mode of apprehending, articulating, and qualifying the infinite—and infinitely elusive—aspects of existence. So although justified primarily by revealing the dimensions of existence that require and support the sense of the presence of the divine, religion is for the sake of the total man. "The sabbath was made for man, and not man for the sabbath." Therefore religion must also be validated by its compatibility with other significant or indispensable forms of experience and judgment and in the light of its contributions to stability and progress in the career of man in the world.

ON HOW RELIGIOUS JUDGMENTS MAY BE FALSE

The greater the radius of light the greater the circumference of darkness.

ARABIAN PROVERB

One religious perspective or mode of judgment may of course be invalidated by the inquiry that justifies another. Yet this is not necessarily or always the case. Life is not an obviously consistent pattern of experience, and the very qualities and commitments required in one situation may be impossible or inappropriate in another. Consequently judicial forms are frequently and in many respects appropriately paradoxical. The psalmist could both profess that "Though I walk through the valley of the shadow of death, I will fear no evil" and cry in anguish, "My God, My God, why hast thou forsaken me." The ideals, qualities, and commitments which the various forms of judgment express, enhance, or encourage must vary from one time and situation to another or else neglect important elements of the kaleidoscopic range of experience through the realms of the actual, the ideal, the necessary, and the possible. Even as the law cannot be made to fit every social or moral problem, so no particular religious mood or doctrine, no single vision of excellence, and no one lyric which may veil our losses and loneliness with beauty is in every circumstance an appropriate or effective expression of the choices, requirements, and qualities which are disclosed in or may belong to the conviction of being in the presence of the holy. Both the thunder of anger and the soft flowing of tears may be expected in the pursuit of qualities demanded by any vision of supreme worth. And no doubt the Bible, for example, is congenial to so many radically different groups and occasions at least partly because it reflects and nurtures the most varied experiences and thus includes many paradoxes and conflicts.

Although *logically* considered the paradoxes and conflicts within and between the various religions are both serious faults and frustrating facts, such logical difficulties (not unlike the specious conflicts between two different sciences or between scientific and religious judgments) are, in a genuinely pluralistic world, by no means in all instances conclusive or even important signs of the falsity of a religion. But neither is it necessary to follow—at least not all the way—the contemporary religious existentialists whose apparent delight it is to heap paradox on paradox, to seek paradoxes where none can be found, and to insist that the prevalence of puzzles which inquiry and reason cannot solve is itself significant evidence of the existence of a wisdom and reality which transcend and ultimately reconcile the various forms of experience.

There is of course mystery; and perhaps no one can explain or explain away, now or ever, the curiously perplexing paradoxes of a Pascal ("I hold it equally impossible to know the parts without knowing the whole, and to know the whole without knowing the parts in detail")[104] or the antinomies of a Kant concerning the absolute incomprehensibility of either finite or infinite time and space or the apparent necessity of complementarity in physics. Yet the metaphysical or epistemological significance of such paradoxes, or limits of reason, is by no means obvious or clear. The notion current in some circles that the profundity of a thinker is in direct proportion to the number of paradoxes he admits, discovers, or invents may be no less indicative of a morbid sense of perplexity than of any genuine interest in increasing the scope and relevance of judgment. Nothing in fact is more evident than the insufficiency of present conceptual and symbolic forms and powers to articulate, reconcile, or account for the most common events and features of experience and existence. Judgment is limited in form and scope, though perhaps infinite in possibilities, and paradoxes abound. But a paradox is not necessarily either a permanent and unscalable wall or a humiliating reminder of human frailty. In many instances the paradox has indeed served chiefly as a specific and extraordinary challenge to the development of new forms and powers of judgment. Nor are the limits of understanding the foundations of religion. In one sense the unknown, with the burden of wonder and curiosity, conflict, need, and paradox which it

---

[104] Blaise Pascal, *Pensees*, No. 1. There are several editions of this work, which was first published in 1670, eight years after the death of Pascal.

brings, is of course the setting if not the inspiration of religion. But it is also in the same sense the setting and the challenge of all our arts and sciences. Neither more nor less than science is religion an attempt to chart the shores of the unknown; it is only a very different way of noting and articulating and thus sometimes discovering and communicating the quality and structure of what would otherwise remain unrevealed and without influence in culture and judgment.

Generally in fact it is not religious judgment at all but airy and uncritical speculation on religious symbols and activities that is puzzled and frustrated by paradox and contradiction. The intrinsic quality and the qualitative consequences of religious vision and activity, not their logical and remote metaphysical implications, are the heart of religion. Philosophy must of course take seriously, but without presupposing its conclusions, the logical and metaphysical significance of religious experience, claims, and activities. But religion itself prospers by giving its own attention primarily to the expressive and revelatory powers of its symbols, though surely both metaphysical beliefs and ethical requirements are among the matters which religions may articulate symbolically. And as paradoxical and contradictory as religious ideas and practices often are, it would nonetheless be more surprising and more truly paradoxical to find a high degree of consistency in the symbolic products of men whose circumstances, passions, interests, capacities, and needs are so multiform and subject in some measure to change simply by choice. Yet such paradoxes may signify little or nothing, except the obviously pluralistic character, about either the ultimate structure of existence or the possibilities of success in solving social, economic, political, and moral problems by rational methods. Contrary to much current and popular opinion, it seems quite clear that neither the deliberate cultivation of paradox for its own sake or the neglect of reason can aid or support the search for religious truth. The only legitimate paradoxes in religious literature and symbolism are due primarily to the reasonable effort to achieve appropriate and effective response to the many faces of the divine.

And although not itself a product of reason and not fully comprehensible to reason, the response to the divine can be regarded as completely nonrational only by identifying reason with inductive and deductive processes but ignoring that primal insight into the nature of existence and the choice or conclusion which asserts, at least implicitly, that matters of extraordinary worth are dependent on some degree of consistency in thought and action. In a fundamental sense of the word, it is plainly no less *reasonable* to trust the sense of worth than to trust the sense for consistency or sensory experience and induction. For unless the sense for the status and worth of both fact and value, united in choice or decision, is essentially reliable, then science as well as the arts and religions are basically only haphazard guesses about the images and patterns we shall next impose (or suffer) in the perhaps formless flux of existence. On the other hand, if existence has an actual and discoverable character, and our sense of worth—of fact and choice—is not illusory, aspects of this character surely may be recognized and communicated in religious judgment. And the scope and reliability of religious judgments may presumably be extended by critical attention to its characteristic methods, claims, and functions.

Therefore, even though wholly false religions are no doubt more rare than either the dogmatic sectarians or the antireligious are inclined to imagine, a defense of religion must nonetheless indicate how a religion may be false. For surely if religion is genuinely judicious, religious truth is not the product of every ill-informed and enthusiastic zealot.

In the first place, then, although brief and even startling successes may sometimes come to those whose vision is narrow, intense, and distorted, the evidence of sustained and critical experience suggests clearly that existence is many-dimensioned and that the search for enduring truth in any area or manner requires discipline and scope as well as enthusiasm and depth. In spite of its essential autonomy, truth in religion can hardly be expected where other dimensions of experience and modes of judgment are thwarted or misdirected. Not only false gods but also false views of the physical world and man's relation to it, poverty in the arts, or social and economic systems which defeat or warp human potential may help to convert the sense of the presence of the holy into desperate confidence in nonexistent powers or into a fanaticism which refuses to recognize either the limits of the religious forms of judgment or the necessity and excellence of certain other forms. Fanaticism, whether the product of blindness and desperation or enthusiasm, is apt to increase its errors in proportion to its intensity. And a religion is almost bound to be fanatical, and therefore false, when it denies, whether implicitly or explicitly, that other modes of judgment sometimes have priority and are also autonomous or when it fails to see that its own claims and powers are always severely limited and partial.

In other words, a religion is false when it demands the serious and unnecessary neglect of other interests and needs of the individual, or hinders some crucial dimension of community life, or warps critical powers of the mind and vital functions of the body. Some degree of such falsity is clearly inevitable in a religion which supposes that fundamental changes in society and scientific knowledge can never demand radical shifts in religious doctrines and practices. For autonomy does not imply isolation, and the presence of the holy abrogates no genuine needs or values. But a false religion alienates the people it pretends to serve from their own greatest good and encourages peace of mind, old habits, or fanaticism when what is needed are imagination, generosity, and interest in new methods of solving unprecedented problems. A false religion stands in the way of increasing the scope and intensity of the vision of the divine; its symbols and practices deceive the credulous rather than encourage and enlighten the weary and ignorant.

But a religion is perhaps most obviously false when it is merely habitual and formal, a facade to hide the vacuum where no vision creates or sustains a genuine sense of the presence of the holy, a mere pretense of sharing the convictions and concerns of an authentic tradition. Such formal and essentially false religion serves chiefly selfish and nonspiritual aims and is characteristic of individuals and groups whose common interests are economic and social rather than spiritual and judicial. Genuine religion can never be wholly indifferent to the conditions which prevent others from sharing both its vision of the holy and every available form of the good. But formal and false religion is exclusive and uncharitable. Its vision is limited and so its fears are many. Such religious hypocrisy—the use of religious symbols, concepts, and manners to mislead others and even oneself in regard to beliefs, intentions, motives, and values—is the most mendacious practice within the religious community. The fanatic may be dangerous but he is not devious or dishonest. But the hypocrite seeks the rewards without the dangers and duties of attending to a genuinely religious interpretation of existence. He speaks of a vision he has not seen and claims powers and virtues he does not possess. And although the established religion of a community is only rarely false by being altogether hypocritical, both individuals and groups, in defense of the status quo in social and economic prerogatives, often practice some degree of religious hypocrisy. Yet hypocrisy is clearly a deadly enemy, not only of religion but of all the forms of the search for truth or of judgment and value.

Ultimately, then, the religious person and not only religious concepts and symbols, must be evaluated. And although actions do perhaps speak louder than words, even actions themselves are nonetheless subject to dissimulation and may be radically misinterpreted. For this reason alone the problem of evaluating a religion is terribly complex and involves two opposed dangers to a degree that is perhaps rare—though not altogether absent—in the arts and sciences. On the one hand, and due partly to the moral necessity of respecting the rights and privileges of the individual, is the danger of an indiscriminate tolerance which can discover no significant differences between the various religious perspectives, claims, and actions. On the other, partly because of limited knowledge and imagination, is the perhaps greater danger of arbitrary authority and exclusiveness which lead eventually to fanaticism and to inevitable and irreconcilable conflict and tension. Yet the religions and the religious philosophers must either face squarely the problem, not only of justifying religion in terms of its historical and expressive functions, but also of distinguishing fanaticism and hypocrisy, as well as sentimental religiosity, from genuine insights and values, or they must abandon the claim that religion does in fact contribute to the moral and intellectual development of man.

But it is surely easy and no doubt morally dangerous to mistake one's own views and preferences for the whole truth or

one's own blindness and lack of sympathy for the inadequacy or
falseness of another's vision and commitments. Such lack of per-
spicacity is perhaps due chiefly to animal bias and poverty of
imagination in which all men share. But it is also apparently supported and encouraged by largely remediable ignorance or by the
refusal to examine seriously and carefully the actual basis and
functions of various judgments. Such claims, for example, as that
there is a hell to shun and a heaven to gain are not necessarily
religiously false, even if man is unqualifiedly mortal. The terrors
of hell may truly represent and warn against the dangers, both
quantitative and qualitative, which constantly threaten to turn
life into a wasteland of terrible sorrows and regrets where all worship would be absurd. And heaven may be the only adequate
symbol for passing judgment on the intrinsic joys and potentialities
of existence as it appears in the light of the holy. The judgments
which express and inspire or sustain religious experience need not
be limited to articulating the actual, magnificent as the actual is.
The most imaginative vision may embody the wisdom as well
as the beauty of experience. Therefore, no matter what the *post
mortem* facts, the religious liberals who attempt to discount completely the doctrine of hell and heaven have not necessarily found
a truer religion. Rather, their religion also is a singular but still
symbolic and limited judgment of the qualitative possibilities
presumably open in an actual or ideal world. Their own vision of
the sacred and of what it forbids and requires must also be judged
by its compatibility with other interests and necessities of life, by
what it contributes to the total quality of experience and especially
by its success or failure in arousing, fulfilling, and sustaining the
sense of the presence of the holy amidst the awesome and terrible
exigencies of individual existence.

The existential conditions and requirements of men are, however, apparently so diverse that nothing demands more sympathetic
insight and careful reason than the attempt to influence or change
a person's religion. To declare that the religion of another is false
or otherwise unjustified is no doubt to risk the most serious error
in regard to all that contributes to and flows from his sense of the
holy and inviolable. Indeed nothing is more difficult than to
judge justly the experience of others. Yet such judgment, hazardous

as it is, is inescapable. For even if it is only a dramatic exaggeration to say that man is "condemned to be free" and must therefore choose himself and his values, the refusal to judge is nonetheless already a judgment. A practice ignored is a practice accepted. Religion is of course not simply the public and practical duties which may accompany the sense of the holy and influence directly the life of the community but equally, and even more basically, a personal vision of splendor illuminating the necessary and often oppressive details of the search for excellence in saying, doing, and making. And presumably false religion must be replaced by such vision, not reformed by harsh judgment. But even so the demands or duties of the religious life do not end, but only begin, in the presence of the holy. *By their fruits*, then, *ye shall know them*. And though the fruit may indeed be often as difficult to judge as the tree, the religion which is obviously without any distinctive or beneficent results in the lives of individuals can never be seriously regarded as true.

SOME SUMMARY REMARKS

There is no common measure applicable to the works of a poet, an artist, a philosopher, a scientist, and the simple kindness of heart of a plain man. Humanity needs them all.

DUNN AND DOBZHANSKY

Man stands, be he scientist, artist, prophet, or philosopher, face to face with what Robert Oppenheimer has called "the edge of mystery"[105]—an uncharted immensity, both quantitatively and qualitatively, which almost defies and always in some measure eludes his instruments, patience, imagination, and labor. Yet as scientist, artist, prophet, or philosopher he must not treat this immensity altogether as a mystery but also as an object of judgment, amenable to exploration by the diverse and magnificent

[105] Robert Oppenheimer, *op. cit.*

powers of sense, imagination, experiment, and reason. The mystery is inescapable but need not wholly baffle or terrify man—though surely one need not apologize at all for feeling occasionally as Pascal apparently did when he confessed to being frightened by his own existence. The mystery is perpetual and awesome, yet must not discourage judgment in whatever modes are possible and fruitful. The mystery should, however, keep every person modest as he encounters and inevitably passes judgment on either the magnitude or the microscopic details of the universe.

And if a person has the courage to be modest and yet aspire, to confess his ignorance and yet continue to search, to attempt, as Henry James put it, to be a person on whom nothing is lost and yet admit that he has found but little, or as Newton thought after a lifetime of inquiry, only pebbles on the shores of the infinite ocean of existence, he will surely not need to make great use of the word *truth*. If he uses the word at all, he will do so aware of the tentative and partial nature of all judgments. The word will, however, no doubt continue to be used in many senses. When man measures, calculates, and manipulates the quantitative and relational aspects of himself and his environment to some purpose and with admirable, though limited, precision, *truth* may and will be used to indicate the success of such judgments. But when he is concerned with other matters, with the dynamic and pulsating qualities of experience, *truth* will no doubt continue to be used in a vaguer but nonetheless appropriate and necessary sense to indicate the artistic products, philosophical claims, and religious symbols which evidently reveal and enhance as well as guide and sustain the search for judicial excellence in qualitative matters. If existence is complex, many-dimensioned, and many-splendored, and experienced from many perspectives and in infinite degrees of involvement and detachment, the judicial description of *what is* must then certainly be in several conceptual and symbolic modes and in many variations in each mode. Truth is a quality that may belong not only to one form of language but to all judgment and is as various and complex as the many possible combinations of objects, perspectives, and judgments.

Only when there are special and narrow interests and causes to plead does the idea arise that truth is the monopoly of one

group, one method, one language, or one perspective. *Truth* is
then given a special and question-begging definition, and the
sciences or, as the case may be, the arts, or certain, if not all, religions are envisaged as always radically but inexplicably less than
modes of critical and discriminating discernment and articulation
of significant matters. But the fundamental difference between
religions is not that one is the whole truth while the others are
false. Rather each form of authentic religion is a distinct instance
of worshipful judgment expressed within the particularity of a
specific, and more or less comprehensive, perspective. And the
difference between religion and other modes of judgment, including the sciences, is not that the one is merely superstition
or the expression of emotion while the other provides accurate, if
not complete, accounts or descriptions of objective reality. All
modes are means of genuine discovery, and yet each may sometimes hinder the pursuit of truth and excellence. Each arises within
and may also affect the direction of human affairs. For each is a
unique but not isolated way of assimilating and manipulating or
judging the richly various materials of experience, and thus concerned with particular but interdependent aspects of *what is*. The
modes of judgment, whether scientific, artistic, religious, or philosophical, are not totally independent one of another; and the
dialogue between them must never end. Yet the attempt to equate
one to another or to explain or understand one wholly in the
terms of another is altogether as futile as describing the rainbow
to a man born blind or the wonderful excellence of language to
a creature that knows no language.

Apologia

. . . and so far as this divine particle is superior to man's composite nature, to that extent will its activity be superior to that of other forms of excellence.

ARISTOTLE

At the last day, I presume, that is, in all future days, when we see ourselves as we are—man's only inexorable judge will be himself, and the punishment of his sins will be the perception of them.

NATHANIEL HAWTHORNE

No reader will suspect that the writer defends the perspective of any current religious sect or tradition. Yet those who dismiss all religious activity as so much superstition or nonsense are, I hardly doubt, more seriously mistaken than the sectarians. Religions are of course particular. Yet their particularity—though it is the very condition of their existence—is inevitably a limit on their cogency and relevance in many situations. And unless religious men recognize and transcend (when the occasion demands it) this particularity and the limits imposed by it, the most genuine religious commitment may be transformed into idolatry and misplaced passion. But in spite of new and happy signs to the contrary, contemporary religion generally remains tragically unable—because its vision of man is so severely circumscribed and limited by dogma—to recognize its own particularity and transcend its own requirements.

But it remains nonetheless true that there are religious

phenomena, incommensurably different from moral and aesthetic experience, artistic creativity, utilitarian pursuits, and philosophic or scientific curiosity and inquiry, which must be fitted into any relatively complete geography of the human spirit or into any account of the different methods by which man discovers and qualifies the conditions of his existence. In summary terms I have called the presumed ground of these phenomena the sense of the presence of the holy, the sacred, the awesome and awe-full, the divine, and the order of splendor.

Yet it must be admitted that these terms do not so much describe the immediate and undeniable qualities of my own experience as the qualities which are apparently the source—and the outcome—of so much of man's unique history of observing and articulating the world and his own reactions to it. However, the love of life, of persons and objects, and halting efforts to give expressive form and substance to a few matters of importance have led me to admire ever more certain achievements of men and to wonder what depths and heights of insight and experience are required to call into existence such works, for instance, as the Winged Victory of Samothrace, *Genesis, The Book of Job,* the sustained magic of Shakespeare and Chaucer, or the overwhelming but essentially peaceful and comforting beauty of Beethoven's symphonies. Surely in the face of such celebrations of the splendid and awesome even our profoundest moral obligations, to say nothing of our preoccupation with practical matters, may sometimes rightfully seem altogether trivial. And it is perhaps appropriate to repeat here some brief poetic examples which seem, personally, both to signify and to call forth essentially a religious quality. Of course no brief statement can exhibit the persuasive grace and power of a larger whole. But the writer of *The Book of Job* comes close when he asks, in the supposed words of God, about matters which, though common sense knows an answer, are nonetheless eternally puzzling:

> Where wast thou when I laid the foundations
>   of the earth?
> Declare, if thou hast understanding.
> Who determined the measures thereof, if
>   thou knowest? . . .

Or who laid the cornerstone thereof;
When the morning stars sang together
And all the sons of men shouted for joy?

Or Joseph Addison in his "Hymn":

What though in solemn silence all
Move round the dark terrestrial ball;
What though no real voice nor sound
Amidst their radiant orbs be found?
In Reason's ear they all rejoice,
And utter forth a glorious voice;
Forever singing as they shine,
'The Hand that made us is divine.'

Or William Wordsworth in "Lines Composed a Few Miles Above
Tintern Abbey":

And I have felt
A presence that disturbs me with the joy
Of elevated thoughts; a sense sublime
Of something far more deeply interfused,
Whose dwelling is the light of setting suns,
And the round ocean and the living air,
And the blue sky, and in the mind of man;
A motion and a spirit, that impels
All thinking things, all objects of all thought
And rolls through all things. Therefore am I
          still
A lover of the meadows and the woods
And mountains.

And Gerard Manley Hopkins in "Pied Beauty":

Glory be to God for dappled things—
For skies as couple-colored as a brinded cow;
For rose-moles all in stipple upon trout that swim;
Fresh-firecoal chestnut-falls; finches' wings;
Landscapes plotted and pieced—fold, fallow,
          and plow.

All the arts, as well as both moral and speculative philosophy, and
the nontechnical reflections of the scientists, provide similar examples which bear witness to or call forth the conviction that in

certain very basic respects the only appropriate response to or judgment of existence is worship, "a joyful noise," thanksgiving, and praise.

But surely no person in search of truth can wholly fail to understand also, in the inevitable moments of unexpected darkness, the cry, "My God, why hast thou forsaken me?"—a cry of immeasurable distress that echoes across the centuries of human history and which may intensify as well as reveal the sometimes unutterable loneliness and the constant uncertainty of man's being in the world.

Yet in spite of the anguish and uncertainty, it seems nonetheless incredible that any person with normal sight and hearing, not constantly beat down by pain and sorrow, should not occasionally regard the world as essentially an altar or a temple. It is of course also equally incredible that some can apparently justify their own vision and the sense of the presence of the holy only by formulating beliefs which make irrelevant the worship by those whose vision of the world is different. To regard any particular vision or symbol as complete or exclusive surely tends to introduce either a vapid tranquility or a tragic militancy into life. And as Karl Jaspers has said, "Man can seek the path of his truth in unfanatical absoluteness, in a decisiveness that remains open."[1]

Indeed any form of judgment that does not remain open—which flees all doubt and agony and anxious inquiry—does not reveal but hides from man his own condition. As Moses Maimonides observed in The Guide for the Perplexed, "We are like those who, though beholding frequent flashes of lightning, still find themselves in the thickest darkness of night."[2] This is hardly less true today than in the twelfth century when Maimonides wrote it, except to the extent that we are now able to take advantage of the recorded accounts of what others have seen when the lightning flashed for them. And so we walk in the darkness by the maps others have made. Philosophy and science, religion and the arts, or all the forms of judgment and wisdom, still begin and end in wonder—for only through wonder and trial and error

[1] Karl Jaspers, Reason and Existenz, trans. by William Earle, New York, Noonday, 1955, p. 76.

[2] Moses Maimonides, The Guide for the Perplexed, New York, Dover, 1956, p. 3.

do the powers and the mystery of the various forms of judgment become available. So wonder, like mystery, is clearly not simply darkness or curiosity and puzzlement. Our curiosity is often satisfied and our puzzlement may disappear or get resolved by increased intellectual powers and knowledge of facts. But in wonder as in mystery we confront the irreducible fact of existence, the darkness and the flash of light which illuminates but is not itself illuminated, the inexplicable circumstance that some of our judgments are indeed reliable.

But we do not discover the causes of wonder, even as we do not discover the cause of causes; and so we name it: Nature, Existence, the Eternal, the Absolute, the Everlasting, the Awe-full, the Last Judgment, God. Clearly one may prefer the name Nature, neutral and benignly indifferent. But there is not necessarily any less superstition, and evidently often less imagination and less justice to many of the most impressive dimensions of experience, in the use of the word *Nature* than in the use of the word *God* as the name of the most comprehensive and sustaining context of man's existence. It is no doubt true that we live in Nature; but it is no less true that our thoughts go beyond Nature—to the possibility of the end of Nature in a cosmic catastrophe or to the ground of Nature in a cosmic accident or in God. But God regarded as the sustaining context of existence is surely not the last refuge of ignorance, a friendly cop on the corner, or a celestial sponge that wipes away the tragedy and failure of mankind. He is rather the light and the challenge, the splendor and the judge, or the terrible source of obligation which has moved the great knowers and reformers throughout history.

Someone has aptly said that it is indeed a foolish philosopher who stands before the world in wonder and sees nothing but mystery. Yet it seems an equally or even more foolish one who sees no mystery at all, and is not occasionally engulfed by extraordinary surprise at the fact that tears and pain and love and hate and beauty and laughter—especially beauty and laughter—should darken and brighten the void that was before the beginning. Isn't it possible that, in spite of the cogency of the many and various ways of judging the world, all that science has discovered and all that the arts, religions, and philosophy have disclosed and suggested are no more than very minor clues to what we are and the character of the universe we inhabit? How bold to imagine that our concepts hold—that our symbols echo—the vast forces, patterns, and implications of all existence! How utterly presumptuous if our ideas and decisions are ultimately *only* the conditioned reflexes of a chance-produced organism adjusting to an environment! And if we are more than that—if, as the existentialists so plausibly claim, we cannot discover ourselves in the conditions of our existence, if we are truly underived, unconditioned, a category rather than a species—then both ourselves and our responsibility for ourselves may be awesome indeed.

No candid mind, in any case, has reason to believe that modern man is safe from destruction by either self-inflicted violence or the slow atrophy of his vision, self-respect, and dignity. We live, as has now been said many times, in an age of total danger—a danger increased by the very anxiety and despair which it generates. And it would of course be foolish to suggest that religion can save us. The problems of modern man are both technical and humanistic, methodological and visionary, conceptual and symbolic. But we may at least hope that the religions (along with the arts and philosophy) will speak in this time about matters of inviolable worth, and that as a consequence even our most technical and methodological problems will be approached, not as means only, but also as genuine possibilities for realizing and demonstrating concretely the magnificent spirit, and not only the great skill and power, of the creature that gains more from giving than from getting. The religions, however, instead of being preoccupied, as they so often are, with *telling man what he must do to be saved* must first help *to show man what he is.* For presumably only the man who knows himself will also discover the specific requirements of his vocation as a person. And in such discovery the holy may also be present in new and still unanticipated forms.

Bibliography

Each of the following books has influenced, in one way or another, a substantial portion of this work. The edition listed is the one to which the footnotes in the text refer. When the reference is to any standard edition, only the author and title are given.

Ayer, A. J., *Language, Truth and Logic*, rev. ed., New York, Dover, 1946.
Buber, Martin, *The Eclipse of God*, New York, Harper & Row, 1952.
———— *Between Man and Man*, trans. by R. G. Smith, Boston, Beacon Press, 1955.
Buchler, Justus, *Towards a General Theory of Human Judgment*, New York, Columbia, 1951.
———— *Nature and Judgment*, New York, Columbia, 1955.
Cassirer, Ernst, *An Essay on Man*, New Haven, Yale, 1944.
———— *Language and Myth*, trans. by S. Langer, New York, Harper & Row, 1946.
———— *The Philosophy of Symbolic Forms*, trans. by R. Manheim, New Haven, Yale, 1953 and 1955, Vols. One and Two.
———— *The Problem of Knowledge*, trans. by W. Woglom and C. Hendel, New Haven, Yale, 1950.
Collingwood, R. G., *Speculum Mentis*, Oxford, Oxford University Press, 1936.
Dewey, John, *A Common Faith*, New Haven, Yale, 1934.
———— *On Experience, Nature, and Freedom*, R. Bernstein, ed., New York, Bobbs-Merrill, 1960.
Heidegger, Martin, *Existence and Being*, Chicago, Henry Regnery Company, 1949.
———— *An Introduction to Metaphysics*, trans. by R. Manheim, New York, Doubleday, Anchor Books, 1961.
Hook, Sidney, *The Quest for Being*, New York, St. Martin's, 1961.
Hume, David, *Dialogues Concerning Natural Religion*, New York, Hafner, 1948.
Huxley, Julian, *Religion Without Revelation*, New York, Mentor Books, 1958.
James, William, *Essays on Faith and Morals*, New York, Meridian Books, 1962.
———— *Pragmatism*, New York, Meridian Books, 1955.
———— *Some Problems of Philosophy*, New York, Longmans, 1931.

———— *The Varieties of Religious Experience*, New York, Longmans, 1928.
———— *The Will to Believe*, New York, Dover, 1956.
Kant, Immanuel, *Religion Within the Limits of Reason Alone*, trans. by T. Greene and H. Hudson, New York, Harper & Row, Harper Torchbooks, 1960.
Kierkegaard, Søren, *Fear and Trembling* and *The Sickness Unto Death*, trans. by L. Lowrie, New York, Doubleday, Anchor Books, 1954.
Mill, John Stuart, *Nature* and *Utility of Religion*, New York, Liberal Arts, 1958.
Nietzsche, Friedrich, *The Birth of Tragedy* and *The Genealogy of Morals*, trans. by F. Golffing, New York, Doubleday, Anchor Books, 1956.
Otto, Rudolf, *The Idea of the Holy*, trans. by J. Harvey, New York, Oxford, Galaxy Books, 1958.
Peirce, C. S., *Collected Papers*, C. Hartshorne and P. Weiss, eds., Cambridge, Harvard, 1934-1935.
Randall, John H., Jr., *The Role of Knowledge in Western Religion*, Boston, Starr King Press, 1958.
Russell, Bertrand, *Mysticism and Logic*, New York, Doubleday, Anchor Books, 1957.
Santayana, George, *Interpretations of Poetry and Religion*, New York, Scribner, 1900.
————*Reason in Religion*, Vol. III in *The Life of Reason*, New York, Scribner, 1905.
———— *Winds of Doctrine*, New York, Scribner, 1913.
Smith, John E., *Reason and God*, New Haven, Yale, 1961.
Taylor, A. E., *Elements of Metaphysics*, London, Methuen, 1903.
Tillich, Paul, *Dynamics of Faith*, New York, Harper & Row, 1957.
———— *Systematic Theology*, Vol. I, Chicago, The University of Chicago Press, 1951.
———— *Theology of Culture*, R. C. Kimball, ed., New York, Oxford, 1959.
Whitehead, A. N., *Modes of Thought*, New York, Putnam, Capricorn Books, 1958.
———— *Process and Reality*, New York, Macmillan, 1929.
———— *Religion in the Making*, New York, Meridian Books, Living Age Books, 1960.
———— *Science and the Modern World*, New York, Mentor Books, 1948.
———— *Symbolism*, New York, Putnam, Capricorn Books, 1959.

OTHER BOOKS MENTIONED IN THE TEXT

Ames, E. S., *The Psychology of Religious Experience*, Boston, Houghton Mifflin, 1910.
Aristotle, *The Nicomachean Ethics*.
Arnold, Matthew, *Literature and Dogma*, New York, Macmillan, 1898.
Baier, Kurt, *The Moral Point of View*, Ithaca, Cornell, 1958.
Bergson, Henri, *The Two Sources of Morality and Religion*, New York, Doubleday, Anchor Books, 1954.
Berkeley, George, *A Treatise Concerning the Principles of Human Knowledge*.
Bertocci, Peter A., *Introduction to the Philosophy of Religion*, New York, Prentice-Hall, 1951.
Blanshard, Brand, *The Nature of Thought*, London and New York, Allen & Unwin and The Humanities Press, 1964, 2 Vols.
—— *Reason and Goodness*, London and New York, Allen & Unwin and The Humanities Press, 1961.
Bradley, F. H., *Appearance and Reality*, New York, Macmillan, 1899.
—— *Essays on Truth and Reality*, Oxford, Oxford University Press, 1914.
Braithwaite, R. B., *An Empiricist's View of the Nature of Religious Belief*, Cambridge, Cambridge University Press, 1955.
Bridgman, P. W., *The Logic of Modern Physics*, New York, Macmillan, 1927.
—— *The Way Things Are*, Cambridge, Harvard, 1959.
Camus, Albert, *The Myth of Sisyphus*, trans. by J. O'Brien, New York, Knopf, Vintage Books, 1959.
Cassirer, Ernst, *The Myth of the State*, New Haven, Yale, 1946.
—— *The Philosophy of the Enlightenment*, trans. by F. C. A. Koelln and J. P. Pettegrove, Boston, Beacon Press, 1955.
Collingwood, R. G., *The Principles of Art*, Oxford, Oxford University Press, 1938.
Dewey, John, *Experience and Nature*, London, Allen & Unwin, 1929.
Existentialism From Dostoevsky to Sartre, Walter Kaufmann, ed., New York, Meridian Books, 1956.
Faith and Logic, Basil Mitchell, ed., London, Allen & Unwin, 1957.
Feuerbach, Ludwig, *The Essence of Christianity*, New York, Harper & Row, Harper Torchbooks, 1957.
Freud, Sigmund, *New Introductory Lectures on Psycho-analysis*, New York, Norton, 1933.
From Descartes to Kant, T. V. Smith, and M. Green, eds., Chicago, The University of Chicago Press, 1940.

326 BIBLIOGRAPHY

Hamilton, Edith, *The Greek Way to Western Civilization*, New York, Mentor Books, 1948.

Harrison, Jane, *Ancient Art and Ritual*, New York, Holt, Rinehart and Winston, 1913.

Hick, John, *Classical and Contemporary Readings in the Philosophy of Religion*, Englewood Cliffs, N. J., Prentice-Hall, 1964.
——— *Faith and Knowledge*, Ithaca, Cornell, 1957.

Hobbes, Thomas, *Leviathan*.

Hook, Sidney, *Education for Modern Man*, New York, Dial Press, 1946.

Hospers, John, *An Introduction to Philosophical Analysis*, New York, Prentice-Hall, 1953.

Hume, David, *An Enquiry Concerning Human Understanding*.

Husserl, Edmund, *Ideas: General Introduction to Pure Phenomenology*, London and New York, Allen & Unwin and Macmillan, 1931.

Jaspers, Karl, *Reason and Existenz*, trans. by William Earle, New York, Noonday, 1955.

Kaufmann, Walter, *Critique of Religion and Philosophy*, New York, Doubleday, Anchor Books, 1961.

Leibnitz, Gottfried, *The Philosophical Works*, trans. by G. M. Duncan, New Haven, Tuttle, Morehouse & Taylor, 1890.

Logic and Language, Antony Flew, ed., New York, Philosophical Library, 1951.

Maimonides, Moses, *The Guide for the Perplexed*, New York, Dover, 1956.

Malinowski, Bronislaw, *Magic, Science and Religion*, New York, Doubleday, Anchor Books, 1954.

Malraux, Andre, *The Voices of Silence*, New York, Doubleday, 1953.

Mill, John Stuart, *Utilitarianism, Liberty and Representative Government*, New York, Dutton, 1910.

Moore, G. E., *Principia Ethica*, Cambridge, Cambridge University Press, 1960.

Munitz, Milton, *The Mystery of Existence*, New York, Appleton-Century-Crofts, 1965.

New Essays in Philosophical Theology, Antony Flew and Alasdair MacIntyre, eds., London, SCM Press, 1955.

Nietzsche, Friedrich, *Beyond Good and Evil*.

Pascal, Blaise, *Pensees*.

Plato, *The·Gorgias*.
——— *The Phaedo*.

Randall, John H., Jr., *The Career of Philosophy: From the Middle Ages to the Enlightenment*, New York, Columbia, 1962.
——— *Nature and Historical Experience*, New York, Columbia, 1958.

Readings in Philosophy of Science, Philip P. Weiner, ed., New York, Scribner, 1953.

Readings in Twentieth Century Philosophy, W. P. Alston and G. Nakhnikian, eds., New York, Free Press, 1963.

Santayana, George, *The Letters of George Santayana*, Daniel Cory, ed., New York, Scribner, 1955.

———— *Realms of Being*, New York, Scribner, 1942.

———— *Reason in Science*, Vol. V in *The Life of Reason*, New York, Scribner, 1906.

———— *Scepticism and Animal Faith*, New York, Scribner, 1923.

Schleiermacher, Friedrich, *On Religion: Speeches to Its Cultured Despisers*, Harper & Row, Harper Torchbooks, 1958.

Tawney, R. H., *Religion and the Rise of Capitalism*, New York, Mentor Books, 1947.

The Age of Analysis, Morton White, ed., New York, Mentor Books, 1955.

The Creative Process, Brewster Ghiselin, ed., New York, Mentor Books, 1955.

Toulmin, Stephen, *Reason in Ethics*, Cambridge, Cambridge University Press, 1961.

Whitehead, A. N., *Adventures of Ideas*, New York, Macmillan, 1933.

Whitman, Walt, *Complete Prose Works*, New York, Appleton-Century-Crofts, 1908.

Wittgenstein, Ludwig, *Philosophical Investigations*, trans. by G. Anscombe, New York, Macmillan, 1953.

————*Tractatus Logico-Philosophicus*, London, Kegan Paul, 1922.

Woodbridge, F. J. E., *An Essay on Nature*, New York, Columbia, 1940.

———— *Nature and Mind*, New York, Columbia, 1937.

Index